COMMUNICATIONS AND INFORMATION IN CHINA

Regulatory Issues, Strategic Implications

Xing Fan

University Press of America,® Inc.
Lanham · New York · Oxford

Copyright © 2001 by
University Press of America,® Inc.
4720 Boston Way
Lanham, Maryland 20706

12 Hid's Copse Rd.
Cumnor Hill, Oxford OX2 9JJ

Library of Congress Cataloging-in-Publication Data

Fan, Xing.
Communications and information in China : regulatory issues,
strategic implications / Xing Fan.
p.   cm
1. Communication and traffic—China. 2. Communication and
traffic—Government policy—China. I. Title.
HE278 .F36   2001   384'.0951—dc21   00-069062 CIP

ISBN 0-7618-1950-9 (cloth: alk. paper)

⊖™ The paper used in this publication meets the minimum
requirements of American National Standard for Information
Sciences—Permanence of Paper for Printed Library Materials,
ANSI Z39.48—1984

Acknowledgements

I would like to extend my genuine and special thanks to Ambassador Diana Lady Dougan, Senior Advisor and Chair of International Communications Studies Program, CSIS, William B. Garrison, Jr., Director of International Communications Studies Program, CSIS, G. Russell Pipe, Deputy Director of Global Information Infrastructure Commission (GIIC), and Gerrit W. Gong, Chair of Freeman China Studies and Director of Asian Studies Program, CSIS, for their gracious support, unique inspiration, and persistent encouragement, without which this in-depth book could not have been completed.

Anthony G. Oettinger, Chairman of the Harvard Program on Information Resources Policy, deserves my profound gratitude. Professor Oettinger was my project director when I did my earlier studies and research at Harvard University. He has been exceedingly supportive to my work. His insightful and continued intellectual guidance has been an important resource to me in the whole process of writing this book.

My cordial and warm thanks also go to Christopher and Rita Foss, close friends of mine, for their dedicated and professional assistance in formatting the draft manuscript and making this book ready for print.

Finally, a personal word of deep appreciation is given to my family for their caring and understanding when I worked long hours away from home. Their contribution is always hidden, yet, never forgotten.

Xing Fan

Center for Strategic and International Studies
Cyber Century® Research Fellow
Washington, D.C.

General Table of Contents

Communications and Information in China: *Regulatory Issues, Strategic Implications*

A "dragon" with thousands of years of history and tradition, China now finds itself stricken by a strong beat of "cyber" forces. The country, within a relatively short period of time, has traveled a long way and arrived at the threshold of the "Information Age." The significance and implications of this spectacular move are profound and immeasurable. Communications advancement and IT applications will transform the face and the heart of China, as it happens to most other countries. Yet, how this dragon will manage rapid changes and struggle to balance its social, political, and economic muscles against its deep-rooted legacies, only time can tell.

Xing Fan
Center for Strategic and International Studies
Cyber Century® Research Fellow
Washington, D.C.

Foreword

In China, market realities (both positive and negative) have little correlation to the statistical extrapolations of economists or central planners. Of course, China is not alone on that score. Even the most open market countries are hard pressed to understand the new Cyber Age that is much more than the dawn of a new millenium. Unlike the Industrial and Information Ages that were shaped by infrastructure and technology, the new age, the "Cyber Century®", will be shaped by "who" and "what" has access, use or control of information. No where is this more critical than China where its resources in people and capital are already being unleashed by economic restructuring.

It is a mistake to interpret China's situation along the simplistic demarcations of the "digital divide" separating developing from industrialized countries and infrastructure-rich from infrastructure-poor. Indeed, as this book illustrates, while China still lags behind most industrialized countries in telephones or computers per capita, in actual fact, China is already a world leader in many areas. By 2000 China already had more cell phones than the UK, France, Germany, and Italy combined, faster computer growth rate than all of Latin America, and a higher percentage of digital phone lines than the U.S.

Xing Fan's book provides much more than an in-depth presentation of China's complex infrastructure and regulatory underpinnings. It reflects a unique vantagepoint. In the mid 1990's, I enlisted his talents to help with joint government-industry initiatives I was spearheading for the Center for Strategic and International Studies in Washington as well as the Chinese Academy of Social Sciences in Beijing. Since that time, Xing has been invaluable to our unique success in getting key experts from often warring bureacracies and always competing industries to contribute vital intellectual capital to cutting-edge policy projects under the resulting Center for Information Infrastructure and Economic Development. This book is very much in the spirit of our objectives. It is also "must-read" for those who want to understand how information technology is already shaping China's future.

DIANA LADY DOUGAN
Chairman, Cyber Century Forum, Washington, DC

Part One: Dynamic Landscape

Profile and Prospect

Fast-Paced Development:

For the past decades, China has distinguished itself in two ways: its internal economic restructuring, which featured economic liberalization, decentralization and marketization, and its opening up to the outside world, which has resulted in a large inflow of foreign investment and a boom in foreign trade. China's economic advances have been paralleled by a spectacular "revolution" in communications and information, which, taking place at an accelerated rate, is characterized specially in the area of telecommunications. The industry's substantial investment, fast expansion of networks and services, and expeditious upgrading of technology have brought to the country better communications capabilities and easier access to information resources.

Only a decade ago, China's communications system was largely featured by the use of such technologies as high frequency point-to-point radio, open wireline carrier, microwave radio relay, coaxial cable transmission network, earth satellite station, electron-mechanical telephone exchanges, analogue mode dominated long distance networks, and wired broadcast for the vast Chinese rural territories. However, the pace with which the Chinese telecommunications industry advances its technology and improves its services quality and management is exceptionally impressive. By 1978, China had only 4.06 million lines of the total public exchange capacity, 3.69 million telephone sets, 19,000 long distance circuits that were predominantly open wires, and a national telephone density of 0.38 percent. Over a period of ten years (1980–1990), the public telephone switching capacity and the number of telephone sets both increased threefold, the number of long distance circuits fivefold, and telecommunications traffic sevenfold.[1]

China's telecommunications sector has achieved remarkable growth in network construction and communications facilities. Noted changes have taken place in the areas of telecom equipment, communications capacity, and scope and scale of services. Old equipment is replaced or upgraded, overloaded long-distance lines are relaxed, and overall capacity is largely expanded. The country's information and communications system and technologies are undergoing a significant transformation from analog to digital, circuit switch to packet switch, narrow band to broad band, and wired networks to a network hybrid composed of wireless mobile, satellite, microwave and fiber optic cable. Information and communication services are upgraded from plain old telephone services (POTS) to more advanced, more value-added, interactive and multimedia services. By the end of 1998, users of digital data network (ChinaDDN), packet switched network (ChinaPAC), e-mail service, and other data communications mushroomed from virtually zero five years earlier to more than 189,000, 106,000, 1.5 million and 560,000 respectively. China's public network's switching capacity had exceeded 110 million lines,[2] second only to the United States. By 1999 the country's national teledensity grew from 0.5% in 1985 to 12.5%, total fixed line subscribers went

---

[1] In 1980, China's telephone exchange capacity was 4.35 million lines, with a nationwide penetration rate of 0.5 per cent. China experienced a dramatic growth in fixed-line telephone users between 1992 and 1997: from 10 million to 93 million.

[2] This achievement is made three years ahead of the targeted timeframe (2000) set by MPT in its ninth five-year plan. In September 1998, China's total telephone exchange capacity reached 121 million lines.

up to more than 110 million, with 22 million new subscribers added to 1998's figure. Wireless paging and mobile phone subscriptions each surpassed 40 million.[3] In the middle of 2000, China's fixed line telephone users climbed up to 125 million, and its wireless mobile subscribers were numbered close to 60 million. These figures are quickly updated.

China has realized the nationwide connection of analog mobile networks; the country's digital GSM mobile networks have covered 95% of the country's cities and towns. Roaming services are made available in the majority of the national territories and across almost 35 countries. The annual growth of mobile telephony averaged 175% between 1987 and 1998, three times as high as that of the wired phone subscription growth. Wireless mobile telephony is stepping away from its initial high-priced and high social-status service for primarily well-to-do business people and ranked government officials to that of communications tool for the general public. New and emerging communication services offered range from 200 security card service, 800 toll-free business phone service, magnetic calling card service, voice mail (166) service, to virtually all kinds of value-added and telephone information (160/168) services. Domestic and international teleconferencing (2Mb/s) via satellite and microwave communications networks and high-speed (64Kb/s-1.544Mb/s or 2Mb/s) data transmission or messaging services are also made available in many big cities and urban areas. Internet applications in China have presented an especially spectacular uphill growth: in a period of fourteen months (October1997-December 1998), for instance, the international gateway capacity of the four major national service providers (CHINANET, CERNET, GBNET, and CSTNET) swiftly upgraded from 25.4 Mbps to 143.25 Mbps, domain names grew from 4,000 to 18,400, WWW sites climbed from 1500 to 5300, and the subscription jumped from 600,000 to 2.1 million. The same

---

[3] China has become the third-largest mobile market in the world. USA and Japan are currently positioned the first and the second in terms of mobile phone subscription. China's mobile teledensity by 1999 remained less than 4% nationwide, as compared with that of USA, 22-25% (15-18% in 1998), and Japan, 15-20% (10-12% in 1998).

stunning growth kept its momentum in 1999 in which total network gateway capacity reached 351 Mbps, domain names expanded to 48,695, WWW sites rocketed to 15,153, and Internet subscription climbed to 8.9 million. Between 1998 and 1999, Internet subscription, domain names and WWW sites in China experienced a 100% growth every six month.[4] Meanwhile, a group of Chinese Internet service/content providers (ISPs/ICPs) has emerged as fairly sizable and high-profiled players.[5]

During the past few years, China's annual telecom industry growth averaged around 35%, three times higher than the nation's GDP growth. Share of telecom revenues in GDP rose from 0.41% in 1992 to 4.9% in 1998. Installation of new phone lines grew by more than 20 million in peak years.[6] This yearly added exchange capacity is equivalent to the size of an US regional Bell operating company, or to the total capacity of Australia's national network. By 1999, China had built up the second largest wired communications network and the third largest wireless mobile network in the world. The core objectives set by China's Ministry of Post and Telecommunications (MPT-MII) for the year 2000[7] include construction of telecom networks that are advanced in technology, effective in operation, and multifunctional. These networks should have an overall exchange capacity of more than 174 million lines, with a nationwide teledensity of at least 13 percent (30-40 percent for urban areas), which

---

[4] Data provided by China Internet Network Information Center (CNNIC) in January 2000. The latest CNNIC survey indicated that, as of June 2000, China's Internet subscribers reached 16.9 million, websites expanded to 27,289 in number, and the total international gateway capacity rose to 1,234 Mbps.

[5] Most well-known ISPs/ICPs include SinaNet, Sohu, Yeah, ChinaInfo, Chinabyte, Netease, 163, 263, 21cn, Goyoyo, ChinaWeb, Beijing Online, Shanghai Online, cpcw, and Shenzhen Online.

[6] In the U.S. telecom history, the highest annual growth was 7 million lines.

[7] MPT was restructured into the Ministry of Information Industry (MII) in 1998, but MPT remains the core of MII. To avoid confusion, "MPT" is used throughout this book unless "MII" is otherwise necessary to appear.

translates into one telephone line for every household in cities and basic telephone access for all rural villages.[8]

Despite all these achievements, China still has a long way to go before the country can meet the enormous demand for telecommunications and information services. In terms of general network systems and equipment technology, China is catching up quickly, but in terms of network management, telecom operation productivity and industry efficiency, China remains significantly behind the developed countries. According to a study in April 2000 by China's State Statistic Bureau, China's countrywide information capacity was by then only 8.6% of that of the United States in terms of China's ability to develop and use IT and information resources, and in terms of China's status of IT professionals out of the country's general population.[9] Serious concerns are geared toward China's still low teledensity and PC availability nationwide, limited penetration of basic telephone services into vast remote and rural areas,[10] a growing disparity in telecom development and IT applications between China's east and west regions, and between the big urban and coastal cities and the rest of the country, and financial and regulatory barriers to the deployment of value-added and advanced telecom networks and technologies. China's task for development is enormous, but, in an unprecedented change of market and technologies, the strategic and regulatory challenges China faces in fulfilling this task are all but overwhelming.

---

[8] Counting the Chinese population, one percentage of teledensity increase is significant: it means over 12 million new phone subscribers added to wireline and mobile services.

[9] The study specified 29 indicators from four areas, analyzed and compared data collected from 28 developed and developing countries. The US, Japan, Australia, Canada and Singapore were ranked the top five.

[10] However, some observers argue that expansion of telecom services to rural and remote areas in China may not be economically rational and efficient as people there tend to be too stuck to their old way of life to use telecom services, or too poor to afford the expenses.

Growth Trends:

China's telecom investment as a share of GDP grew from 0.26% in 1989 to approximately 2% in 1995. Since then, telecom investment has been growing steadily above the 2% figure. However, as a percentage of the nation's total investment, China's telecom investment climbed up sharply to approximately 6% in 1998. Main sources of China telecom investment included: telephone installation fees and service charges (40%-45%),[11] depreciation on fixed assets (18-20%), domestic and international loans (25%), state budget 1-2%, and others (5%). With an increased pressure to reduce installation fees and service rates, domestic commercial loans and market-based funding may soon become a more important source of capital. Specific indicators of China's telecom development over the past years are listed and described below:[12]

Telecom Investment (US$ million)[13]

Year	(US$ million)	Year	(US$ million)
1988	397.7	1995	10,840
1989	545.9	1996	11,800
1990	648.76	1997	13,500
1991	939.18	1998	18,500[14]

---

[11] This percentage will become smaller as installation fees are lowered under increased pressure.

[12] Source: Adapted from MPT/MII annual reports, with adjustment. All data for the year 2000 are estimates.

[13] China's investment is divided approximately 10% and 90% for post and telecom sectors respectively. The figures here have excluded the investment for postal services. They are converted from RMB based on the current exchange rate of roughly 8.3. However, historical exchange rates (middle level) since 1981 have varied significantly: 1.70; 1.89; 1.98; 2.33; 2.94; 3.45; 3.72; 3.72; 3.77; 4.78; 5.32; 5.52; 5.76; 8.62; 8.35; 8.31; 8.29; 8.28. For 1996-2000, more than US$65 billion is planned to be invested for network construction and technical renovation, of which about 9.4% is for mobile networks development. Around

Year	(US$ million)	Year	(US$ million)
1992	1,761.9	1999[15]	18,290
1993	4,810	2000	24,000
1994	8,214		

Telecom Service Revenues (US$100 million)[16]

Year	US$100 Million	Annual Growth Rate (%)
1991	24.5	31
1992	35	42
1993	56	59
1994	84	50
1995	118	41
1996	150	26
1997[17]	200	32
1998[18]	252	25
1999	304	21
2000	370[19]	20

70% of the investment may come from installation fees, depreciation, and profit reinvestment; domestic commercial loans also act as an important source. International loans and foreign supplier credits are encouraged. According to MPT, at least 15% of the total investment is expected to come from foreign sources.

[14] This figure is the adjustment of the Chinese official data. US$360 million was reallocated from China's treasury bonds to the nation's telecom industry in 1998. It is estimated that communications investment accounted for 6.1% of China's total fixed asset investment in 1998.

[15] Between 1996 and 1999, investment in wireless mobile sector, as a percentage of the total, accounted for 24%, 28%, 39% and 47% respectively.

[16] *China Daily* (Jan. 23, 1999) officially announced that total output in 1998 from the nation's telecom industry was about US$29 billion. China Telecom's service revenue was US$18 billion (about 95% of the total), while Unicom's was only US$880 million (about 4% of the total). In 1999, China's telecom services revenue took more than 3% of the country's GDP.

[17] In 1997, ratio of revenue from local, long-distance, and wireless mobile services are 1, 1.04, and 0.99, each taking about one third of the total.

[18] China Unicom's mobile market share in 1998 was less than 5%, and its revenue in the same year was US$187 million, less than 1% of the total.

MPT Telecom Revenue Breakdown (%)

	1996	1997	1998
International and domestic long-distance[20]	45.41	38.62	37.5
Local	24.9	28.49	30.5
Mobile	22.89	24.73	25
Paging	6.2	7.4	6.2
Telegraph, Fax, Telex etc.	.59	.76	.8

Up to 1999, revenues from data communication, Internet, multimedia, and other value-added services remained fairly small, approximately 4-5% of the total, even though the growth of the users was high.

	1993	1994	1995	1996
Nationwide Teledensity (%)[21]	3.2	4.6	6.33	6.8
Total Exchange Capacity (million lines)[22]	29.84	49.26	62.61	85.1
Number of Phone Subscribers (Wireline and Wireless, in million)	14.07	22.19	35.7	54-55
Internet Users (000)	1.7	5-100	120	150
Data Communications Users[23] (000)	N/A	8.5	28	108

---

[19] MPT in 1993 projected that China's telecom revenues for the year 2000 would be US$24 billion. In 1995, the figure by projection was raised to US$30.8 billion. Later, the figure was once again raised to US$37 billion.

[20] China's 1999 domestic long-distance call traffic reached 58.5 billion minutes, and its international long-distance traffic was 1.7 billion minutes. The growth of China's long-distance calls is about 20% per year.

[21] Teledensity in China stands for total number of phone (wired and wireless) lines per 100 people. China's wireless mobile phone penetration by 1999 was only 3.5%.

[22] China had only about 10 million lines of total exchange capacity in 1991, but in August 1997, the figure reached 100 million.

	1997	1998	1999[24]	2000
Nationwide Teledensity (%)	8.07	10.54	12.5	16-17
Total Exchange Capacity (million lines)	93.19	119[25]	158	240
Number of Phone Subscribers (Wireline and Wireless, in million)	110	123	153	200
Internet Users (000)	680	2100	8900	18-20 million
Data Communications Users (000)	195	330	426	N/A

Wireless Mobile Communications[26]

Year	Cellular Phone Users		Radio Paging Users
	(10,000)	Growth (%)	(million)
1988	0.32	357	N/A
1989	0.89	178	N/A
1990	1.83	106	N/A
1991	4.75	160	N/A
1992	17.69	272	0.64
1993	63.82	261	5.6
1994	156.6	145	10.3
1995	362.7	132	17.4
1996	684.8	89	25.4
1997[27]	1,325[28]	93.5	30

---

[23] Data communications in mainland China currently takes only about 2% of the total IT market, but it is likely to grow at approximately 35% per year (compound annual growth rate) into the next century.

[24] Urban teledensity in 1999 reached 28.4%.

[25] 99% of the long-distance exchange capacity is in the form of automatic program control, and long-distance exchange is 98% digitized (in 1998).

[26] Public wireless mobile service was initially offered in China as a supplement to wired phone service in 1987 when a national youth sports meet was held in Guangzhou.

[27] In October 1998, the number of wireless phone users reached 20 million, with the ability to roam among 35 countries. Pager users reached over 36 million.

Year	Cellular Phone Users		Radio Paging Users
1998	2,498	88.8	39
1999	4,324	75.4	46
2000	6,500	52	50

Major Drivers for Development:

China's official explanation on the fast growth in telecommunications is that the industry has been fueled by the favorable government policies and incentives[29] concerning taxation, loans, use of foreign currency,[30] zero customs duties for the import of telecom equipment, installation fees, equipment depreciation, and service charges, the enthusiastic deployment of advanced technologies from abroad, the support from local government organizations and military forces,[31] and hard work of the industry people. In fact,

---

[28]Guangdong Province leads the way in China's telecommunications: towards the end of 1997, it has over 10 million telephone subscribers (teledensity: 16.4%, compared with 7.3% nationwide), of which about 3 million are mobile phone users (far ahead of Shanghai which has 0.5 million mobile phone users in Sept. 1997). Five Chinese cities that have the highest figures of mobile phone subscription are Guangzhou, Shanghai, Beijing, Shenzhen, and Tianjin.

[29] Between 1982 and 1988, China's telecom industry enjoyed a three 90% policy (dao san jiu) set by the central government, i.e., (1) as much as 90% of the central government loans for telecommunications could be deferred for repayment; (2) Provincial Telecom Administrations could keep 90% of their taxable profits; and (3) MPT could keep 90% of its foreign currency earnings from international traffic. This preferential policy was revoked in 1995. However, favorable treatment in taxation, loans, and foreign exchange for telecom and IT sectors have remained to some extent.

[30] Diversification of investment sources is encouraged by an official strategy called in Chinese borrowing money to buy hens, and then paying money back by eggs."

[31] For example, MPT often receives generous support in manpower from the People's Liberation Army for constructing long distance fiber optic cables (*e.g.,*

strategic changes in industry ideology and in government development priority,[32] along with other factors such as large investment,[33] MPT organization and policy initiatives, the enormous market demand, and the competition in equipment supplies (domestic and international) and services from Unicom and other non-MPT players, should have played very critical roles.

China's unique momentum to develop its information and telecommunications industries is triggered by both domestic and international pressure. Domestically, China faces an urgent need for economic growth. China's expansion of telecommunications infrastructure and growth of its national economy seem to be significantly correlated and mutually reinforcing. Overseas, China has realized that a well-built national information and communications infrastructure will be decisive to the country's social, economic and political future.[34] China must respond with timeliness to the challenges of the worldwide Information Revolution, as the country cannot afford the heavy price it has to pay if it loses the opportunity to play catch-up and to achieve strategic competitiveness in the world.

---

from Lanzhou to Urumqi and from Lanzhou to Lhasa), and the use of land for laying communication cables is often at little financial cost.

[32] For many years before China's Economic Reform, public post and telecommunications in China was regarded by the government as political tools to support official governance and maintain social stability, not as an essential infrastructure for economic development and public welfare (*People's Post & Telecom Journal*, September 1998).

[33] In early and mid-1980's, China invested a yearly average of US$250-300 million, or around 30% of the revenue, for telecom infrastructure, resulting in a net industry growth of 13-14% annually. Since 1990's, China has significantly increased investment in telecom sector and greatly pushed up telecom growth.

[34] China's leader Jiang Zeming has urged the Chinese government and Communist Party officials to embrace the Internet. He is reportedly quoted as saying " Internet technology is going to significantly change the international situation, military combat, production, culture, people's daily lives and all economic aspects."

Competition has been officially recognized as having many advantages over monopoly.[35] The enormous and soaring market demand, both potential and apparent, for telecom products and services drives the government to seriously rethink its policies and strategies regarding China telecommunications industry. Since mid-1990s, both the State Council and the MPT have increasingly been pressured by government organizations and industry entities to open up telecom services for competition, the arguments being that if the old MPT monopoly were protected to proceed without making essential accommodations or changes, the long-standing gap between supply and demand would widen, the desired political and macro-economic control over the nation would remain primarily unattainable, and the present momentum of economic development would soon be crippled. China has also learned from overseas practices that telecommunications operated by corporatized or competing entities provide better and cheaper services while generating larger and quicker profits than ponderous government ministries in a monopolistic context have been able to. Emerging competition in China over the past few years has sped up telecom development, lowered prices, and improved quality. It has gradually reshaped China's telecommunications industry growth from a government and policy pushed build-out to a demand and technology driven model. The introduction of competition to China telecom market has other merits as well. By having a centrally controlled competition between China Unicom and China Telecom of the MPT, market forces may set in to (*i*) rationalize the telecom industry structure; (*ii*) reallocate resources for more efficient utilization; and (*iii*) diversify and facilitate telecom financing.

China's telecom equipment supplies have been open to both domestic and overseas competition since the early 1990's. To encourage services competition on a limited and regulated basis, the central government in 1993 opened nine areas of information and

---

[35] Chinese President Jiang Zemin, in one of his recent public speeches, stated that China will gradually phase out monopoly in telecom industry.

communications services for domestic competition among state-owned or collectively-owned enterprises, while privately owned firms and individuals in China were banned from any involvement in these services.[36] These nine areas are:[37]

- Radio paging
- 800 MHz dispatch service
- 450 MHz mobile communications service
- Domestic very-small-aperture terminal (VSAT) communications service
- Telephone information services
- Computer information services
- E-mail service
- Electronic Data Interchange (EDI)
- Videotex service

These nine areas were defined by MPT as value-added services that could be less controlled by the government. In the 2000 telecom regulation drafted by MII and approved by the State Council, basic and value-added telecom services are re-classified. Basic telecom services include fixed line long-distance and local telephony, wireless mobile voice and data services, fixed and mobile satellite communications services, Internet and other public data transmission services, leasing and sales of network, bandwidth, wavelength and other network related elements, international network facilities and communication services, radio paging, and network subcontracting and basic service resale. Value-added services include e-mail and voice mail, online data storing, processing, retrieving and trading,

---

[36] In March 2000, Bao Yujun, Vice Chairman of China's Industrial and Commerce Federation, stated that China should allow domestic private firms to enter telecom service market before the country enters the WTO. He estimated that at least 100 big private firms in China have enough resources to compete in the telecom market.

[37] MPT required that, as a precondition, providers of radio paging, 800 MHz dispatch, 450 MHz mobile and domestic VSAT get service licenses and other service providers get approvals from MPT or MPT local offices.

EDI, value-added faxing, video-conferencing, and Internet access and information services.

Industry Structure and Key Players:

Changing Status:

In 1996-1997, China had a total of 406 enterprises operating in telecom and postal industries, with 188 being state own enterprises (SOEs), 51 being Sino-foreign joint ventures, and 167 in collective or other business structures. Total number of MPT related industry employees was more than one million. The 1999 structure of the industry players in communications service operations was considerably changed, as summarized below:

<u>Structure of Telecom Public Service Sector in China</u>

Service	# of Operator	Competition	Ownership
Intl long distance	1	Virtually none	State monopoly
Domestic long distance	2	Limited	State own
Local	2	Limited	State own
IP phone	4	Intense	State own
Telegraph	1	None	State monopoly
Data comms/Leased line	3	Limited	State dominant
Cable TV	1	None	SARFT monopoly
GSM900/1800 mobile cellular	2	Limited	State own
Radio paging[38]	1763	Intense	Varied[39]

---

[38] China Telecom paging operator Guo Xin alone takes a lion's share (60%) of China's paging users, while more than 2000 other paging service providers struggle to compete for the rest of the paging market. In fact, competition is so intense among these non-China Telecom operators that a significant number of them are going out of business. Thus, this figure is shrinking. In 1999, China had

Service	# of Operator	Competition	Ownership
800 MHz radio dispatch	110	Relative[40]	Varied
450 MHz wireless mobile	25	Relative	Varied
Telephone information[41]	410	Intense	Varied
VSAT	27	Relative	Varied
E-mail & voice mail	54	Intense	Varied
Database	100	Relative	Varied
Internet service providers (ISPs)[42]	520	Intense	Varied
EDI	8	Relative	State dominant
Videotex	11	Relative	Varied
Multimedia	8	Relative	Varied

23 operators offering inter-provincial paging services and 6 operators providing 2-way paging services. Because of the fierce competition among paging operators and between paging and cellular phone services, the number of paging providers has dropped sharply from about 5000 to current 1763. Paging providers in China are trying to upgrade their networks and offering value-added services such as news release, e-mail notification, stock updates, voice mail and messaging to revive their competitiveness.

[39] "Varied" indicates that ownership varies from MPT (&PTAs), ministries, local business entities, to even PLA business entities. But most of these operators are still "state owned" in a genetic sense.

[40] MPT licensing or approval is required for offering different competitive services.

[41] In 1999, only 11 of these 410 firms were able to provide inter-provincial telephone information services.

[42] Those ISPs are MPT/MII licensed operators. 520 indicates only the license receivers, not necessarily the actual operators. In 1999, some 300 ISPs were offering services in the market, out of which 77 ISPs were able to provide inter-provincial services. These 300 ISPs included the licensed MPT-MII agents that provide Internet access services. Non-MPT operators have invested about 1.5-2 billion yuan. The services they provide include access installation, E-mail, training, maintenance, value-added database or online information, or promoting CHINANET services as China Telecom's business agents. By 1998, ISPs in China were numbered 204.

Service	# of Operator	Competition	Ownership
Satellite communications[43]	3	Limited	State own
Domestic frame relay[44]	2	Limited	State own

Compared with the previous years, the structural change was significant in value-added and non-basic segments, as domestic competition in service areas such as paging, telephone information, IP phone, voice messaging, and Internet access grew rapidly. But the lion's share of China's telecom market remained monopolistic. That is, dominant proportion of the telecom services in terms of traffic, revenue, and subscription was continuously provided by MPT/MII controlled China Telecom and its local carriers (PTAs) that operate networks for international, long-distance, local voice telephony, satellite communication, data transmission, and wireless cellular services. China Unicom's services were constrained practically to wireless mobile and radio paging, with less than 5% of the market share. JiTong and China Netcom were only fledgling players offering data and Internet services to a marginal number of business and individual users.

Reforms Underway

China's telecom monopolistic status has been increasingly challenged or confronted by Chinese consumers and institutions. Lack of competition has resulted in high prices, few choices, and low service quality. Pressure, from both lower levels and upper authorities, has continually mounted on MPT to liberalize the market by relaxing its control for competition. In December 1998, MPT

---

[43] China's three major satellite communications operators are China Communications and Broadcast Satellite Corporation, China Eastern Communications Co. Ltd., and Xin Nuo Satellite Communications Co. Ltd.

[44] Two companies that offer this service are JiTong and Zhong Yuan Financial Datacom Ltd.

vetoed the suggestion for a geographical or geographical-functional split off of China Telecom[45] and proposed a plan to restructure the monopoly player into four independent national operators along the service sectors of paging, wireless mobile, fixed wireline, and satellite communications. In March 1999, the State Council approved this restructuring proposal to split China Telecom, but the initial State Council endorsement was only given to paging and mobile sectors. The restructuring implementation was scheduled for completion by the end of 1999, but it has lingered well into the year 2000. Upon the completion of this plan, China's major telecom network operators will include China Telecom, China Mobile Communications, China Unicom, China International Broadcast and Satellite Communications, JiTong Communications, China Network Communications, and possibly China Railway Communications.[46] All of these companies are presently state owned and they perform under the auspices of the State Council's "Leading Committee for Large State Enterprise."

In June 2000, China drafted some new regulations that intend to encourage more competition in the communications market by treating China's domestic telecom firms with different policy measures. More established companies with larger market shares will be subject to more strict government regulations on their market performance, while smaller and newer players will be given more freedom and access to market entry.[47] Unfair and predatory practices of the dominant companies are to be officially targeted and regulated.

---

[45] Argumentation against this scheme is that geographical split will weaken the country's telecom competitiveness, especially when foreign players enter the market and harm incentives to develop remote and rural services which require higher investment but have lower or no returns.

[46] China's national wireline and wireless mobile companies declared their official establishment in April 2000, with Zhou Deqian, former vice minister of MPT-MII, and Zhang Ligui, former China Telecom's president, appointed general managers for these two telecom groups.

[47] Some non-state companies in Beijing, Shanghai and Guangdong have indicated that they are financially prepared to enter mobile, Internet and value-added services market once they are allowed and the problem of network interconnection with China Telecom is solved.

The government also plans to divide telecom firms into two categories. One, those who own and operate communication networks. They must be legally established enterprises in which the State has majority shares. Two, those who provide services on communication networks. These firms are not subject to the specific requirement of the State control.

The paging company "Guo Xin," which used to be part of China Telecom, will be merged into China Unicom. China Telecom will become a national wireline services carrier, with more than 500,000 staff, operating local and long-distance voice and data communications, as well as managing the country's backbone networks, while China Mobile Communications will act as the nation's largest wireless mobile service provider with more than 100,000 employees. The immediate issues these two companies will have to address are traffic harmonization between wireline and wireless networks, and the determination of network interconnection or lease fees. China's satellite operator will be composed of current China Satellite Communication and Broadcast Corporation, which used to be under China Telecom, and China Oriental Satellite Communication Ltd., which is still a business entity of the military supported Baoli Group.

Because of the rapid technology and network convergence, the initial division of service areas for each of these companies can hardly be maintained. As a result, these companies will most likely go across the predetermined service borders and compete head to head. The restructured China Telecom, for instance, is already aggressively seeking for a wireless mobile license to compete with China Mobile Communications, even though its official mission is providing fixed line telephony and data services. These six or seven players may in 21st century create a new competitive marketplace figuratively referred to as China's ancient "Warring States." Some of the services they operate will be divided or specialized, while others will be overlapped and competitive with one another. It is until then that China's telecom monopoly by China Telecom will be broken in a real sense, and most of the service areas including international and domestic long-distance telecom services will be opened for domestic, as well as international competition.[48] The official objectives behind the China Telecom separation are obviously to break up China Telecom's monopoly, encourage competition, and prepare the Chinese telecom operators for the international competition that is ushered in with China's accession to the WTO. Public concerns, however, have surfaced that this initiative may not create a real competitive market, but may simply bring up new monopolies at sectorial levels, giving little or no benefit to the consumers.

The Internet "Stir-fry"

In the Internet arena, highly dynamic market forces are stirring up a structural change that has never occurred within China's communications and information industries. As a matter of life and death, some 500 robust ISPs presently compete for venture capitals, sales revenues, market share, and information resources among themselves and against traditional media. The "marriage" between China's ISPs/ICPs and financial institutions, both Chinese and foreign, and the fast trend in which telecom, computer, and media players all struggle to get involved in China's Internet marketplace are creating a more sophisticated industry scenario.[49]

In February 2000, China International Trust and Investment Corporation (CITIC), one of China's most high-profile financial institutions, announced that it had taken 10% strategic stake in ChinaWeb,[50] a leading online financial information and e-business

---

[48] Beijing Telecom Vice President Wang Fu Le stated in December 1999 that international telephone service would be open for competition in 2000 among the six major Chinese domestic players.

[49] *China Daily* reported in February 2000 that more than 700 news outlets in China had registered for online domain names and 270 China's news papers and journals had set up their own web sites for news release, but they tend to be slow in updates and inefficient in operations compared with the new born commercial ISPs/ICPs who are armed with better technologies and operate very efficiently to update information around the clock.

[50] ChinaWeb runs two popular financial information and e-business sites, i.e., Chinaweb.com in English and Homeway.com.cn in Chinese.

transaction firm. CITIC also indicated that it had made some other telecom deals including a joint project with US Lucent Technologies to develop CDMA systems in China and purchase of 60% stake of a joint venture involving acquisition of fiber optic networks from China's military forces for approximately US$250 million (Yahoo News, Feb. 13, 2000). At about the same time, Legend Holdings Ltd., China's largest computer company, released its plans to acquire foreign and Chinese Internet service providers via mergers, buyouts, and other forms to launch web services and business-to-business electronic commerce (e-commerce).

While China's Internet online services face a strong competition from the traditional media such as newspapers, radio broadcast, and television, they have posed a growing challenge to their strong "older brothers" who are trying to protect their positions by launching their own network information services, or by reaching alliances with ISPs/ICPs. To safeguard and empower the official information flagships, the Chinese government decided in February 2000 to provide funding and network support to the web development of the five state central media organizations including Xinhua News Agency (*xinhua.org*), *China Daily* (*chinadaily.com.cn*), *People's Daily* (*peopledaily.com.cn*), China Internet Network Information Center (*china.org.cn*), and China Radio International (*cri.com.cn*).[51] Government financial support may come directly from the state budgetary allocation, or through a government share holding mechanism. The online services of the state controlled media, however, are encouraged to operate financially independent of their

---

[51] *China Daily*, the China's official English paper, set up its web page in 1995. It claimed to have six million web hits per month in March 2000. The web site received US$1.5 million by 1999 from the state government to fund its operations. Funding has increasingly become a serious issue and the management has decided to develop two sections for the official news and information release and for commercial business. The latter is positioned to invite foreign investment. Radio China International is fully government funded, non-commercial radio broadcasting service with more than 30 news reporting bases and programs in 43 languages. China.org.cn serves the State Council's News Office. It is also a non-profit, non-commercial government function.

parents, set up cooperative partnerships with other ISPs/ICPs, and absorb foreign capital when permitted. To this end, state and Beijing municipal government organizations[52] pushed in March 2000 for the launching of a new official online multimedia portal, "Twenty-first Century Dragon News Network" (www.21DNN.com) which taps into information resources of Beijing's nine top media groups, namely, *Beijing Daily*, Beijing Youth Daily, Beijing Morning Daily, Beijing Evening News, Beijing Economic Daily, Beijing TV Station, Beijing Radio Station, Beijing Cable Broadcasting Station and Beijing Broadcasting and TV Weekly. The network operation is endorsed to Sparkice Information Technology Co. and Beijing Si Hai Hua Ren international. Shanghai, in the same mode, has launched its www.Eastday.com.cn site which has the support from both the government and local newspaper and media. This strategic move among rising Internet players and traditional media will considerably affect the structure of China's communications and information market.

Evolving Communications Infrastructure

General Background:

China has four large communication networks at work: (1) MPT's extensive nationwide public networks; (2) Chinese Military Forces' (People's Liberation Army) specialized networks; (3) Nationwide television and broadcast networks operated by China's TV and radio broadcast sector; (4) Ministry of Railway's dedicated networks, with 1999 assets totaling US$10 billion.[53] In addition, about 70 long-distance private/dedicated networks and close to 3000 local private

---

[52] These government organizations include the Propaganda Department of the Chinese Communist Party, State News Agency and Beijing Municipal Government.

[53] In comparison, China Unicom's network assets in 1999 were only about US$2 billion in value.

networks are in operation. Private networks have a considerable amount of spare capacity which can be utilized to supplement MPT's public networks. The debate in China has long focused on how this spare capacity can be utilized: should it be allowed for commercial public services that compete with China Telecom, should it be confined to dedicated use only, or should it be brought under MPT's control if allowed to offer public services?

China's public communication networks are designed, built, and managed by MPT and its PTAs at inter-provincial, provincial, prefecture, and county levels. Funds for the network development, operation, and maintenance are raised mainly from MPT and PTA sources, or from local government budgets or commercial bank loans. MPT public networks consist of basic backbone networks (PSTN and ISDN, *e.g.,* China PAC, China DDN and ChinaNET) for long-distance voice, telegram, fax, data, and video transmissions, local telecom networks, and support and management networks to enhance network functionality and performance, and to improve overall transmission qualities. With the introduction of new technologies from abroad, China's public networks have undergone dramatic changes in both quantity and quality. Fiber optic cables have been replacing the symmetrical cables and coaxial cables. 98.6% and 99% of long-distance transmission and central office switching systems were digitized in 1998.[54] In the same year, the fixed assets of China's public communication networks accounted for more than RMB600 billion yuan (US$72 billion). The figure climbed to approximately RMB800 billion yuan (US$96.4 billion) in 1999, dominantly out-weighing all other dedicated network assets. The value of China Telecom's public network assets was only surpassed by that of China's television and broadcast networks which accounted for almost US$200 billion.[55]

MPT-China Telecom runs both national and local public communications networks while dedicated networks are usually built and operated by different government organizations and industry

---

[54] Source: MPT's official report.

[55] Source: Reports by MPT and the Ministry of Radio, Films and Television.

entities, with or without MPT's technical assistance or supervision.[56] Most important dedicated network operators include China's armed forces, railway industry, electric power plants, financial and banking sector, air and space industry, petroleum industry, transportation firms, foreign trade enterprises, customs control, taxation administration, public security agencies, CCTV, Xinhua News Agency, and the State Information Center. In 1997-1998, long-distance dedicated networks had a combined data transmission capacity more than that of the MPT-controlled China Telecom's, but their telephone (voice) transmission capacity was only about 10% of the MPT's. This capacity situation has changed significantly since both China Telecom and dedicated network operators have upgraded their technologies and expanded their network capacities. The relationship between public and dedicated networks is in principle defined as that of cooperation and coordination, but in reality, conflicts of interest have often occurred with regard to network construction, interconnection, tariffs, and applications.

Fiber Optic Backbone Networks

By 1999, China had built up about 213,000 km of broadband (PDH144Mbps or SDH 2.5 Gbps) fiber optic trunk networks of 22 main lines, which accounts for approximately 75% of the country's long distance circuits. These fiber optic trunk lines connect all

---

[56] In response to the SWIFT network system used by many multinational banks, China's financial and banking industry has engaged in developing a national financial network (CNFN) using Java, ActiveX, DCOM (Distributed Component Object Model), and other advanced technologies to provide services for business-to-business online electronic commerce, stock exchange, bank settlement, and various financial transactions. The CNFN project is a joint venture between MPT and six China's major state banks,[56] in cooperation with AsiaInfo, a Sino-US systems integrator and software developer. The project is managed by Zhong Yuan Financial Data Network Co. The network's Frame Relay backbone connected over 200 cities, it was planned to reach 400 cities by 1999.

provincial capitals, 95% of the major cities and regions, and 50% of the lower-level counties.[57]

Meanwhile, China has been building international submarine and underground optical fiber networks, in an effort to satisfy the surging demand for international telecommunications. China-US Trans-Pacific Submarine Cable Project,[58] with an investment of approximately US$1.1 billion, initially involved the cooperation of about 14 big international telecom companies from China, the United States, Canada, Japan, Republic of Korea, Malaysia, Indonesia, Australia, Taiwan, Hong Kong, and Singapore. Upon its planned completion by December 1999, the 30,000 km, 80-gigabits-per-second digital optical fiber cable will provide about 960,000 telecom circuits[59] for transnational communication services.[60] This project is an indicator of China becoming a principal player in building trans-ocean submarine network systems involving multinational efforts.

---

[57] China reported in September 1998 that it had installed 820,000 km of fiber optic cables, of which 150,000 km is long distance trunks. 2.5 Gbps SDH technology is used for the trunks.

[58] Contracted network suppliers include Alcatel Submarine Networks, Fujitsu Ltd., KDD Submarine Cable Systems, NEC Corp., and Tyco Submarine Systems Ltd. The cable will contain 4 main segments: (1) Northern TransPacific, linking Bandon, Ore., to Chongming, China, with additional landing points in South Korea and Japan; (2) Southern, linking San Luis Obispo, CA, to Shantou, China, with additional landing points in Okinawa, and Guam; (3) Eastern, connecting the Bandon and San Luis Obispo US landing points; and (4) Western, connecting the Shantou and Chongming China landing points. Tyco, Alcatel, and Fujitsu will jointly supply the southern and eastern segments. KDD-SCS and NEC will jointly supply the northern and western segments.

[59] This capacity is enough to handle 4 million phone calls simultaneously. China's total international fiber optic capacity after the year 2000 will be more than 100 Gbps.

[60] This cable system will be owned and operated by AT&T, China Telecom, Hong Kong Telecom, KDD, Korea Telecom, MCI, KDD, NTT, SBC, SingTel, Sprint, Teleglobe USA, Chunghwa Telecom (of Taiwan), Telekom Malaysia, and Telstra. Additional 30 companies have signed the construction and maintenance agreement as non-voting capacity owners.

Since 1989, China has joined hands with other countries in developing several international optical fiber networks, such as China-Japan cable system between Shanghai and Miyazaki; China-Korea cable system between Qingdao and Taean; SEA-ME-WE 3, linking Europe, Asia, and Oceania; the Trans-Asia-Europe (TAE) ground cable network starting from Shanghai and expands all the way to Frankfurt; and the ground fiber optical cable that connects China, Vietnam, Laos, Thailand, Malaysia, and Singapore.

Deployment of fiber optic technology has significantly upgraded China's network transmission capacities and speed, and laid a good basis for network digitalization.[61] Major satellite earth stations grew from 6 in 1992 to 40 in 1997, offering a wide range of wireless network connections. With the operation of three national backbone telecommunications networks, China's availability to offer public data communications services for market activities and business transactions is considerably expanded and strengthened. These three backbone networks are:

1. *ChinaPAC*: a packet switching data communications network composed of fiber optic cables and backed up by satellite communications networks. It covers more than 90% of the Chinese cities and counties above the township level, and has been connected with 44 packet switching networks in 23 countries and regions. Its international gateways are established in Beijing, Shanghai, and Guangzhou, and its network management center is located in Beijing. Tandem offices are set up in seven other major Chinese cities. ChinaPAC has provided leased lines for more than 20 central government organizations to build their national dedicated networks for data transmission and value-added services such as E-Mail, EDI, and Videotex.

---

[61] For instance, relay stations needed for optic-fiber cables are 100-120 kilometers apart, while older technologies require relay stations be built every 6-8 kilometers along the transmission lines.

2. *ChinaDDN:* an optic fiber-based public digital data network which has connected all the provincial capitals and major cities. With more than 70,000 ports in 500 cities and a capacity of 776 circuits of 2.048Mbps, it provides leased digital circuits with 2.4Kb/s to 2Mb/s for frame relay, compressed voice/G3, fax, virtual private networks (VPN), and teleconferencing services. ChinaDDN will connect 2000 cities and act as a platform for China's public switched data networks and for various private networks that need to perform digital data transmission.

3. *ChinaNET:* China's MPT controlled commercial data transmission network connected with the global Internet. It is planned, constructed, operated, and managed by the MPT's Data Communications Bureau. The network is connected with ChinaPAC and ChinaDDN, interfaced by both English and Chinese languages, and has 8 management centers and 31 key nodes across the country. The initial ChinaNET public services were launched in May 1995. The subscribers can have access to worldwide Internet for E-mail, UseNet News, Global Telnet, file transfer protocol (FTP), Gopher, the World Wide Web (WWW), Archie, and wide area information server (WAIS) services.

Wireless Mobile Networks

Since China launched its mobile telecom services on analogue networks in 1987, the average growth rate of subscription has been over 150% per year.[62] Wireless mobile network development has been

---

[62] Between 1998 and 1999, more than 10 million new mobile phone subscribers were added annually. In 2000, about 25 million mobile phone users and more than 18 million fixed line users are projected to sign up for services. Mobile phone users in Beijing, Guangzhou, Shanghai and Wuhan may soon surpass fixed line users. By 1999, China's GSM network had become the world largest while mobile phone users had become the third largest, next to the U.S. and Japan.

strikingly fast. Coverage has spread to most of the Chinese cities. Paging service has realized a nationwide roaming, with over 38 million users by 1996. In early 1996, MPT adopted Motorola's high-speed *Flex* system as the national paging standard. At about the same time, Motorola (System A) and Ericsson (System B) analogue systems of cellular phones were connected, representing the making of the largest analogue cellular networks in the world. In December 1997, China Telecom signed an agreement with Lucent Technologies to jointly construct a public wireless data network backbone, which would initially have three principal nodes located in Beijing, Shanghai, and Guangzhou. The network adopts cellular digital packet data (CDPD) technology that is based on TCP/IP protocol with an open platform and interface.

By 1999, all the big and medium-sized Chinese cities, plus 96% of the counties and towns, had been covered by a system of wireless mobile networks (GSM900, DCS1800 digital, TACS analog, and trial CDMA) operated by China Telecom, China Unicom, and Great Wall Communications. Total switching capacity of the mobile phone network exceeded 60 million lines. Network capacity growth in the year 2000 and beyond is predicted to be around 20 million lines per year. To meet China's growing need for wireless access to Internet, China Telecom in early 2000 initiated the construction of China's national wireless access protocol (WAP) based backbone network (CMNET), which would cover majority of the Chinese cities and regions, with a 155 Mbps x 3 bandwidth international gateway, to offer virtual private network (VPN), general packet radio system (GPRS)[63] and other wireless mobile Internet access and data transmission services. With WAP network in place, users of mobile phones (e.g., Nokia 7110, Motorola A6188 and L2000www, Ericsson R320 and R380, and Siemens C35 and S35), pagers, personal digital assistants (PDAs), and palm-sized personal computers (PPCs) will be

---

[63] GPRS enables the current GSM system to upgrade toward the 3rd generation mobile. It raises the access speed from the current 9.6Kbps to 115Kbps. Users of GPRS do not need to dial up for connection, therefore, they pay less for online applications.

able to access online information[64] and value-added services via WAP-based websites such as "172" www.wap.chnmobile.net.

In 1998, China became one of the pioneering countries outside the United States to massively deploy dense wavelength division multiplexing (DWDM) technology across its major cities and regions. With the rapid growth of voice and data traffic and ever enlarged telecom and Internet subscriber base, plus the lowered tariffs resulting from competition, the demand for China's communications infrastructure, both wired and wireless, has continually increased.

China's Near-term Network Development Focus

1. Cross-country backbone public switched telephone networks (PSTNs) and local access networks (including ADSL, N-ISDN, and Cable Modem technologies) digitally transmitted and switched.
2. Wireless mobile networks, with analog mobile networks interconnected for nationwide roaming, GSM (Global System for Mobile Communications) digital networks gradually expanded and interconnected for automatic roaming. GSM/SCDMA dual applications and R&D of the Third Generation wireless mobile systems have been on the official agenda.
3. Public packet-switched data networks (*e.g.,* ChinaPAC, ChinaDDN).
4. Narrow-band integrated services digital networks (N-ISDN), which will be integrated with PSTN and public-switched data networks.
5. Intelligent networks (INs), aimed for nationwide services.
6. An advanced communications support system to provide services and support for the operations of PSTN, N-ISDN, and IN which is expected to significantly improve the management of networks at both national and regional levels.

---

[64] Charges for this service will include three parts: phone line use, Internet access and online information browse.

7. Fiber optic networks and systems for long-distance and local telecom transmissions (4x2.5Gb/s or 8x2.5Gb/s). International communications network based on submarine fiber-optic and satellite communication technologies.

8. Broadband digital networks for multimedia and interactive applications, deploying the technologies of asynchronous transfer mode (ATM) switching, synchronous digital hierarchy (SDH) transmission, dense wavelength division multiplexing (DWDM, e.g., 32x2.5Gb/s), and Internet Protocol (IP).

Despite the fast-expanding coverage of the networks, the communications infrastructure in China faces many critical issues. Operating productivity and efficiency are siginificantly low. According to the MII study, China's ratio of network output and input averages only 1.14 to 1, lower than the US ratio of 7.7 to 1 and the world average of 3.3 to 1. With only 40% of the installed transmission capacity being employed, China's network capacity is strikingly underused, as compared with the world average of 70-80%. Uncoordinated installation of network and equipment systems has created problems in network structure, interconnectivity, delays of project implementation, compatibility among different systems, and high rate of connection errors. These problems are most apparent with ISDN, X.25, DDN, VPN, ATM platforms and frame relay networks and their applications.

Internet Initiatives

Status Review

China's major initiatives to build its global Internet-linked networks are launched and funded by key research institutions and government organizations. China Telecom, Chinese Academy of Sciences, China JiTong Communications Corp., China Netcom, China Unicom, and some key Chinese universities under the Chinese Ministry of Education have constructed and operated China's Internet backbone networks designated as CHINANET, CSTNET, CHINAGBN, CERNET, CNCNET and UNINET. CSTNET and CERNET are operated on non-commercial terms, while CHINANET, CHINAGBN, CNCNET and UNINET are authorized to market Internet services to institutional and individual subscribers or lease lines to smaller Internet service providers. In October 1999, China Netcom (CNCNET) was officially added to China's big Internet player's list. Growth over the past three years in China's Internet network capacity (international gateways), domain names, connected computers, WWW sites and overall subscription were all extremely phenomenal (Data based on China Internet Network Information Center's reports):

International Gateway Capacity (Mbps)[65]

	2000[66]	1999	1998	1997[67]
CHINANET	711	291	123	18.768

[65] Their outgoing lines link China with U.S.A., Germany, England, France, Japan, Korea, Australia, and Hong Kong. China plans to set up several domestic Internet data exchange centers to link the backbone networks of the major Internet providers due to the current slow traffic flow (at 2-8Mbps) between them, as compared with the traffic going through international gateways. Initially, traffic through these centers will be transported at 155 Mbps. Development of wireless mobile connection to Internet was also put on the official agenda in early 2000.

[66] All the listed data for 2000 was released by CNNIC in July 2000. CHINANET's total capacity consisted of 170Mbps for Beijing, 214Mbps for Shanghai and 327Mbps for Guangzhou. CHINAGBN's total capacity consisted of 49Mbps for Beijing, 12Mbps for Guangzhou and 8Mbps for Shengzhen. UNINET's total capacity consisted of 47Mbps for Shanghai and 8Mbps for Guangzhou. CNCNT of China Netcom was added to the calculation of China's Internet international gateway capacity but not listed as an entity here. Its total capacity was reported by CNNIC as 377Mbps consisting of 4Mbps for Beijing, 365Mbps for Shanghai and 8Mbps for Guangzhou. By then, China's international IP phone bandwidth was 56Mbps.

[67] 1997 data were collected in October, two months short. The same is true of other items listed for domain names, linked computers, WWW sites, and subscription.

	2000[66]	**1999**	**1998**	**1997**[67]
CHINAGBN	69	22	8.25	2.256
UNINET	55	20	N/A	N/A
CSTNET	10	10	4	2.128
CERNET	12	8	8	2.256
Total	1,234	351[68]	143.25	25.408

Domain Names
(including "com," "net," "gov," "org," "edu," "ac" and administrative divisions)

2000[69]	**1999**	**1998**	**1997**
99,734	48,965	18,396	4,066

Internet-linked Computers (million)

	Dialup	**Dedicated Line**	**Total**
2000	5.49	1.01	6.5
1999	3.09	0.41	3.5
1998	0.63	0.117	0.747
1997	0.25	0.049	0.299

WWW Sites

2000	**1999**	**1998**	**1997**
27,289	15,153	5,300	1,500

---

[68] CHINAGBN reportedly expanded its network gateway capacity to 67 Mbps in April 2000. A Chinese official stated in January 2000 that the total capacity of the international gateways would be expanded to more than 1000 Mbps in the near future.

[69] Chinese domain names were reported as 71,712 out of the 99,734 total in number.

Subscription[70] (million)

2000	1999	1998	1997
16.9	8.9	2.1	0.62

The most popular websites in China, according to the 1999-2000 surveys by China Internet Network Information Center (CNNIC) and *www.consult*, include Sina.com, Sohu.com, Yahoo, Netease (netease.com or 163.com), Capital Online (263.net), Chinabyte.com, China.com, Yeah, Shanghai Online (online.sh.cn), Guangzhou Xinfei (163.net), 169.net (China's public multimedia data network), CCTV.com, 21cn.com (Guangdong PTA) and cpcw.com.[71] China's Internet users are mostly aged between 18 and 35, college-educated, located densely in large urban areas, and are enthusiastic about exploiting the Web for e-mail communication, information browsing, research, and IP telephony. With the rise of the Internet applications in China and the increased competition among some 500 Chinese licensed ISPs,[72] there has been a increased demand for coordination and cooperation, through which ISPs can address critical issues, have their voices heard, and develop strategic relationships in a very competitive marketplace.

This demand for concerted efforts to establish important cooperation among ISPs and between ISPs and government agencies

---

[70] This figure takes account of the people having access to Internet connected computers, which covers shared users and online café surfers. The CNNIC indicated that, in 1999, about three fourths of the China's Internet users got access to Internet services via others who have networked computers, and that more than 50% of the users were in scientific research and academic areas, and only 25.3% of the users access Internet through their home PCs. Annual growth of subscription was more than 300% between 1996 and 1999. In the first part of 2000, however, about 60% of the surfers often accessed the Web through their PCs at home. China had 65.1 million e-mail accounts at work in the first part of 2000.

[71] These numbers are both web addresses and telephone numbers by dialing which users get access to the Internet services.

[72] ICPs were mostly not registered then.

led to an ISP alliance in April 1999 among major Internet service providers. Challenges between ISPs and traditional media in China also brought about serious concerns and requirements for cooperation. In February 2000, major Chinese ISPs and media organizations joined hands in making a declaration for multi-lateral consensus and strategic partnerships. Thirty six ISPs and media organizations signed up for the document, among which Sina, Sohu, Netease, Chinabyte, China.com, Beijing Online, 8848.net, Kunpeng, Legend FM365, China Infobank, Xinhua, ChinaNews, CCTV, Radio China International, *Guangming Daily*, *China Daily*, *Science and Technology Daily*, and *Beijing Daily* were taking the lead.

Issues of Concern

MPT views Internet applications in China similarly to that of telecom services. That is, China should build up a state (MPT) controlled multi-media backbone infrastructure,[73] with information content primarily in the Chinese language. Non-MPT Internet service providers are supplementary to MPT's operations and may eventually wither away because of China Telecom's strong position. Many Chinese government organizations under the State Council think differently. They prefer to see the growth of a multiple Internet network and services environment in which MPT does not play monopoly.

Major bottlenecks to Internet applications in China include the working language, interface, low networked PC density, network capacity, transmission speed, last-mile access connection, data security, cross-cultural compatibility of the content, on-line information resources, and high access charges.[74] Among these, low

---

[73] MPT established a multi-media bureau in 1997 to make plans for the Chinese intranet. China Public Multimedia Information Network (169) is the start of China's broadband communications backbone operated by MPT's Datacom Bureau. It is designed to offer Chinese information resources within China.

[74] MPT's charges for Internet services are higher than many advanced countries or regions such as USA, UK, and Hong Kong, even if the rates have been reduced a number of times since 1998. China's rates for Internet use was again officially

transmission speed (especially local access lines), high usage charges, and relative shortage of online Chinese information resources are ranked on the top. Three factors account for slow dial-up Internet access in China: less standardized website designs and installations by the ISPs, slow operation of the local servers, and the very narrow bandwidth of the "curbside-to-home" links, which works through the old-fashioned copper lines connecting homes to fiber-optic long-distance backbones. Upgrading these "last-mile" connections by ADSL, ISDN, or other technologies is costly in labor and capital. Policy and regulatory issues involved in institutional coordination for network access and management, pricing for leased lines and services, cost and revenue accounting, and network security and oversight also have a significant impact on China's Internet development.

Increasingly, confusions in China's ISPs/ICPs have surfaced because of (1) the corporate structural complexity of the ISPs/ICPs that are either China-based (headquartered in mainland China), such as Sina, Netease, and 21cn, or China oriented (content focused on China, but headquartered outside mainland China), such as China.com (Hong Kong), ChinaWeb.com (Hong Kong), VirtualChina.com (U.S.A.) and ChinaOnline.com (U.S.A.). (2) Political and regulatory battles among different ISPs/ICPs (state-own or private) in a rush of getting their shares listed in the stock market.[75]

---

reduced in 1999. Even so, a 30-hour web search per month on the Net still cost US$25, almost one quarter of the Chinese average monthly income. Since late 1999, China has charged $0.5/hour for dialup Internet access, plus US$0.25/hour rate for the cost of phone line use, which totaled US$0.75/hour for Internet deployment. In comparison, U.S. citizens are charged approximately US$15-20 per month for unlimited Internet access.

[75] China's Internet portals engaged in going public for IPOs in NASDAQ or HK GEM market include Sina, Sohu, Netease, 8848.com, Chinadotcom, Sparkice, Zhaodaola, Etang, Eachnet, Jiaodian, Alibaba, Yabuy, Zhaoyin, ChinaWeb/Homeway, Yinghaiwei, Elong, Chinaren, MeetChina, Legend, Dangdang, Chinanet.com, and China Economic Information Network of the State Information Center.

Currently, companies registered and operating in China (foreign funded businesses included) intending to go for initial public offering must meet the strict requirements set by China Securities Exchange Commission (CSEC), such as earning profits for three consecutive years and having approximately US$48 million worth of net assets. ICPs/ISPs planning to be listed must also have the approval from the Ministry of Information Industry besides the CSEC. MII said in March 2000 that Internet firms planning to go public overseas must have their content-related assets and business separated first. To avoid China's strict regulation on public listing abroad, Sina, Netease, Sohu and some other Internet portals have tactically had their companies registered abroad.[76] (3) Regulatory and security concerns as a result of booming individual homepages that use free space provided by big ISPs to post information online and the growing use of proxy servers and overseas e-mail accounts to bypass China's official oversight.[77] (4) Emerging issues of online content fabrication, business dispute, copyright infringement and intellectual property rights violation.

To facilitate and coordinate the making and implementation of Internet-related policies and regulations, the State Council established a special cross-ministerial leading group called the State Council Informatization Leading Group in early 1996 and then China Internet Network Information Center (CNNIC). The leading group is charged with the nation's Internet related policy making power, and CNNIC, located in the Chinese Academy of Sciences, has the jurisdiction to offer domain name registration and other Internet related information services. The State Council Leading Group is set to address critical Internet issues and propose corresponding Internet policies and

---

[76] China's 1998 directive on firms going IPO abroad did not have specific rules on IT enterprises operating in China but registered abroad. Sina and Netease had part of their assets registered in Cayman Islands of UK. Sohu did the same in Delaware of the U.S. These three firms all have a significant amount of financial resources from international venture capital.

[77] According to CNNIC's report, about 100 China's ISPs provided free space in 1999 for individuals to have their own homepages which could be used for information posting, and a considerable number of the Chinese Internet surfers had developed their personal web pages and were able to deploy proxy servers.

regulations whereas the Ministry of Public Security, the Ministry of State Security, State Administration of Radio, Films and TV (SARFT), and their local organizations are officially charged for network security and online content inspection.[78]

As China Telecom operates most of the Internet related networks and CHINANET takes over 90% of the country's market share, China's Internet market is apparently distorted and market power is unduly concentrated in the hand of China Telecom. Because of the exorbitant charges on leased lines or access fees by China Telecom, most of the China's ISPs (IAPs and ICPs) have been operating with a deficit, since about 70% of their revenues has to be paid for the expenses of using China Telecom's lines. Plus, the current subscriber base for each of non-China Telecom ISPs is quite small, far from that of a critical mass required to generate profits on the basis of the economies of scale. Some ISPs, in order to cut down costs, have tried to lease dedicated networks with unused capacity, or have affiliated with China Telecom to act as CHINANET's sales agents for 169/163 services. Many of these ISPs struggle to survive through posting online advertisements, or conducting projects on web page design, technical consulting, and virtual private network (VPN) development. "To be or not to be," a philosophical question asked by Hamlet, has now turned to a realistic challenge to China's ISP management. Closures, mergers and acquisitions of China's ISPs may soon become more of a norm than an exception.

Because of the high per-minute charges, average web surfers in China had to spend RMB200-300 yuan (US$25-38) per month, which was almost one third of the Chinese average salary. This provoked widespread complaints and led to a group of net users to organize a one-day mass boycott in January 1999, an event that had never occurred in China's telecom history. The boycotters appealed to the government to check out the situation and requested that (1) all unfair charges be eliminated and access fees and phone rates be reduced; (2)

---

[78] On December 30, 1997, Chinese Ministry of Public Security issued a State-Council- approved regulation on security and protection of China Internet-linked networks, endorsing itself as the supervisor and enforcer of the regulation.

transparency of billing processes be improved; and (3) internationally recognized practices regarding telecom and Internet charges be enforced. This consumer effort worked. In February 1999, MPT slashed Internet access fees by half and lowered call rates significantly. However, pricing and rate structure remains an important issue that needs to be further addressed.

Impact of Technology on the Society

With rapid innovation of technologies, wireless access to Internet (e.g., via WAP cell phones), and mobile phone banking have been rolled out in China. Internet telephony and Internet fax are emerging from a potential competitor to a real threat to China Telecom's traditional monopoly in local and long distance services. Although officially designated IP phone service providers are China Telecom, China Unicom, JiTong, and China Netcom, non-MPT operators in several Chinese cities have tried to offer IP-based phone and fax services to customers.[79] The restructured China Telecom (fixed line services oriented) and China Mobile are both looking at the IP phone service as an important area for market competition. IP telephony has, in fact, created one of the most competitive playing fields in China's telecom market because of its adcantages in higher utilization of switching and transmission resources, lower costs of installation and operation, and less sophisticated network management.[80]

In January 1999, two brothers in Fuzhou, Fujian Province, who used their own facilities to offer long distance IP-based call service at

---

[79] In 1999, China Telecom tried IP telephony in 25 cities, while Unicom and JiTong each picked 12 cities for the trial. Rates charged by IP phone services were only about one third of the conventional phone services, that is, RMB 0.30/min vs. RMB1.00/min for domestic long-distance calls, and RMB4.80/min vs. RMB12.00-15.00/min for international calls. MPT-MII regards IP telephony as basic telecom service and therefore it must be regulated accordingly.

[80] IP telephony is a packet-switched service with much higher utilization of the network resources. Its costs for switching equipment, billing system, and overall operation are significantly lower than conventional circuit switched services.

a rate only one third of what China Telecom charged, were caught and convicted. MPT declared that all phone services in China fall under its exclusive authorization, public provision of phone services via Internet by any operators without MPT licenses is illegal "information smuggling," therefore, must be cracked down with a firm hand. Fuzhou Intermediate People's Court of Appeal later overturned the local court's conviction by saying that no Chinese laws or regulations were yet established to give China Telecom exclusive authorization for Internet phone services. This court decision is significant because it is the first time ever that a Chinese court stands up and rules against a Chinese ministry. The event breaks the tradition in China that court rulings are made under government guidelines to serve government policies, not to contradict or confront them. The case is also an indicator that new technologies can challenge existing government regulations and lead China toward adopting into a new regulatory environment.

Internet applications have fostered a vigorous growth of Internet culture in China. As information transported through Internet is based on multimedia and interactive in nature, Chinese people have responded to Internet with wide acceptance and high enthusiasm. Mainstream Chinese printing and television entities have quickly made their presence online to expand or update their service arms, holding no reservation in aggressively competing with emerging ISPs/ICPs. Many Chinese websites have shown an impressive degree of openness, richness, and creativeness in content development, which seems to discredit commentaries of the foreign press on China's strict online information censorship.

Information on China's websites has an extensive encyclopedic coverage ranging from news, economics, politics, law, history, science, technology, entertainment, health, arts, literature, education, religion, business, travel, references, computing, world knowledge, military studies, community service, to electronic commerce. These information resources tend to be distinctively Chinese oriented, even though they contain information from abroad. This, as some studies point out, may imply that the content preference of the Chinese netizens is fundamentally rooted in Chinese cultural values and outlooks, not easily "westernized." Globalization of economy and increased information exchange do not seem to shake or erode the Chinese mentality for cultural and spiritual independence. Multinational Internet service providers, such as America Online and Yahoo, may have to remodel their content resources after the Chinese socio-cultural traits, if they want to enter China and establish their market position there in Internet services.

Track Record

In retrospect, China's Internet-linked milestone networks evolved as follows:

- On September 20, 1987, Qian Tienbai, Head of China's Academic Network (CANET), successfully sent the first electronic mail (at 300bps) through the networks of Italian ITAPAC and German DATEXDP from China to Germany. CANET was a joint project between Beijing Computer Application Institute and German Karlruhe University. CANET began operations in 1988, marking China's earliest network connection with the global Internet. CANET provided E-mail and data transfer services using X.25 technology.
- In 1989, China's State Planning Commission, State Science and Technology Commission, and the World Bank jointly launched a project called *National Computing and Networking Facilities of China* (NCNFC), which aimed at the development of one national supercomputer center and three campus networks, i.e. China Academic and Science Network (CASnet), Qinghua University Network, and Beijing University Network to share their computing facilities in a high speed network environment. These networks were upgraded in 1994 by deploying 64 Kbps satellite technology via the Sprint international router for full Internet access to users. NCNFC was the first high-speed network project, centered in CAS (Chinese Academy of Science). The network later evolved into China's Science and Technology

network (CSTNET), which served more than 120 research institutions under CAS and 200 other research organizations in China by 1999. NCNFC was planned to connect three campus networks, but it later became a hub linkage of the following networks:

- CASnet (Chinese Academy of Science Network)
- Bnet (Beijing University Network)
- Qnet (Qinghua University Network)
- Canet (Chinese Academic Network)
- CRNet (China Research Network)
- IHEPnet (Institute of High Energy Physics of CAS)
- SSTCnet (State Science and Technology Commission network)
- CERNet (Chinese Ecosystem Research Network)
- USTCnet (University of Science & Technology of China campus network)
- NFCwan (National Flood Control wide area network)
- MEFnet (China National Research Center for Marine Environment Forecast)
- BSTISnet (Beijing Science & Technology Information Society)
- IMnet (Institute of Microbiology of CAS)
- Shanghai Regional Network
- Wuhan Regional Network

- *Network of High Energy Physics Institute, Chinese Academy of Sciences,* (HEPINET): HEPINET was initiated in 1993 between China's High Energy Physics Institute and a counterpart research center at Stanford University, USA. Stanford leased a 64Kbps satellite communications network from AT&T and had it connected with CHINAPAC in Beijing. When the US government approved the export of Cisco routers to China in 1994, HEPI also gained the permission to use ESNET in California, which enabled the institute to become connected with Internet. In July 1994, the network was reconnected to a 64Kbps satellite communications channel run by Japanese International Telecommunications. The transmission then was performed via the network of Japan's national high-energy physics lab (KEK) and relayed to the US by a 512Kbps network (or vice versa). Services available at HEPIN include E-mail, Telnet, FTP, FINDER Service, WWW, Gopher, Archie, TALK, and VERONICA and JUGHEAD.

- *China Research Network* (CRNET): CRNET was built in 1990. This network also uses X.25 link to exchange information with the outside world via RARE. There are more than ten research entities connected by CRN. CRN works via an European research network. The network uses X.400 standard, and has 9 network centers located in Beijing (two research institutes under former Ministry of Electronics Industry or MEI), Shanghai (Shanghai Transportation University and Fudan University), Shijiazhuan (MEI 54th Research Institute), Chengdu (MEI 30th Research Institute), and Nanjing Southeast University. The network, linked to Internet through a research institution in Germany (DFN), provides X.400 (MHS) electronic mail, FTAM file transfer, and X.500 directory services.

- *China Education and Research Network* (CERNET): Funded by the Chinese government and managed by the State Education Commission, China initiated a nationwide education and research network (CERNET) project in December 1993, with an objective to build a national backbone network to have all the Chinese universities, research institutes, and most of the schools connected with one another and with the global Internet by the year 2000. CERNET is centered in Qinghua University, Beijing. Its backbone consists of ten key universities which are mutually connected via CHINAPAC (X.25) and extends out to campus networks of China's universities and colleges. Its link to Internet is primarily through NCNFC linked to US Sprint 128Kbps line, a Global One 2Mbps line, and 64Kbps lines of German DFN, Japanese ITJ, and Hong Kong Telecom.

CERNET is co-constructed by Chinese Academy of Sciences, Beijing University, and Qinghua University under the State Education Commission CERNET Leading Group. It was connected to Internet through US Sprint satellite communications network in July 1994. It is now one of the most influential Chinese Internet linked networks because of its rapid growth in users and in database services. CERNET has established, in addition to its national center in Beijing, 8 regional network centers in China, and is planned to connect 1090 Chinese universities, 39,412 secondary schools, and 160,000 primary schools in the foreseeable future.[81] It uses 3 international communications networks (at the speed of 64Kbps, 128Kbps, and 2Mbps) for Internet connection via North American, European (DFNET in Germany), and Asia-Pacific (HARNET in Hong Kong) network gateways.

- *Golden Bridge Network* run by JiTong Corporation[82] (GBNET): To serve the need for state macro-economic control, and to facilitate the sharing of national economic and social information among China's government agencies and business enterprises, GBNET was launched in 1993 with initial funding of US$3 million from a special pool of funding under the Chinese premier's control. It was officially considered as the key national public economic information infrastructure authorized to connect to Internet via a US Sprint 256Kbps line. GBNET is designed as a hybrid computer information network based primarily on satellite networks and terrestrial optic fiber networks interconnecting many other Chinese private networks or virtual networks. Deploying ISDN, Frame Relay, MUX/IDR at 2-8Mbps, and wireless data technologies, GBNET provides diverse

---

[81] By 1999, more than 300 universities and colleges in China had been connected by CERNET.

[82] JiTong Communications Co., with 26 major shareholders, takes charge for the planning, development, operation and management of GBNET. JiTong was established by former Ministry of Electronics Industry. It offers Frame Relay, VPN, VSAT, IP-telephony, and Internet access services.

services, including voice, data, image, IP telephony, E-mail, EDI, online information, electronic emulation, and multimedia, to more than 24 provinces and cities. GBNET has been interconnected with CERNET, State Information Center, Information Center of State Economic and Trade Commission, and National Electronic Press Service Center. In 1998, users of the GBNET services included central and local government organizations, business enterprises, Sino-foreign joint ventures, sole foreign funded firms, media, and key universities and research institutions.[83]

- *China nationwide public network* (CHINANET) run by MPT-China Telecom: CHINANET is a MPT/China Telecom operated commercial Internet network. In 1994 MPT and US Sprint reached an agreement by which Sprint offered its international gateways to China Telecom for connecting China's package switch backbone with Internet. CHINANET is based on NCNFC backbone and has at present three international gateways located in Beijing, Guangzhou and Shanghai. The Beijing gateway is linked with Singapore (128Kbps), Japanese KDD (128 Kbps), U.S. Sprint (256Kbps-2Mbps) and U.S. MCI (2Mbps) while Shanghai gateway is connected with a Sprint 2Mbps line. In 1996, CHINANET began to provide users with DDN, X.25 and dialup access to worldwide Internet for E-mail, UseNet News, Global Telnet, File Transfer Protocol (FTP), Gopher, World Wide Web (WWW), Archie and wide area information server (WAIS) services. CHINANET quickly expanded its international bandwidth capacity from 18.8 Mbps in 1997, 291 Mbps in 1999, to 711Mbps in June 2000. CHINANET was interconnected with CASNET, CERNET, and GBNET in 1997.

---

[83] GBNET clients include, for example, IBM, BellSouth, Sprint, Softbank, and General Electric, *People's Daily*, Economic Daily, and China Infoworld. GBNET's access number for individual users is "167."

- *China Wide Web* (CWW) by China Internet Corporation of
  Xinhua News Agency: Xinhua Internet project is worth
  attention. Xinhua News Agency, China's official news
  authority, formed China Internet Corporation (CIC) in Hong
  Kong in 1995. CIC claims to have Sun Microsystems, Bay
  Networks, New World Infrastructure, Bechtel, Edelson
  Technology Partners, Mittsui & Co., Pointcast, Netscape,
  Oracle, IBM, Cisco Systems, Microsoft, Stone Rich Sight,
  and America Online as its shareholders or technology
  partners. CIC launched China Wide Web (*www.cww.com* and
  www.xinhua.org) in late 1996, aiming to provide an exclusive
  database of the Chinese and the world business information.
  CWW would also provide global e-mail and other services for
  Chinese and international users. CIC intended to become a
  leader in electronic on-line services in Asia, with an objective
  to bridge information gap between the Chinese businesses
  and the international business communities. The unique
  importance of CWW was revealed by the name itself: "China
  Wide Web," as the Chinese government once had a wishful
  hope to build a Chinawide Intranet, or a China specific
  network within the global Internet, to provide information
  online to Chinese audience in Chinese language within
  China's borders, not beyond.[84] Thus the side effect of
  deploying the global Internet might be warded off. Xinhua
  has business relations with Bloomberg, Reuters, Dun and

---

[84] A similar effort was made by Sichuan Zhongcheng Network Development Co.
Ltd. that rolled out China City Interconnected Network, or China C-Net. C-Net,
based on China's domestic network technology, was connected with over 4000
businesses and 60 cities in early 2000. It aimed at offering a nationwide, no
Internet connection, Chinese language information services for comprehensive
information broadcast, online tax return and e-commerce. In March 2000, C-Net
management was split off by the opposing opinions of whether C-Net should
maintain its original plan for independence or whether it should switch to an
Internet-connected network. Some Chinese experts from MII and academic
institutions argued to support C-Net's independence while others said that
having a China domestic network is inefficient and unnecessary.

Bradstreet, Nikkei, Thomson, First Call, Wen Hui Pao, Cnet, Cambridge Scientific Abstracts, and Financial Times. It is powerful not only as a Chinese media, but also as a government function. Over the past few years, Xinhua's stiff political position, however, seemed to have been loosened or somewhat eroded by its commercial interest.

- Ministry-backed ICPs: Along with China's Internet initiatives, some Chinese government organizations have taken steps to lease lines from telecom operators and offer information services either for the benefit of the society or for their own financial gains. China Economic Information Network (CEINET, *www.cei.gov.cn*) operated by the State Information Center of the State Development Planning Commission and ChinaInfo (*www.chinainfo.gov.cn*) endorsed by the Ministry of Science and Technology are two notable examples.

CEINET provides information on macro-economic developments, industries, commerce, investment, education, and entertainment. It also offers Internet services such as e-mail and on-line information retrieval. CEINET collects information from its provincial and local agencies, or from various business establishments that are overseen by the State Development Planning Commission. CEINET's network connects major provinces and cities. Its long-distance transmission relies on a cross-country infrastructure and 24 satellite stations operated by former MPT and MEI enterprises.

ChinaInfo, opened in August 1997, is state-sponsored but commercially operated by China Institute of Scientific and Technical Information (CISTI) under the Ministry of Science and Technology. Wanfang Data Corporation acts as the operating arm of CISTI to develop and manage ChinaInfo's services. ChinaInfo is connected with regional and provincial networks run by local science and technology administrations. Drawing from 100 databases throughout China, ChinaInfo offers a wide variety of information concerning science and technology, economics, finance, education, Internet, policies and regulations, human resources, social and cultural dynamics, and business companies. CASNET serves as ChinaInfo's communication platform. About 30 local science and technology information centers in China are expected to cooperate with ChinaInfo in Beijing. Network management and arrangement of information and profit sharing among different players seem to be crucial to both CEINET and ChinaInfo's future.

Several other government organizations at the central level have also taken early initiatives in allocating considerable amounts of resources to developing their own Internet websites. The most notable ones include the State Council Development Research Center, the State Statistics Bureau, the State Economic and Trade Commission, *China Daily*, the Ministry of Information Industry, the Ministry of Foreign Affairs, and the Ministry of Foreign Trade and Economic Cooperation.

- In 1997, China's State Council Informatization Leading Group authorized the establishment of China Internet Network Information Center (CNNIC) to take charge of domain name (IP address) registration, national Internet directory and database management, and provision of China's Internet policy, regulation, and status information. CNNIC is under the Ministry of Information Industry, offspring of MPT, but it is managed and operated by the Network Computing Center of the Chinese Academy of Sciences. CNNIC has periodically issued official reports on China's Internet development.
- CERNET and CASNET installed satellite-based backbone systems in January 1999, which replaced the IP/X.25 technology. The upgraded networks provide data transmission services at a higher speed for more than 40 cities in China.
- Between 1998 and 1999, two national centers were set up: (a) China Internet Product Safety Testing and Authorization Center, and (b) China National Information Security

Inspection Center. Both centers operate under China's State Council.

Golden Projects and E-Commerce

Golden Projects

China's Golden Projects were spearheaded in mid-1993 when the former Ministry of Electronics Industry announced the development of three nationwide information networks of Golden Bridge, Golden Card, and Golden Customs. The driving forces behind these projects included requirements for rapid national economic and social development, the Chinese government response to the global information infrastructure (GII) initiatives, and the need to interconnect China's existing private networks for efficient, specialized, and nationwide applications.

The core of these Golden Projects is the *Golden Bridge*, as it was expected to be a national web of networks linking other golden projects. The Golden Bridge Project was planned to construct a national public information backbone network which would link major dedicated networks of government organizations, and connect 30 information centers and 12,000 state-run large enterprises across over 400 municipal cities. Golden Bridge was architectured with the support of two mutually connected and supplemented data/voice communications systems: the MPT's fiber optic ChinaPAC, ChinaDDN, and a national satellite-based integrated services digital network, plus some microwave relay transmission lines.

With the Golden Bridge as the backbone communications network, the *Golden Customs/Gate* for foreign trade management and tariff data processing – *e.g.,* statistics, quota, licensing, tariff, tax rebate, payment, account settlement, etc. – communication and documentation processing and the *Golden Card* for electronic financial and banking transactions will link all the dedicated networks of foreign trade enterprises, shipping, tax-collection, customs offices and financial institutions through construction of virtual electronic networks (using China Telecom's leased data networks) and applications of EDI/EFT/E-mail technologies.

Golden Card Project is implemented in 3 phases. First, 1994-1996: experimenting with electronic 30 million bank cards in 10 provinces/cities; second, 1997-1999: issuing 60 million additional cards in 30-50 cities; and third, 2000-2003: popularizing electronic payment and settlement system and increasing the use of bank cards by issuing more cards to 300 million people in 400 cities. Golden Card Project is intended to set a unified standard for China's inter-bank online transactions and payment systems, with which ATM machines in major cities are interconnected and electronic payment across the nation can be implemented. The 10-year project will involve an investment of 37.5 billion yuan (US$4.7 billion). The implementation of Golden Card related projects in different areas is estimated to have a 75 billion yuan (US$9.4 billion) market potential for electronic information industry.

On November 4, 1997,[85] China National Bank Card Switching Center was set up. Its mission is to coordinate different electronic networks run by different banks and financial institutions, and help realize the objective of Golden Card Project of conducting trans-regional and trans-bank business in cyberspace.

As a chain of extensive efforts, China has initiated a number of "golden projects" intended to facilitate the development of many sectors, such as economics, taxation, agriculture, health care, education, commerce, and business management. To name a few, these projects include:

- Nationwide economic information backbone network (Golden Bridge Project)
- Electronic monetary and modern payment system (Golden Card Project)
- Foreign trade information sources network (Golden Customs Project)

---

[85] By then, China's commercial banks had installed 15,000 ATMs and about 120,000 POS systems in major cities.

- Electronic taxation system (Golden Taxation Project)
- Industrial production and circulation information network (Golden Enterprises Project)
- Comprehensive agricultural management and service information system (Golden Agriculture Project)
- Education and scientific research computer network and human resource project (Golden Intellectual Project)
- Health care network system (Golden Health Care Project)

E-commerce

Government Recognition and Initiatives

The "golden projects" launched by the former Ministry of Electronics Industry (MEI) in 1993 created an early appetite for the basic nutrients of China's e-commerce.

Since 1996, the Chinese government has increasingly positioned e-commerce high on its official agenda. Official policies and incentives have been brought out in support of e-commerce. Golden Projects and the program of Government Online are two initiatives mirroring the Chinese government's enthusiasm to embrace electronic business and the information age. Most high-profiled government organizations are the State Council Informatization Leading Group, the Ministry of Information Industry (MII), Ministry of Foreign Trade and Economic Cooperation (MOFTEC), and State Economic and Trade Commission (SETC). Other top-level Chinese government organizations involved in policy making and regulation of e-commerce and network operations include State Development and Planning Commission, State Council Legal Office, People's Bank of China, State Commercial and Trade Bureau, State Customs Administration, State Internal Trade Bureau, State Industry and Commerce Management Bureau, State Taxation Administration, Ministry of State Security and Ministry of Public Security. They each have different and often overlapping jurisdictions.

China's official e-commerce initiatives concentrate on three areas:

1. Inter-organizational and inter-departmental network connectivity. The Ministry of Finance, State Administration of Taxation, SETC, MOFTEC and State Internal Trade Bureau will be networked first to facilitate e-commerce.
2. Network interconnectivity among China's key cities. Beijing, Shanghai, Guangzhou, Tianjin, and Shenzhen will be interconnected by advanced information networks as China's e-commerce hubs.
3. 520 large and medium-sized SOEs will be given initial priority for the construction of e-commerce infrastructure and applications systems for their production, planning, R&D, marketing, and decision making. These networked SOEs will spread out their e-commerce capabilities and services to smaller companies in due time.

MOFTEC, China's foreign trade authority, has played a remarkable role in pushing forward the country's foreign trade oriented e-commerce. The Ministry built up China International Electronic Commerce Center (CIECC) in 1996, which laid a good foundation for China's e-commerce development. CIECC is physically housed in and administratively managed by MOFTEC. It is operated by a team of computer networking experts and trade specialists. CIECC deploys facilities supplied by IBM, HP, SUN and other international companies, and uses ChinaDDN (initially at 64Kbps) as its backbone to connect to global Internet-based trade networks (e.g., UN's GTPNet for ETO services) and to China's major cities and several dedicated networks run by China's government agencies and business sectors. Major MOFTEC branches, local offices, and six trade associations are all connected to CIECC. CIECC network is designed to support multiple protocols including X.25, X.28, X.400, X.435, FTP, OFTP, TCP/IP, and SNA. The services include EDI, electronic bulletin board, GTPNet-ETO, online economic and trade information, processing and storing of trade documents, commercial Web design and publication, data exchange platform, domestic and international e-mail, and e-business training and consulting.

Through its performance and services, CIECC intends to help China minimize foreign trade administrative loopholes as related to tax evasion, corruption and smuggling, streamline the process of foreign trade paperwork, enhance MOFTEC's policy transparency and operational efficiency, and achieve the safety of data transmission between China's enterprises and government organizations. CIECC network will be linked, as planned, with the networks of customs, taxation, banks and foreign exchange control. CIECC runs five Websites: www.moftec.gov.cn,   www.chinamarket.com.cn, www.cecfgc.com,   www.chinainvest.com   and www.techfair.com.cn, each with somewhat different priorities in content and services. CIECC has received approval from the State Council and MPT-MII to become one of China's major Internet access providers. MII also authorized CIECC to establish China International Economic and Trade Network (CIETNet) which will link all government agencies and business companies involved in foreign trade and e-commerce in China and provide them with foreign economic and trade related value-added services.

In 1999, CIECC formed a joint venture with China Infobank, a Hong Kong based website, to issue newsletters and post MOFTEC, the State Council, and other Chinese government policies and regulations on foreign trade to the world. This service is available to subscribers who pay about US$400 per year. In early 2000, CIECC joined hands with another Hong Kong based New ePOCH Information Co. Ltd., who takes 49% of the shares while CIECC holds 51% majority   ownership.   The   Joint   venture   launched www.chinatradeworld.com to enable foreign firms to import goods directly from more than 180,000 factories, farms and production facilities in China. The registered users of this site have access to over twenty industries in China, and they can get information on products and companies making these products. Moreover, surfers can place orders online and get local know-how and customer support from 600 service staff working in 70 Chinese cities.

MOFTEC uses CIECC as its arm to implement online enterprise management operations. The foreign trade ministry requires that, within a short period of time, China's foreign trade enterprises' applications for quota and licenses, foreign trade documentation, verification of foreign currency flows resulting from China's imports and exports and trade statistics calculations should all be conducted via CIECC network and its online services. In 1999, CIECC charged RMB 10,000 (US$1,208) for each permanent membership and RMB550 (US$66.44) for a monthly maintenance fee. CIECC in 1999 also developed China's first patented e-security software for digital signature and digital certificates. The software has been approved for use by the State Commercial Encryption Management Commission and the Ministry of Science and Technology.

Other major e-commerce initiatives supported by government organizations include China Business-to-Business Commerce (www.chinabbc.com.cn), jointly launched by SETC, MPT-MII, and the Ministry of Science and Technology, featuring 500 China's domestic companies; SETC backed Website www.ccec.com.cn; China Commodity Market Information Network (CCMnet) opened by the State Internal Trade Bureau and Beijing VSAT Information Network Corp, and the bilingual www.eChinaNow.com, a joint venture between the State Administration for Industry and Commerce (51% share) and Pacific E-link of Vancouver (49% share).

China's government support for e-commerce can also be seen in the government involvement in and encouragement for incubation industry ("fuhuaqi" in Chinese). Incubation works as a half-way house for innovative enterprises that find themselves between invention and corporation, or as a bridge between new ideas and the resources needed for materializing those ideas in the market. The government realizes that it should set up favorable policies concerning taxation, depreciation, warehousing and funding to help with the establishment of an efficient incubation structure that provides infrastructure, facilities, services, capital and management expertise to newly founded e-commerce and other enterprises. Government officials in Beijing and Shanghai have stated that China's incubation for e-commerce and high-tech industries can be fueled by Chinese entities, foreign investors, or a blend of both.

Key Players

Parallel to government involvement, mushrooming "dotcoms" and some foreign corporations are substantially engaged in e-commerce development. Their performance and growth represent a most active and entrepreneurial part of China's e-commerce.

E-Bookstores

Electronic bookstores, state own or privately initiated, were the pioneers in China's e-commerce. "Bookmall.com" (Shanghai Book City) in Shanghai and Beijing-based "Bjbb.com.cn" (part of the Beijing Book Emporium), "Dangdang.com," "Shikong.com," "Foundbook.com," "Bookoo.com," "Goshoo.com" and Allsages are among the most well-known online booksellers. The Beijing Book Emporium is currently the largest online bookstore that has invested over US$0.12 million for its network-related access, payment and security systems. Monthly online sales in 1999 from domestic and international purchasers averaged US$10,000 since its opening. Shanghai Book City, with its more than 140,000 types of books available online, attracted an average of 1000 visitors everyday in 1999. Its sales amounted to nearly US$8500 per month.[86]

The popularity and business volume of China's e-bookstores are not yet striking as compared with their investment and expectations, but the development of their Web design and online services has been impressive. Many of these bookstores have enriched their Webs with such items as "read online," "book reviews and comments," "new book briefs," "bestsellers' lists," and "readers' reactions," which appeal to many of the online users. "Dangdang.com" has appeared as one of the most successful privately own e-bookstores in China. The company has established a comprehensive book database and operates with the alliance with Science and Culture Book Information Co., China's largest government-approved private book distribution firm (55% foreign-owned), and claims to have listed some 200,000 titles

---

[86] At present, China publishes about 250,000 different books a year and its annual book market is estimated as US$3.61 billion.

online. Through its three rounds of financing, Dangdang.com has acquired funding to set up a new warehouse in Beijing and develop a door-to-door delivery system to 40 of China's cities.

E-Business "Portals"

In terms of general merchandise and comprehensive e-commerce, "8848.net," "Sina.com," "Alibaba.com," "Netease.com," "Sohu.com," "Sparkice.com," "Yabuy.com," "Eachnet.com" and several others are all well-noted to the Chinese and overseas web surfers.

8848.net (Everest E-commerce Network Co., Ltd.) was officially launched in May 1999, with US$145,000 in registered capital and subsequent injection of capital totaling US$12 million.[87] The number 8848 symbolizes the height of Mt. Everest's peak. The name reflects the company's high ambition to become China's best online business. 8848.net is considered one of the success stories in China's electronic online sales due to its monthly growth of 50% in sales with a total revenue of US$1.5 million for the first six months after its inception. 8848.net has about 200,000 types of products and about 100,000 titles of books available for sales online.[88] Its registered members were claimed to be 300,000 in May 2000 and its projected revenue is US$15-18 million for the year 2000.

Although though China's present online PC users are limited, 8848.net believes that most of the users are highly educated with enormous interest and desire to explore and experience new things, particularly in IT and information products. Targeting these users for electronic sales should be a good strategy. The company has upgraded or restructured its existing 260 plus retailing outlets across 160 cities to serve the needs of online business distribution and

---

[87] 8848.net has absorbed investment from Zong Yi Share Holding Company that holds 51% of the total company shares, China People's Insurance Corporation, and IDG's venture capital.

[88] However, 85% of the sales is made out of IT related products, and the rest of 15% are mostly books, CDs, and flowers etc. Many of these 200,000 products have not yet made sales online.

delivery in addition to their traditional sales activities. Besides, 8848 is working with UPS to improve its distribution and delivery systems. In terms of payment, 8848 has developed a number of "innovative" ways for "electronic" or "remote" payment transactions which accommodate the Chinese situation. Customers can pay for their online purchases through credit/debit cards, ATM transfer,[89] postal or bank transfer and cash payment at delivery. 8848 signed a business agreement with Intel for online sales of Intel's micro-processors and network products.

Sina.com has been highly regarded as China's best Internet service (content) provider for its diversified and effective services. Sina.com operates four Websites tailored for the Chinese population in mainland China, Hong Kong, Taiwan and North America, with claimed 16.6 million daily pageviews and 3.1 million registered users worldwide. Sina.com's strong business growth has been a solid basis for its IPO in NASDAQ.[90] Its US$17-priced shares have recently been up by almost 70% during the time when many of the IT stocks were badly hit. In November 1999, Sina.com made a strategic move by expanding its business to e-commerce. "Sinamall," Sina.com's e-commerce Website, was launched to develop a platform for consumers to access information and purchase online. Sina.com indicated that it would form alliances with commercial banks and product suppliers, exploit financial, technology, content and human resources available, and provide its Web users with quality and secure shopping and e-payment services. Sina.com has also joined hands with the Focus Technology Development Co. in starting "Made-in-China.com" which aims to build an online data center for Chinese products, manufacturers and market dynamics. People who log on

---

[89] That is, after the customer makes an order and advises *8848.net* what kind of card is to be used, *8848.net* will provide the customer with an account number for fund transfer, the customer can then go to an ATM machine on which to implement the transfer. This helps to maximize the customer's confidence and minimize the security risk.

[90] *Sina.com* is the first China's Net portal officially approved by China's State Securities Regulatory Commission and the Ministry of Information Industry to list shares abroad. Other top portals listed abroad include Sohu.com and Netease.com.

can get access to information, make pricing inquiries, and carry out efficient and safe online transactions. The near-term objective of Sina.com e-commerce is to achieve a high market share, trading volume and sales revenues via commissions from product providers and renting out "Net sales counters."

Sparkice.com is one of the earliest e-commerce portals established by returning Chinese from abroad. In addition to its operation of the Internet Café in many Chinese cities and e-commerce and Internet training programs, Sparkice intends to become China's leading business-to-business solution provider by bridging the product suppliers in Asia with the buyers in Europe and America. Sparkice has partnerships with Bank of China, China Ocean-shipping Corp., Metro AG of Germany and many other Chinese domestic and international firms. In April 2000, Sparkice and ChinaOnline, a leading US-based but China-focused business information service, formed a strategic alliance to promote product offerings from Chinese manufacturers to ChinaOnline's extensive readership and to develop programs for better use of the information available at both of their websites. The alliance rolled out "One Source E-commerce Trading Service," which offers Chinese enterprises to use "best of breed" online product catalogs, communications and messaging tools, auction and exchange transaction features, and "single point of contact" trading services.

Alibaba.com represents the entrepreneurial spirit of a Chinese teacher of English who pursued his dream out of his earlier career in teaching. Yun (Jack) Ma, the founder and CEO of Alibaba, established a web hosting company and headed the infoshare division of MOFTEC's CIECC before creating his Alibaba.com in 1999. The new e-commerce company rose as the poor woodcutter in the *Arabian Nights*, but soon found entrance to the treasure cave. Alibaba's business strategy is based on the management's 3-component perspective: Eastern wisdom, Western way of operation and the access to the global market, all of which must be integrated and well utilized.

Alibaba runs three interlinked websites: the English site for international trading companies; the China site in simplified Chinese for China's domestic marketing and trade firms; and a global Chinese site in traditional Chinese that serves overseas Chinese business communities in Hong Kong, Taiwan, Asia and other parts of the world. The information on these sites is categorized into 32 industries and 700 product lines. The essence of Alibaba.com is its information platform, which allows information exchange among businesses about their products, services, and themselves. One of Alibaba's business focuses is offering e-commerce solutions to small and medium-sized companies to deploy e-commerce facilities to lower their costs and raise their efficiency. Alibaba also intends to build e-commerce platforms for China's west regions where e-commerce will enable underdeveloped enterprises to grow up and conduct business with other regions in China and internationally. Alibaba claims that it has more than 10,000 clients worldwide. The company has reportedly acquired US$20million worth of venture capital from Japan-based Softbank.

Foreign Penetration

China's rapid growth in e-commerce has attracted multinational corporations to take a share. IBM, Compaq, HP, Oracle and Motorola, to name a few, have put in a considerable amount of resources in developing their e-business activities in China.

Early 2000, IBM reported its partnership with Hong Kong based Sino-i.com Ltd. to launch an e-commerce platform, ChinaEnterprise.com, to explore e-commerce opportunities in Greater China. The partnership would use eMarketPlace, an online transaction solution of IBM's China Research Lab, to offer an interface in both English and Chinese for procurement of 15,000 products with 600,000 registered suppliers in China. In July, IBM signed a contract with Jiangmen City of Guangdong Province to help train e-commerce personnel, build a local e-commerce platform, and provide the latest IT information to local companies. This IBM project is part of the RISE program (Regional Integration for Sustainable Economies) initiated by Asia Pacific Economic Cooperation (APEC) and Pacific Economic Cooperation Council (PECC).

The Hewlett Packard (HP) Company signed an agreement in April with Xi'an Xietong Software Company to set up a US$8-million e-commerce R&D center in western China to develop software and provide services for the e-commerce market. Compaq also formed a joint venture with China's PC maker Fujian Start Group to provide e-business related applications and services such as customized e-business solutions, software and system integration.

In May 2000, Compaq and Oracle allied with China's Ningxia Hui Autonomous Region's city of Yinchuan to offer assistance to build the West China E-commerce Port which will be an important regional e-commerce center to enable electronic trading and financing activities to take place and allow large commodity trading houses in Chongqing, Chengdu, Kunming, Nanning, Xi'an, Lanzhou, Xining, Yinchuan, Lhasa, Urumqi and Hohhot to minimize inventories and obtain lowest procurement prices.

China's first e-commerce virtual company, the Neu-Alpine Oracle E-commerce Virtual Co., or eON, was recently launched by Oracle and Shenyang Neu-Alpine Software Co. to help China's firms employ advanced and practical e-commerce systems. eON will provide marketing, management and technical support services to its customers. The employees of this virtual company are from Oracle and Neu-Alpine, they work simultaneously for both eON and the company where they are based.

In July 2000, an international and Chinese coalition entitled "E-commerce China Forum (ECCF)" was established. It comprises of 36 well-known international and Chinese companies from diverse e-commerce related industries, including Microsoft, General Motors, United Parcel Service, IBM, Motorola, Hewlett Packard, Intel, Lucent, Samsung, Xin De Telecom, Baker&McKenzie, Standard Chartered Bank, America Online, Cable&Wireless, Legend and JiTong. The coalition is set to collaboratively address a broad range of China-related e-commerce issues such as investment, standard, security, encryption, online taxation, advertising, payment, infrastructure, Internet services, distribution, privacy and intellectual property rights. ECCF retains APCO's Beijing office as its secretariat, supporting membership development and coordinating public relations and various activities. It attempts to work with and lobby the Chinese government in formulating policies and regulations for China's e-commerce development in a context of global economic interconnection.

Issues and Implications

The rise of e-commerce has posed a challenge to China's largest import-export trade fair in Guangzhou. This 50-year-old fair is a central-government sponsored bi-annual trading event that involves tens of thousands of China's SOEs and foreign firms and generates significant amounts of China's foreign trade income. Many of the 500,000 China's companies authorized to conduct import or export business used to be present at the Guangzhou Fair, but they had to pay high fees (US$9,600 – $18,000) to rent a space for their products or services. E-commerce provides new trading channels and practices to both Chinese and foreign firms at lower costs and higher speed. It gives trading partners a network platform by which product information, price negotiations, order processing, and business transactions can be efficiently exchanged and settled on a continuous basis.

For those presently involved in e-commerce in China, success seems to reside in a combination of offline brick-and-mortar know-how with online "click" operation competence. That is, rather than having a completely virtual business without any physical presence, e-commerce firms may integrate their real-world bricks and mortar establishments with a strong online presence. Chinese consumers can search information online and walk down the street to purchase what they located on the Web. Cooperation and alliances with conventional retailers and wholesalers tend to be mutually beneficial and serve as a partial solution, temporarily at least, to payment and distribution problems. Franchise and network service providers' leasing web space to traditional offline businesses for online sales in "cyber buildings" are two examples of this linkage between the old and new business practices.

Like the e-commerce market in the world, China's e-commerce market is growing along horizontal and vertical frontiers. The horizontal e-market is a group of websites or service portals that jointly provide an electronic platform for information and trade. Users of this platform can share, post and exchange information. They can conduct business transactions on a large variety of products or services. The vertical e-market is more specialized for specific industry sectors or market segments. Vertical e-market suits the trading needs of high cost, technology intensive and innovative products and services. It is therefore far more applicable to B2B online transactions. The vertical e-market helps to significantly lower the transaction costs.

To initiate and complete a business transaction in both horizontal and vertical e-markets requires the availability of four major infrastructures: information and communications infrastructure to enable the efficient information flow, distribution and delivery infrastructure to transport goods and services, payment and certification infrastructure to ensure safe and reliable financial settlement, and regulatory and legal infrastructure to regulate the market and protect the interest of buyers and sellers. China is in a process of building these four kinds of infrastructure, but apparently China is still behind many developed nations in this regard. Lack or shortage of these infrastructures creates issues and obstacles to China's e-commerce business activities.

Major issues and obstacles existing in China's present e-commerce market include distribution and delivery systems, network security and authentication, information infrastructure, online taxation, regulatory and legal framework, online credit and payment, and venture capital for e-commerce startups.

Distribution and Delivery

China's underdeveloped and insufficient distribution capabilities present difficulties to the development of e-commerce in China in terms of both large-scale business-to-business transactions and small-volume business-to-consumer tradings. Currently, "just-in-time" supply chain management for manufacturing enterprises or major retail outlets is rendered almost impossible by China's limited distribution capabilities. Commodities purchased online have to be transported and delivered by inefficient motor vehicles or manpowered bicycles. Online consumers often have to wait 3-5 days to get what they purchase from a local e-commerce provider. They usually get no commitment assuring when delivery can be made from the online vendors.

Many e-commerce firms have tried to team up with China's postal services (e.g., EMS) for deliveries, but it has proved to be slow and costly.[91] Other e-business companies have tried to link up with China's emerging chain stores to go beyond their primary business lines in order to distribute e-commerce products, or to make deals with express delivery carriers such as the domestic EMS and international DHL to offer faster local delivery. In the context of e-business, China's old and largely uncoordinated and segmented channels of product and services distribution systems are obviously a hurdle to meeting the demand of the e-customers – sellers and buyers – who want quick, efficient and timely transport and delivery of a very sophisticated array of products and services. It is urgent that China establish a computerized system of professional distribution to handle local and national products and services in a timely and cost effective manner, without which e-commerce development will be significantly restrained.

Network Security and Authentication

Network and data security in e-commerce transactions is the number-one concern in China. The majority of the e-commerce participants and Internet users have put security on the top of their priority list. They seriously worry about how data is transmitted and processed online and if their privacy and confidentiality can be protected when they conduct online shopping and e-payment

---

[91] China's State Postal Bureau (SPB) has taken initiatives to play an active role in e-commerce. It signed agreements with 14 large companies, including Haier and Dell, to provide e-commerce logistic services. SPB claimed that it has the country's biggest and best logistic network with 236 large delivery centers nationwide which link more than 2300 cities and localities. SPB also claimed that it has a network platform of its own, an e-commerce website "183" and a customer service center "185" to offer Internet and phone-in services.

transactions. With the increased alarms of hacker attacks, virus raids, cyber crimes, online fraud, and the reports that 80% of China's computer networks have security loopholes and 40% of China's Websites have been invaded by hackers, this concern about e-commerce security is intensified and justified.

Network security, in fact, concerns all parties involved: the government, the businesses and the individuals who are engaged in network related activities. Experience in other countries also denotes that when the e-commerce market takes off in earnest, there is a primary need to address network and data security issues. All parties involved should have the facilities to authenticate identities and ensure the integrity of information transferred online. Aside from providing connectivity and Web-enabling applications and transactions, e-commerce services should establish secure transaction protocols and supply adequate digital measures to assure their customers of the transaction security.

To foster the growth of e-commerce, China has made noted efforts to address the issues of network security. The government has issued a number of rules and regulations on network security. Specific initiatives by government agencies and businesses include:

- People's Bank of China (PBC), the country's central bank, has cooperated with 12 commercial banks and major network operators to establish a national credit card and online payment certification authority (CA). This CA, equipped with 128-byte encryption technology, is capable of digitally verifying user and vendor identities that safeguards online payment and inter-bank transactions. The CA has two sub-systems, SET of Visa/MasterCard and Non-SET of PKI. IBM, Sun Microsystems and Entrust were among the major international companies selected to provide technology and help build these systems. The PBC CA has been opened for operation since July 2000.
- China Telecom announced in May 2000 that it would roll out a network interface system for China's digital certificate to facilitate e-commerce activities.

- The CIECC of MOFTEC has reportedly developed a set of public key and encryption technologies based solutions for e-commerce.
- Shanghai E-commerce Certificate Management Center has created an online business security system.
- Hunan Post and Telecom Bureau and MII's Telecom Research Institute have jointly developed an e-commerce secure payment system that has been approved and accredited by MII and the State Commercial Encryption Management Commission.
- Several Web operators have opened websites to provide information on security. They also offer security related technical solutions and evaluation to online surfers. Most notable of these websites include *ccidnet.com*, *net120.com.cn*, *cnns.net*, *rising.com.cn* and *Chinabyte.com*.

Technology tends to be key to e-commerce security. The difficulty, however, lies in the government decision to choose from different technologies developed by either foreign firms or Chinese companies, and in how applications of security technologies can be coordinated among many different government and industry players. China's policy position is to encourage domestic R&D institutions to develop advanced network security products and solutions to meet e-market demands. The dilemma, however, is that it takes time and financial and human resources to develop world class security systems while China does not have such a large pool of resources available, nor can the country afford to wait. China needs to strengthen its domestic technological R&D in areas of fire wall, cryptography, digital signature and authentication, virtual private network reliability, network filtering technology, data identification, anti-virus software, safety scanning and gateways, and network operation monitoring. This cannot be done without coordination among different domestic interest groups and international cooperation.

Information Infrastructure

Over the past years, China's information and communications infrastructure has greatly improved. Both telephone and data transmission networks have undergone significant upgrading. National Golden Project initiatives and inter-provincial network development efforts have resulted in a rapid increase of trunk lines and exchange capacity. China Financial Data Network (CFDN) in 1999 had 1975 PVC circuits and more than 2000 ports connecting 80 large clients in banking, insurance, and stock exchange. The third-phase upgrade of CFDN is presently underway, which will lease more PCM and DDN lines and install more Cisco made ATM/SDH switches and routers 134 cities and towns (in addition to the previously linked 200 cities and towns) across China's 25 provinces to provide financial and banking related data services.

In terms of the overall network technology and scale, China is close to the developed countries, but in terms of network management and efficiency, China remains far behind. Network infrastructure bottlenecks to e-commerce include connectivity among different networks, last-mile access capability, narrow bandwidth of the local networks, and high charges on leased lines, data transmission, and Internet and phone usage.

E-commerce development requires Chinese government and industry players to seriously address these infrastructure bottleneck issues. Because of the industry restructuring, competition in network construction and management by China Telecom, Unicom, Jitong, China Netcom, China Information Highway Corporation and Zhong Yuan Financial Data Network Co. and local operators will likely increase, which may provide the market with better platforms, more alternatives for access and backbone networks, and greater incentives for e-commerce growth.

For e-commerce to thrive, adequate information infrastructure needs to be in place and network services provided need to be reliable with sufficient bandwidth and high quality. In addition, network services need to be reasonably priced to ensure that e-commerce transactions are commercially viable and appealing. The weak competitiveness among China's domestic Internet service providers and the reluctance on the government's side to allow foreign companies to compete in China compound the issue of China's inadequate information infrastructure for e-commerce development.

Currently, China's online consumers are significantly held back by two things: narrow network bandwidth which causes very slow web search and high charges for going online which keeps away many people who can hardly afford. Except for Sina, Sohu and China.com that respectively offer 300Mbps, 200Mbps and 100Mbps in bandwidth, most of the other e-commerce portals operate on networks with a very narrow bandwidth (e.g., 10Mbps for 8848, 2Mbps for China Commodity Trading Center, and 128Kbps for Shanghai Commercial Net.) For e-commerce firms to upgrade or lease more bandwidth from China Telecom, the incurred cost is terribly high.[92] The charge (for Web access and phone line use) on individuals to access the Internet is another barrier to e-commerce. If an individual in China goes on line for one hour per day, 30 hours per month, he/she has to pay RMB 200-250 yuan (US$25-30), which is more than a quarter of the Chinese average monthly income (US$100 -120).[93]

Online Taxation

Rising e-commerce will have an important impact on China's tax regime. Levying taxes on China's infant e-commerce may negatively affect the growth of online information and trade services. The government position, however, has indicated that, to protect tax sovereignty and provide a level playing field, online business activities should be equally treated as non-electronic offline business activities in terms of tax obligations. Challenged by emerging issues of tax collection and tax evasion in cyberspace, the State Taxation Administration (STA) has set up a special task force to conduct serious studies and make policy recommendations for e-commerce taxation. The general principle seems to be that China will not exempt e-commerce transactions from taxation to boost the growth of e-

---

[92] For example, leasing dedicated lines from China Telecom's DDN costs RMB 53,000/month for a 1Mbps line, RMB80,000/month for a 2Mbps line, RMB13,000 for a 128K line, and RMB7,000/month for a 56K line.

[93] As a comparison, Americans pay about US$20 flat fee a month for unlimited Internet access, which is only 1-2% of the average monthly income.

commerce, as some developed countries strongly advocate;[94] no new tax category should be created for online transactions: tax neutrality should be maintained for both online and offline tradings. China intends to apply network technologies to simplify and improve the process of tax collection, and at the same time, minimize tax evasion. A new regulatory framework on the enforcement of e-commerce taxation is reportedly being drafted by the central government. It may come into effect prior to the end of 2000.

In a transition period from a conventional tax system to an online tax system, e-taxation in China would mean two things: e-taxation on online transactions and electronic taxation on non-online transactions. Specifically, e-taxation is a two-step process of electronic tax declaration and electronic tax settlement. The first step requires that taxpayers use network systems to send their tax declaration information to the relevant tax offices. The second step means that upon the receipt of the taxpayers' declarations, tax offices contact the related banks and financial institutions, where the taxpayers have accounts, to collect taxes electronically. Both steps involve no flow of paper documentation, and the information and tax payment are transported online to the appropriate destinations. Electronic taxation raises efficiency, effectiveness and accuracy. It also cuts costs of manpower and other resources involved in the tax processes.

Specific concerns regarding online taxation that China's tax administration has expressed are:

a) *Cross-Border Jurisdiction and Mandate of the Taxation Authorities* Under the emerging e-commerce circumstances, tax agencies of different levels and different geographical regions need a new division of jurisdiction and distribution of responsibility. In conventional tax practice, domestic cross-regional tax rules are determined by the Chinese government while cross-border tax rules are set through bilateral

---

[94] The United State government favors the policy of tax exempt for online business while some European countries have proposed levying online business taxes based on the volume of the electronic bit flow or cash flow.

agreement between China and other countries. With the rise of e-commerce, traditional concept and practice of taxation and tax regimes are faced with a severe challenge. How a standing agency can be reorganized in cyberspace becomes a complex issue. OECD in 1963 denoted that if a non-resident standing agency – a physically fixed body representing business entities – conducts trading transactions, it must pay taxes according to the rules set by the country where the agency is located. In the e-commerce market, such a standing agency is no longer needed. Business transactions are conducted electronically without the physical presence of people or agencies. When a Chinese organization purchases goods or services via a web or ISP on Internet, which may have no physical presence in China, what can be done to this virtual agency regarding taxes?

b) *Transfer of Taxes with Online Commerce* Because of the discrepancies in tax rules and practices in different countries or regions, consumers of high tax countries/regions can purchase goods or services through electronic networks from low-tax countries/regions, thus the issue of tax transfer or arbitration occurs. China currently relies on the practice of distributed responsibility for tax collection. That is, local taxes are collected by local tax authorities and central taxes by central tax regime even if tax rates and tax categories are determined by the state tax administration. Assignment of tax collections and varied favorable policies for tax collecting and re-distributions in different localities are also likely to be incentives for tax transfer under e-commerce circumstances. Transfer of taxes will lead to unfair competition between different nations or regions.

c) *Indirect Tax* (e.g., value-added tax and sales tax) Lack of tax rules and management for business transactions online creates confusions such as how to define buying or selling points for tax purpose, what country's tax rules to follow if the transaction is international, and what to do with the tax money if the goods purchased are returned for refund.

d) *Paperless Documentation* E-commerce is conducted online without conventional contracts, documents, invoices, and other transaction records. This paperless practice makes away with the traditional tools for accounting and tax tracking, monitoring, and auditing. Chaos within tax regimes may arise before an e-commerce compatible system is established. Tax evasion and the black economy take advantage of this system transition due to loopholes in enforcing tax rules.

e) *Managerial and Operational Issues* E-commerce enables the producer and seller to have direct connections. The role of intermediaries for levying taxes is weakened or even eliminated and there is no record for stamp tax. It is therefore hard to distinguish between transactions and services that should or should not be taxed.

Regulatory and Legal Framework

In spite of the efforts made by China's MII and a few other government bodies, the regulatory and legal framework for e-commerce remains largely behind the market development. At the National 1999 People's Congress Assembly, many representatives pushed for the drafting of China's e-commerce law to regulate e-market related activities. Creating a regulatory environment for e-commerce is urgently called for by not only government agencies but also by industry and consumer organizations. Yet, the challenge is that no tried and tested precedent regulating this e-commerce market exists, and the rapid evolution of Internet and communications technologies and applications tends to leave China's lawmakers and government officials trailing in its wake. Feeling the way ahead seems to be the norm, not the particular. Furthermore, E-commerce and the Internet applications concern so many different fields of activity that a broad range of China's government entities are entitled and required to involve themselves in the regulatory process. However, their vested interest allows for no easy and smooth coordination and consensus in this complex policy and regulatory process.

Although China urgently needs to set up a legal and regulatory environment good for e-commerce activities, the government is simultaneously concerned that, given the dramatic changes in technology and market, hastened enactment of cumbersome and impractical legislation may create an undesired situation that is risky and problematic. This, in part, speaks for why the government has been hesitant in issuing new rules and regulations.[95] It also reinforces the view that China still lacks a well-grounded legal and regulatory framework to safeguard and lever economic and social development.

E-commerce growth has to be nurtured in a sound and effective legal and regulatory environment. Like many other countries, China must make its best effort in drafting and enforcing new rules and regulations that cover such issues as online contract, security and certification, infrastructure, IPR, privacy and confidentiality, taxation, e-payment, dispute resolution, consumer protection, and self-regulation by service providers.

Online Credit and Payment

Another critical obstacle to China's e-commerce transactions is credit and payment. Currently, China's online credit and payment system remains underdeveloped and credit card use remains low. Even though China has issued more then 100 million bank cards to date, most of these cards are debit cards (only about 10% of them are domestic credit cards[96]) and their use is quite limited. The majority of these bankcards cannot be used for e-commerce transactions because many stores are not yet electronically connected with the banks and because inter-bank network connections remain largely non-existent.

---

[95] To date, few rules and regulations have been issued by the government. These rules and regulations concern online advertising, online dealing in audio-visual products, online securities trading, encryption, content, data security, and business registration. Beijing E-commerce Notice by Beijing Municipal Administration for Industry and Commerce is one of the examples.

[96] One of the true credit cards is the Great Wall Consumer Credit Card issued by the Bank of China. The card gives a 50-day no-interest grace period for repayment. After this period, 0.05% interest will be charged per day.

Interoperability between various e-payment centers and servers differs from region to region and city to city. The penetration of universal ATMs and point-of-sale (POS) sites is still in an embryonic stage. Furthermore, China's traditional preference for cash-based retail transactions for "peace of mind" remains very strong, particularly in less developed regions and cities. China's government strict financial control over foreign exchange and cross-border financial settlement also considerably diminish possibilities for easy and efficient international transactions.

Despite the fact that the People's Bank of China (PBC) – China's central bank – has taken the lead and cooperated with China's eleven commercial banks to set up a secure inter-bank certificate authorization (CA) system, no nationwide network system for financial data management is established yet, through which corporate or individual credit can be verified. Without a reliable and efficient CA system, online payment transactions are both risky and inconvenient. However, PBC's effort has met with resistance because of divided views among China's banks and financial institutions in technology standards, alliance formation and network interconnection.

E-commerce firms have to take measures adaptable to China's situation. The methods of payment they accept include real credit cards (VISA, MasterCard, American Express);[97] bank cards issued locally by China's banks such as Yikatong and Yiwangtong by Merchant Bank, Great Wall Ka by Bank of China, Long Ka by Construction Bank, Mudan Ka by Industrial and Commercial Bank, and Golden Grain Ka by Agriculture Bank;[98] payment by bank or

---

[97] It is said that only those who have a foreign currency deposit account with Bank of China, Industrial and Commercial Bank of China, or Guangdong Development Bank can be apply for an international credit card.

[98] When people use these cards to purchase products online, verification process may take as long as two weeks before delivery can be made. Besides, service fees of 2-5% charged by banks and geographical restrictions are also major issues to those who use credit/debit cards for online payment.

postal transfer; and cash payment upon delivery at the door.[99] China Merchant's Bank (CMB) seems to be moving ahead of other Chinese banks in constructing its own online intra-bank payment platform. It set up China's earliest online banking system in April 1998 and had taken over 90% of the online market. CMB claims to have garnered most of the major online accounts including 8848.net, Sina.com, Alibaba.com, and Eachnet.com.[100]

Venture Capital

Many of the e-commerce service providers in China are non-state own Internet service firms that emerge into the market with entrepreneurial initiatives. Because of the high market risks and a severe shortage of capital, they have to overcome numerous difficulties in order to grow. According to Morgan Staley Dean Witter and other analysts, only 10% of these new ventures will be successful, 20% will barely survive, and 70% face a strong probability to go bankrupt. Other businesses involved in e-commerce in China are non-Internet companies that are moving their operations online. Both of these entities are confronted with a shortage of capital that is required to enable them to initiate online e-commerce.

Venture capital (VC) seems to be one of the most viable sources of funds to support the growth of China's e-commerce enterprises. China's government has over the past years tried to pull in different efforts to set up venture capital funds for IT and e-commerce related firms. In 1998, Shenzhen Venture Capital Ltd., a government-backed venture fund, was launched. Beijing and Shanghai followed up and set their government-supported venture capital funds a year later. Each of these government funds manages about US$50 million. Guangdong, Jiansu, Tianjin, Shanxi and Shenyang have also pushed out government-supported venture capital funds. The total assets of

---

[99] Cash on delivery is presently the most popular method of payment (more than 30% of all B2C e-retailing business in 1999 was paid this way.) It suits many Chinese consumers' preference in payment and it does not require verification.

[100] Because of the lack of interbank system, business firms and individuals may have to get more than one account at different banks to meet their needs.

these VC funds amount to over US$500 million (source: *Deloitt & Touche*). These government funds are far from enough to support China's e-commerce firms. China's small and medium-sized e-commerce start-ups may never have access to these funds.

VCs to China are something new, something on trial. No established legal, regulatory, financial or managerial infrastructure or expertise has ever existed in China to facilitate and protect the operations of VCs. This means China's home-grown VCs, international VCs, or Chinese-foreign hybrid VCs, all face various constraints, particularly the constraints from China's current legal and regulatory framework. These constraints are mainly reflected in the following aspects:

- Government agencies in charge of corporate regulation and records remain largely non-transparent and inaccessible to the public;
- Prohibition or restriction against lending by non-financial and private institutions;
- Restriction against disposition of VCs' shares on the open market upon IPO of the invested firms;
- No formalized law governing or sanctioning the formation and operation of VC funds originating from the private sector;
- Foreign investors face considerable uncertainties and risks when making investment in China's unclearly-defined "encouraged," "permitted," "restricted," and "prohibited" industry sectors.

At an impressive pace, China is making strategic inroads into a network-based digital economy. The country, however, has to overcome a number of hurdles which crucially hold back China's e-commerce development. Product distribution and delivery system, online credit and payment, secure electronic identity verification, accessible and affordable high-speed network infrastructure, efficient value-chain and transaction platform and appropriate legal and regulatory environment are all fundamental building blocks China has to work hard on. Besides, e-commerce growth depends very much on a new cultural and conceptual framework regarding business and commercial activities. China faces a big challenge on this.

Unlike many other countries, China apparently has the advantage of strong government support and enthusiastic involvement by both government and non-government sectors in pushing forward e-commerce. The key opportunity for China seems to rest upon if and how the country's conventional industries will embrace the emerging network economy, and if and how the new IT-based e-commerce will interact with and transform China's existing economic system. Foreign investment and international participation are important driving forces for China's e-commerce development, but they may only be best employed with China's increasing market liberalization and persistent improvement of the legal and regulatory environment.

Computer Industry

Overview

Between 1990 and 1995, China's computer and IT industries experienced an average annual growth of 31.5%, much higher than the country's GDP growth. In 1997, China's overall information technologies market was somewhere between US$25 billion and US$30 billion.[101] The figure climbed to US$52 billion in 1999.[102] It may go beyond US$70 billion in 2000, representing a 24% compound annual growth.[103] With a burgeoning market demand and increasing

---

[101] MEI reported that China's 1997 electronic information industries had a production output value of RMB380 billion yuan (US$45.8 billion), up 24.9% from 1996, ranking the seventh in the world. IT sales reached RMB250 billion yuan (US$30 billion), up 15%, profit from IT sales was RMB 12 billion yuan (US$1.5 billion), up 13.2%, and tax levied on IT industries was RMB65 billion yuan (US$7.8 billion).

[102] US$39 worth of China's IT products was exported, taking 20.6% of China's total export revenues in 1999. MII estimated that the figure may reach US$45 billion in 2000.

domestic and international competition, China's IT market size may expand to US$100 billion in the early part of 21st century.[104]

Similar to telecommunications and Golden Projects that play critical roles in the country's information and communications development, China's computer industry and computer market have developed rapidly. International involvement, rise of the Chinese players, Internet applications, and reduced sales prices have all fueled China's remarkable growth in computer related sectors.

In 1996, there were about 15,000 Chinese business companies and state institutions involved in computer industry and relevant information services. Domestic computer industry players were segmented into:

Segment	Players	Employees
Manufacturing	1000 plus	100,000
PC Makers (licensed)[105]	176	N/A
Software Development	1,000	80,000
Marketing and Services	13,000	120,000
R&D	50	N/A

In the subsequent years, the number of Chinese companies involved in the production of computers increased, but the growth is most noted in their increased production scales and capabilities. In 1998, China had about 18,000 firms involved in computer business, but 90% of these firms engaged in the business of computer marketing and sales, only a small proportion of companies worked in the fields of

---

[103] The figure includes IT market in Hong Kong. In 1997, Hong Kong took 24% of the total, whereas in 2002, the proportion will likely drop to 17%. This percentage change does not necessarily mean Hong Kong's IT market decline, but it indicates mainland China's rapid growth. Out of the US$25 billion, IT equipment (mainly computer hardware) spending is about US$8.5 billion. The figure will likely reach US$28.6 billion in 2002, representing a 27% compound annual growth.

[104] Source: Business Weekly, *China Daily*, April 12, 1998.

[105] PC makers in China are about 170 in 1997, approximately 30% of which manufactured unbranded clone PC models.

computer R&D, production, and technical services. According to the data from the former Ministry of Electronics Industry and the Ministry of Information Industry, China's computer industry output value and total market sales experienced a rapid growth:

	Output Value[106]		Market Sales	
	100 million RMB yuan	Growth (%)	100 million RMB yuan	Growth (%)
1991	70	40	70.4	26.85
1992	134	91.42	198.95	182.6
1993	205	52.98	284	42.7
1994	395	92.6	407	42.25
1995	500	26.6	520	27.5
1996	N/A	N/A	800	30
1997	1300	N/A	1120	40
1998[107]	1480	13.9	1400	25
1999	1750	18.2	1720	22
2000[108]	2000	15	N/A	N/A

From 1991 to 2000, the number of PCs sold in the China market is approximately:[109]

Year	Set of PCs (000)	Year	Set of PCs (000)
1991	120	1996	2,100
1992	280	1997[110]	3,000

---

[106] Note the varying exchange rates between the Chinese currency and U.S. dollar in those years.

[107] In 1998, China's computer hardware sales reached RMB115.5 billion, up 11% over 1997's; software sales were RMB32.5 billion, 25% higher than 1997's.

[108] The figures for 1999 and 2000 are estimates.

[109] PCs are sold in China either bundled with operating and application software or with DOS but no other software ("naked PCs" as put in Chinese). Since 1999, some vendors began to market "free" PCs to customers who must sign a long-term contract with an ISP for Internet access. Pentium-II PCs were marketed in 1999 by some Chinese vendors for about US$600.

[110] By then China became the second largest PC market in Asia, next only to Japan. China took 3.9% of the world PC market share in 1999, and the country may have 6-8% of the global PC market share in 2000.

Year	Set of PCs (000)	Year	Set of PCs (000)
1993	500	1998	4,200
1994	800	1999	4,910
1995	1,000	2000 (target)	7-8,000

Out of this figure, the total sales of home PCs were:

	Market Sales (100 million yuan)	% of the Total
1991	18	25.57
1992	37.5	18.85
1993	63.4	22.32
1994	110.8	27.7
1995	160	30.77
1996	220	34.38
1997	315	43.2

Since 1996, most important vendors, Chinese and foreign, for desktop PCs, home PCs, notebook PCs and PC servers in China's computer market have been Legend, Great Wall, Founder, Compaq, IBM, HP, AST, TRUAIT, Toshiba, Acer, Twinhead and MAX Station. Changes in the pattern of top PC sellers (in terms of PC units sold) in China show that Chinese firms such as Legend, Great Wall and Founder are climbing up quickly, surpassing big international players like Compaq, HP, IBM and Toshiba. In 1998, Chinese computer vendors increased their sales by 65%, taking 71.9% of the Chinese market, while many foreign vendors, for the first time in history, experienced a negative growth. Top international companies' sales in China increased by only 15%, with their market share dropping from 21% to 19%. Sources predict that, in the early 21st century, the share of foreign PC vendors may decline to well below 30%.[111]

---

[111] Currently, foreign firms generally serve high-end corporate and institutional clients, while Chinese vendors tend to pinpoint low-end corporate segment and home PC market, with significant differences in technology and price. A

Ranking of Top PC Vendors in China

	1995	1996	1997	1998	1999
Legend	4	1	1	1	1
Great Wall	7	7	5	6	4
IBM	3	2	2	2	3
ACER	8	9	10	10	9
Compaq	1	3	3	4	6
AST	2	4	6	N/A	N/A
HP	5	5	4	5	5
DEC	6	6	N/A	9	N/A
Founder	N/A	N/A	7	3	2
Dell	N/A	N/A	9	8	10

1999 saw an increase of 16.2% in China's PC sales. Foreign brands dropped to 25-30% of the market share while China's brands and clones took about 70%. Legend remained on the top for a succession of four years. With foreign brands dropping further, Founder and Great Wall climbed significantly higher in the rank. Since 1992, China has seen an annual growth in PC unit sales between 35% and 50%. In terms of laptop and notebook computers, Toshiba, IBM, Legend, Compaq and NEC have been strong vendors. Top server suppliers in 1999 were HP, IBM, Compaq, Legend, Langchao and Dell. Opportunities in this rapidly expanding market have attracted many computer multinationals. It has also provided stimulus for China's domestic IT industry to grow and gain a bigger market share.

Over the past eight years, China's export and import of computer peripherals, components and PCs have grown significantly, which is reflected by the following numbers (MEI-MII data):

---

different source estimated that 1997 market share was: Legend 18%, Compaq 17%, IBM 13%, AST 12%, Great Wall 7%, Founder 5%, Acer 5%, and Tontru 2%.

	Export		Import	
	US$100 million	*Growth (%)*	*US$100 million*	*Growth (%)*
1991	4.5	124.3	4.1	10.2
1992	10.67	137.1	9.85	140.2
1993	15.6	46.2	14.77	49.95
1994	28	79.49	20.2	36.76
1995	49.6	77.1	27.5	31.2
1996	64.7	30.4	34.2	29.1
1997	87.3	34.9	44.3	29.5
1998[112]	68.9	-21.1	26.9	-39.2
1999[113]	119.3	73.9	74.5	177

About 80% of these exports consist of major computer components, half of which fall under the classification of HS 874160, primarily computer display units, keyboards, mouses, and printers. Around 40% of the exports are components such as CD-drivers and disk drivers (HS 847170). Complete sets of computer make up only a small proportion of the exports. The major destinations in 1998 for China's computer related exports include U.S. (33%), Netherlands (19%), Hong Kong (14%), and Japan (7%). China's computer related imports are concentrated on IC chips. Principal sources of these chip imports in 1998 were Japan (34%), Taiwan (18%), U.S. (13%), Hong Kong (10%), and Korea (7%).

China's national plan for the application of computers in the upcoming years focuses on such areas as PC usage and access density, Internet-based applications, electronic commerce, CAD,

---

[112] China's 1998 total value of computer product import-export was US$9,580 million, representing a drop of 25.2% from the previous year. The value of computer based import-export, as a percentage of China's national import-export value, declined from 4% in 1997 to 3% in 1998.

[113] Foreign-funded enterprises or joint ventures accounted for almost 75% of the 1999 computer-related exports. State enterprises, however, accounted for most of the imports. U.S.A. was the country that took the largest shares of the exports and imports (28% and 24% respectively).

computerization of financial and banking industries, brokerage
business, telecom operators, air traffic control programs, computer
information systems for energy, transportation, iron and steel,
petroleum, chemicals, and machinery industries, EDI system for
foreign trade, customs, and taxation sectors, Golden Projects, Three
Gorges Project, and networked computer data services. During 1996-
1999, China claimed to have invested at least 30 billion yuan (US$3.8
billion) to fuel the development of the country's domestic computer
industry.

The Development Track

The development of China's computer industry has undergone a
fast-paced evolutionary process. In the late 1980s, the State Science
and Technology Commission launched the "Torch Program" to
encourage the commercialization of high-tech based industries and the
adoption of a more flexible attitude toward international partnerships.
Meanwhile, the Ministry of Electronics Industry (MEI) was charged
to vitalize China's computer industry, and the State Education
Commission (SEC) spear-headed the nation's endeavors to spread
computer applications, with a goal to add 11 million PCs for local area
networking for 25% of the China's 900,000 universities and schools
by 2002.

A group of the MEI affiliated research institutes and organizations
thus received "green lights" and official instructions to transform
themselves into market oriented companies. They formed China's
pioneering computer firms. But they lacked business skills and
advanced technology to compete in the market. A few foreign firms,
such as Hong Kong-managed AST, had the advantage to dominate the
market from the 1980s until the mid-1990s.

Chinese firms, Legend, Founder, and Stone, for example, then
adopted a business strategy to distribute foreign brand products by
deploying the government policy support (*e.g.,* loans and reduced tax
treatment since 1993), the knowledge of the market demand, lower
costs and prices, access to local distribution channels, connection
with local government organizations, and strength in Chinese language
software development. As a result, these Chinese players successfully

traded market access in exchange for the expertise, skills, and technology needed for corporate growth. While distributing foreign brand products, these Chinese firms built up their sales and service networks and started to market their own lines of desktop PCs.

Many Chinese firms, however, still lack core technologies for computer production. Their operation is low value-added with small profit margin (approximately US$13 per PC unit), and their competitiveness in the market remains relatively weak. Generally, Chinese firms have strength in the manufacturing of power devices, computer hard frames, keyboards, and some other non-critical parts, whereas central processing units (CPUs), high-speed micro-processing integrated chips (IC), operating systems (OS), hard drives, color monitors, and other critical components still need to be imported from foreign companies like Intel and AMD. China's financial input for computer industry's R&D remains significantly behind what is needed. According to China's official statistics, only about 6-7% of the computer sales revenues is re-allocated for the R&D of the computer industry, much lower than China's average R&D expenses (14%) for other high-tech sectors. Shortage of venture capital and slow commercialization of technology innovations are also negatively affecting China's computer industry.

The market share for PCs domestically made, not by Sino-foreign joint ventures, reached 65% in 1996. The figure climbed to over 75% by the year 1999. However, a significant proportion of these "domestically made" PCs is still locally assembled using foreign components imported. Only 20-30% of the parts is locally sourced.[114] China's computer market has experienced keen competition among domestic and international players. Most of the big-name international computer vendors have made strong efforts in marketing and producing computer products in China. They have sold computers of their brands either through Chinese distributors or by their own local outlets. International firms have increasingly focused on localization

---

[114] In 1997, China's PC market is about evenly split among foreign brands, domestic brands, and non-branded clone PCs. Clone PCs are 25% cheaper than domestic brand PCs, and about 30% cheaper than the foreign brand PCs.

in R&D, manufacturing and sales to achieve lower operating costs and higher sales volumes.

China is keen on new products. Several Chinese research centers started the R&D of network computers (NCs) as early as 1996. The first China-produced NC prototype, STAR-910, made its public appearance in early 1997. The prototype is developed by the Fuzhou-based Star Group, with the technical standards accepted by Oracle, Sun Microsystems, Apple, IBM, and Motorola. The STAR-910 is equipped with high-speed 32-bit CPU, 4M ROM, 256K flash, and 1M VRAM. It supports both English and Chinese display in Internet e-mail and browser applications.

Key Players

More than twelve Chinese computer companies have been listed on Shanghai or Shenzhen stock markets, while Legend, Stone, and Founder have been listed on Hong Kong Stock Exchange. In regard to asset/liability ratio, earnings per share, and increase in net profit, these companies are more strongly positioned than many other Chinese enterprises. Since 1997, China's computer market has been marked by the rise of a number of domestic companies such as Legend, Founder, Great Wall, Tongchuang, Langchao,[115] Changjiang, Stone Group, Sea-star, Shida, Ziguang, and Taiji. Their total output of computers in 1998 reached more than 2.55 million. In addition to these top players, more than 30 second-tier Chinese computer firms are also active in the niche market. They produce local brand computers and have them marketed with a comparative price advantage (RMB 2000-5000 yuan lower than well-known foreign brands) to households through direct-sale channels. Local brand computers are assembled mostly with Intel chips and Seagate hard-drives.[116] The sales of mainline local-brand computers reached 402,800 units in 1998.

---

[115] These five Chinese firms receive priority support from the Chinese government.

[116] Apart from Seagate (with 52.4% of the 1998 market share), Quantum (23.1%), Fujitsu, Western Digital, and Maxtor are also widely used.

Legend Group has ranked, overall, number one computer vendor in China since 1997, with its 1999 PC sales taking over 20% of the China's domestic market share. It is also positioned the top vendor in Asia-Pacific region outside of Japan,[117] with sales taking 8.5% of the market share in 1999, exceeding IBM's 7.8%. Since 1999, Legend has made efforts in gradually integrating its PC business with China's Internet related and e-commerce services.[118] In April 2000, Legend released its plan to restructure the company by dividing its operations into Legend Computer and Legend Shenzhou Digital China to focus on two business entities focusing on Internet services, electronic commerce, PC, and information products.

Legend was established in Beijing in 1984 by a group of 11 members from the Chinese Academy of Sciences. It was originally called the New Technology Development Company of the Computing Technology Research Institute. Prior to 1995, Legend primarily involved in distribution of HP, IBM, and AST products in China. The company draws managerial expertise and technology skills from HP and other world class computer players and went through a series of organizational and business restructuring. Shorter supplier delivery lead time, higher inventory efficiency, and stronger business management have enabled Legend to slash prices to 30-40% lower than its competitors. The company's new efforts are focused on competing upfront with foreign and domestic players in the market, rather than passively following them as it used to. Since 1995, Legend has been aggressively marketing its own brand PCs, with revenue reaching US$1.5 billion in 1997, US$2.1 billion in 1998, and US$2.4 billion in 1999. Legend's core business includes manufacturing and

---

[117] The PC market size in Asia-Pacific (excluding Japan) in 1999 was 14.1 million units (IDC data).

[118] In February 2000, Legend developed an alliance with Hong Kong-based Pacific Century CyberWorks (PCCW) to involve in co-branded Legend-NOW (Network of the World initiated by PCCW) Internet services in Asia-Pacific. Pacific Century CyberWorks had just beaten down its competitor Singapore Telecom and acquired 54% of the shares of C&W Hong Kong Telecom for US$38 billion. Legend was also reportedly to invest 1.6 billion RMB for Internet related services.

distribution of PCs, distribution of foreign brand computer related products, networking and systems integration, and the production of modems, projectors, laser printers and motherboards.

Legend targeted China's embryonic computer market earlier than most of other Chinese companies and plans to sell 1.2-1.5 million PCs in 2000.[119] Based on the study that China has more than 100 million families in cities and at least half of these families with children at secondary school age are inclined to buy computers, Legend's marketing strategy focuses on urban families with teenagers who are part of the first Chinese generation that have access to computer training courses at school and whose parents believe that PCs will promise their only child a competitive advantage for the future. Legend business also include distribution and reselling of computer products of 27 different vendors by its 300 first-tier distributors throughout China. Legend management has decided to merge its Beijing subsidiary with a Hong Kong company and expand its sales and support operations into Hong Kong and Asia in 1998, a move marking the Legend's new business strategy abroad.

Founder is another well-known Chinese player based on the talents and resources of Beijing University. The company markets different PCs, printers, network systems, and develops Chinese application software. Software development is Founder's butter-and-bread business while home PC is also one of the company's targeted market segments. Many of the Founder's PC models are configured with modems and Internet access to hit the market stride. Founder first came into being with the central government endorsement for the projects on Chinese character processing, office automation, and electronic publishing systems. Drawing on a wealth of technological and human resources from Beijing University, the company is a pioneer in developing Chinese character processing card and long-distance satellite paging transmission system for China's newspapers.

Founder engages in software development and system integration for publishing, banking, retailing, and public security. It also makes

---

[119] Legend distinguishes itself as the top vendor by taking 10% of the China's PC market share in 1997 and 18% in 1998.

PCs of its own brands and distributes computers for multinational firms such as Digital, Unisys, Agfa, Wyse, Creative and Hewlett Packard. The company now has a network of 36 branch offices or subsidiaries and over 300 distributors spread out in China, Hong Kong, Japan, Malaysia, Macau, Taiwan, South Korea, Canada, and USA. In 1998, 80% of China's desktop publishing system market was taken by Founder. Founder had an impressive sales growth of 98% in 1999. Ernst & Young acts as Founder's certified public accountant. In November 1997, Founder was selected by the Chinese government as one of the six state companies to be supported to rise to the world-class status.[120]

Great Wall Group is a large computer firm previously under the former Ministry of Electronics Industry that makes and market computers and software. Business strategy of the company is based on the management view that most users in China regard PCs as consumer products and that Chinese buyers are very much concerned about upgrading of computer models, i.e., they care a lot about features and prestige found in high-end models. Great Wall suffered from a declining market share in 1996-1997, but picked it up in 1998.

Tontru Information Industry Group was set up in Nanjing in December 1995. It grows out of Nanjing Creative Co. and is enthusiastically catching up with other Chinese computer leaders like Legend to become one of the largest domestic PC vendors. Tontru's 1997 revenue was more than doubled to US$130 million. With support from Jiangsu provincial and Nanjing city governments that hold about 31% of the company shares, Tontru has been doing well in Shanghai and southeast regions. The company's PC manufacturing capacity is reportedly expanded from 500,000 units in 1998 to approximately one million units by 2000. Tontru has set up 29 offices across the country which control 1000 local PC distributors.

---

[120] The six companies selected are Baoshan Iron and Steel, Haier Electronic Group, Changhong Electric, North China Pharmaceutical, Jiangnan Shipyard, and Founder. They will each receive policy support and over US$2.41 million government funds for technology innovations.

Langchao Electronic Information Group was established in 1989 by the Shandong branch of the MEI and is supported by the Shandong provincial government. In 1999, the company had 20 subsidiaries or branches, 200 distributors, and 22 various joint ventures. It was staffed with 3,000 employees, 70% of whom work on IT related business operations across a number of Chinese provinces.

Changjiang Computer Group was set up in 1987 by the Shanghai branch of the MEI. Staffed with 4000, it is one of the key Chinese PC manufacturers and distributors in Shanghai.

Sea-star was founded in 1988 by the Xi'an Communication University. It has become a major force of IT sales and distribution in northwest China.

Taiji Computer derived from the North China Institute of Computing Technology in 1987. Taiji acts as one of the principal bases for China's research on computer technology, development of new products, and systems integration for major national information projects.

Software Sector

China's software sector has emerged from virtually nothing. In 1999, about 2000 firms were involved in software development, of which more than 100 were foreign funded or sino-foreign founded joint ventures. The annual growth for the past few years has been close to 50%, with 1997 sales reaching US$1.57 billion. To a considerable extent, China's domestic software sector is not involved in direct competition with international firms, because they focus mainly on the market of 56k encryption software products, system integration, specialized and niche software, and Chinese language systems. In 1998-1999, Microsoft took almost 96% of China's PC operating system market. China's office management operating software is dominated by Microsoft's Office, IBM's Notes, LotusNotes, Computer Associates, and Unicenter. Oracle, SQL Server, DB2, Informix, Sybase take a lion's share in China's database software market. In 1999, application software took 62% of the market, while support software and system operating software had about 27% and 12% of the market respectively.[121]

The US Embassy in China estimated the 1996-1998 status of China's software industry as follows:[122]

	1996	1997	1998
Market Size (US$ million)	1,350	1,900	2,600
Local Production	415	650	870
Exports	35	50	70
Imports	970	1,300	1,800
Imports from U.S.	800	1,100	1,400

In contrast, MII's estimates on the country's software market tend to be more modest:

	1996	1997	1998	1999
Market Size (US$ million)	1,150	1,400	1,720	2,274
Growth (%)	35.3	21.74	23.21	31.88

China's software sector is estimated to grow by an average of 28% in 1999, 2000 and beyond. In 1999, China's market for domestic-made software was about US$1.2 billion, taking half of the total maket. The total software market there may grow to US$3.6 - 4 billion by the year 2001, which alone may expand the Chinese economy by US$6.2 billion and create more than one million jobs.[123]

By the year 2005, China Software Industry Association predicts, annual sales of computer information services and software will grow

---

[121] Application software serves management information systems, file management, CAD/CAM, education and entertainment. Support software is used for database management, networking and communications, language and development tools, anti-virus, and translation.

[122] Source: Report by U.S. Embassy in Beijing, December 1998. The figures do not include software used in telecom networks.

[123] This is estimated by Price Waterhouse Coopers and the Research Center for Computer and Microelectronics Industry Development.

up to US$21 billion, accounting for 2.2% of the world's total. The Association also forecasts that China's firms will take 60% of the domestic software and related services market. China's targeted areas for software development cover network security, Linux-based operating and application systems, enterprise management, home appliance systems, e-commerce, wireless mobile communications, Internet access and applications, Chinese language information processing, and information and communication intelligence applications.

In 1998, some 5,000 Chinese firms,[124] about 30% of them owned by the state, were involved in the computer software business. 80,000 professionals were working with these firms on software R&D. Top Chinese companies involved in software development and marketing include Ziguang, Stone, Yongyou, Legend, China Software, Wangma, Hope, and Founder. Main product lines these companies manufacture cover information processing, MIS, word processing, software tools, financial management, antivirus, spreadsheet, Internet connection and services, home PC, entertainment/games, and other application areas.[125] In 1997, China's domestic software firms took about 40% of this particular market.

Despite the progress, China's domestic software industry remains small because of the financial and structural weaknesses.[126] A joint study in the late 1998 by Beijing University, Qinghua University and Chinese Academy of Sciences shows that China's investment for

---

[124] Most of these firms are rather small, with fewer than 50 employees.

[125] Main software products Chinese firms developed (or developed jointly with foreign partners) by the mid-1997 included UC DOS, Richwin, Chinese Star, Hanshen, Chinese Windows, WPS, CCED, Hanwang, Qinghua, Wentong, Jinshan, Haima, Lide, Qingsong, Jindie, Yongyou, Wanneng, Anyi, Jinzhuzhu, Hope, Yaqi, QuickMIS, Wangte, KILL&KV300, AV95, Ruixing (Lucky Star), Zelin, Zexing, Gaolin, Hanshen Hanbridge, Liandao, Shitong, Tongze, Roboword, Internet Treasury, Nice&Easy Ready Word, Kelihua, Bitter Cloves, Wuzitong, Nurture of Men, Ant's Nest, Qishilu, Quandu, and Submit a Problem for Resolution.

[126] In 1999, the output of the China's software industry made up less than 1% of the world's total and China's software exports accounted for only one twentieth of the India's.

computer software development lagged far behind that for hardware infrastructure. In 1996-2000, the study estimates, a total of only US$181.4 million would be invested for computer software development, as compared with a big sum of US$120.9 billion for hardware.[127] In addition to funding, or software R&D venture capitals, to support innovative projects, major challenges China's software industry faces include widespread piracy and copyright infringement, updating of software development know-how, industry management expertise, and training and maintenance of human talents involved in software development.

In an attempt to support China's software development, the Chinese government has made preferential policies concerning taxation[128] and investment to encourage investment and industry consolidation. Support from the Chinese government to foster software industry's development includes an increase in investment and favored loans, preferential policies for venture capital, stock listing and taxation, measures to crack down software piracy and to protect software intellectual property rights, and priority for domestic software developers in government initiated projects and government procurement contracts. Meanwhile, China's software industry leaders seem to have realized the importance of resources and good strategies in software development. Early 2000, about 30 Chinese software developers, including Beijing University, Qinghua University, the Chinese Academy of Sciences, Star Computer, Langchao Electronics and China Software Project Center, established China Software Development Alliance in Beijing with an aim to create an open and effective environment for sharing of information and pooling of resources to enhance China's software industry strength.

Software is gaining more importance in China, as indicated by the changing software-to-hardware market ratios. The 1996 ratio of China's computer software to hardware (plus the related services) was approximately one to eight, in terms of sales. The ratio altered to

---

[127] Source: *Zhongguo Shang Bao* (China Commercial News), January 12, 1999.

[128] For example, in 1999, Beijing lowered the value-added tax on Zhongguancun software companies from 17% to 6%.

one to four in 1998. China's PC market shares in 1999 for software (plus the related services) and hardware were roughly 77% and 23%, up two percentage points for software over 1998. In terms of the hardware and software output value by China's domestic firms, the gap remained strikingly large. In 1999, China manufactured about US$12 billion worth of computer hardware products while software products were only about US$1.2 billion.

Estimates of China's Computer Hardware and Software (plus the related services) Sales:

	Software (US$billion)	Hardware (US$billion)	Total (US$billion)
1999	4.90	16.4	21.3
1998	3.92	14.5	18.42
1997	1.57	12.5	14.07
1996	1.108	8.615	9.723
1995	0.86	4.84	5.7
1994	0.62	3.75	4.37

China's official prediction for the country's computer industry in the year 2000 is as follows:

	Sales (US$ billion)	Growth (%)	As % of Total
Hardware	18.9	15.7	73.6
Software	2.8	27.8	11.0
Related Services	3.94	32.1	15.4
Total	25.64	N/A	100

As China becomes increasingly cautious of the Microsoft monopoly power and security flaws imbedded in Microsoft operating systems (Windows),[129] Linux, an alternative operating system invented by Finish scientist Linus Torvalds, has been seriously regarded by the

---

[129] Patent expense to Microsoft Windows in 1998 was 3-10% of the total sales price of a computer sold by Chinese vendors, which amounts to more than US$120 million paid to Microsoft in that year. Security back doors embedded in Windows were discovered in several cases.

Chinese government and computer industry as an alternative to Microsoft Windows because of its potential for China's future software applications. Linux, with its source code open, offers Chinese software industry an opportunity to develop new operating and applications software that meets China's development needs but leaves little room for information security "back doors." In view of this advantage, some Chinese software firms have worked to develop Linux-based products such as Xteam Linux, Cleek for Linux and other server and network solution software. The most notable player is the Red Flag Software Development Co. Ltd. of the Chinese Academy of Sciences. Red Flag is jointly invested by the Software Research Institute of the Chinese Academy of Sciences (60%) and Shanghai Lianchuan Investment Management Corporation (40%), with a startup investment of US$6 million. Red Flag has openly declared that its development model is America's Red Hat that develops and markets Linux products plus related technical support in the market of servers, PC and embedded computer equipment.[130]

National Informatization Program

China's unique development strategies for information and communications are reflected by the country's attempt to achieve a national "informatization," a process to extensively apply advanced information technologies for the enhancement of economy, trade, finance, sciences, education, culture, business management, and government performance and administration. This national informatization is government initiated and is apparently led by a few Chinese urban cities such as Shanghai, Beijing, Guangzhou and Tianjin. Both central and local government organizations in China have been enthusiastic and supportive to this informatization drive. Shanghai, for instance, has designated information technology as the

---

[130] Jiang Mianhen, son of the Chinese President Jiang Zemin, is Vice President of the Chinese Academy of Sciences and Chairman of the Board of Directors of Shanghai Lianchuan. He is directly involved in the Red Flag.

most important industry sector and has proclaimed that using network-based information technologies is becoming a life necessity. For the first time ever, more than half of the new terms embedded in Shanghai's 1999 government work report are IT-specific, such as "Shanghai Infoport Framework 1520 Project," "3C products," "IC cards," "network security systems," "IP broadband experiment networks (fiber optic cable, 100Mbps)," "access networks (using ATM, IP, ADSL, CATV-HFC technologies)," and "integration of computer, communications, and CATV networks."[131]

China's informatization program stems primarily from two strategic recognitions, namely:

1. As an important part of the world economies, Chinese economy should become increasingly modernized and globally engaged, which requires that China achieve a high level of economic competence and competitiveness based on electronically networked information systems. The great potential of the information technologies will provide China with a powerful cutting-edge instrument to carry forward and manage the process of China's economic modernization and globalization.

2. It is crucial that Chinese economy be fundamentally transformed from the traditional model that is product-based and labor intensive into an information-based system that is capital, intelligence, and technology intensive, and that is no longer restricted by time and distance. The new information-based economy will create an effective mechanism for adjustment and rationalization of China's industry structure, market supply and demand, financing and investment, equity ownership, operation management, and inter-regional economic activities.

---

[131] These terms refer to Shanghai's broadband information network project ("1"); five backbone network projects ("5"), i.e., interactive information network, social welfare network, international economic and trade EDI network, community service network, and Golden Card and payment network; twenty key information application systems ("20"); computer, communication and consumer electronics products ("3C"); and integrated chip cards ("IC Card").

While the country does not seem to be fully aware yet that national informatization will ultimately involve a large scale of fundamental adjustments or restructuring in social, political, and economic sectors, China understands that informatization plays a key role in the nation's overall development. Informatization promises both opportunities and challenges. It provides an enabling power by which China will catch up with or leapfrog over many industrialized nations, but at the same time, China can be left further behind if it does not have a good strategy to meet the challenges of the global information revolution. China also recognizes that informatization is a complex process involving integrated performance of six key elements: advanced information technologies and communications networks, capital investment, computer hardware and software, information resources (*e.g.,* content and database), regulatory and legal regime, and the people who innovate and operate on information technologies.

Chinese academics have worked on establishing a model to measure the development status of informatization. They have drawn upon the methodologies developed by Japan, International Telecommunication Union and International Data Corporation, and come up with a revised measuring system that takes more than 40 variables for analysis and assessment. These variables include, among other things, information consumption (*e.g.,* telephone traffic, penetration of publications, Internet access time), unit availability of information facility and equipment (*e.g.,* teledensity, Internet servers, PC, radio and TV penetration), user numbers of wired and wireless communication services, infrastructure status (*e.g.,* length of backbone and access networks, technology, coverage of various networks), revenue and employment percentages of telecom industry, information services, information oriented manufacturing, and expenses on information and communications as a percentage of national expenditure. A study based on 1995 data shows that China, compared with other countries, was ranked 21, 27, 28, and 27 respectively in terms of communications facilities and equipment, information resources development and usage, government input for information development, and general capacity of information and communications.[132] This ranking may have been considerably higher, given China's progress since 1995 in these four areas.

The conceptual framework of China's national informatization program is composed of four essential building blocks:

1. *Information Infrastructure* that includes advanced electronic wireline-wireless networks such as telecommunications networks, computer information networks, and media (TV and broadcasting) networks; information resources; and information transmission and processing equipment and facilities.
2. *Information Supporting Construct* that refers to information and communications industry, information technologies, R&D, information services, and human resources that work for information related sectors.
3. *Information Applications* that encompasses market supply and demand, effectiveness of information services, pricing, impact of information on micro- and macro-economic realities.
4. *Social and Regulatory Environment* consisting of such factors as government policies, legal framework, market regulation, information management, education and training, and socio-cultural values on information and communications.

This conceptual framework dictates that China will concentrate its resources on the following nine areas in achieving its informatization objectives:

- Construction and upgrading of advanced information networks that are digitized, integrated, pervasive, and well managed
- Development and deployment of information resources
- Wide-spread applications of computer-based information systems

---

[132] This study was done by China State Statistics Bureau.

- Manufacturing, import/export, and installation of information and communications equipment and facilities
- Innovation and development of information technologies
- Growth of information related industries
- Nurturing of information market and information services
- Education and training of human resources for information and communications
- Establishment and implementation of regulations and laws for information and communications

The substantive informatization objectives China visualizes for the year 2000-2010 include:

- *Communications Infrastructure:*

  - To build and upgrade communications networks - composed mainly of fiber optic, satellite, wireless mobile, and microwave technologies - and facilities (not including equipment-manufacturing sector). To meet this target, China has invested over US$60 billion from 1996 to 1999. A projected US$24 billion will be invested for the year 2000.
  - By the end of 2000, national teledensity grows to 15-16%, and fiber optic trunk lines reaches 240,000 km. Telecom exchange capacity increases to 180 million main lines; mobile telecom channels climbs up to 1.05 million, and data communications network capacity, 800,000 nodes.
  - Development of ISDN ATM/SDH/IP and IP based broadband networks which are world-class in functions, performance, and capacity, capable of providing high quality voice, video, data, and multimedia services. Public communications platforms will serve China's various socio-economic information applications such as Golden Projects and E-commerce.

- Broadcast and TV coverage rises to 95% or more of the population nationwide.

- *Electronic Technology and Equipment Manufacturing Industries:* Moving into 2000 and beyond, China has designated electronics industry as one of the key (pillar) industries and is targeting to have the industry's GDP share rise to 5% and its production climb to 8% in the nation's total industrial output value. China focuses its IT R&D and manufacturing efforts on several areas, including:

  - Semiconductor Industry: upgrading the manufacturing capability from current Integrated Circuits (ICs) of 4/5-inch wafers with 3/4-micron and 1.2/1.6-micron line widths to that of 6/8-inch wafers with 0.35/0.25/0.18 micron line widths; expanding the annual production capacity to 2.5-3 billion units by 2000.[133]
  - New-generation Electronic Components: *e.g.,* CPUs, monitoring and demonstrating devices, light-electron appliances, photoelectric devices, and other advanced IT components.
  - Computers: mainframes development bases, PC and peripherals production lines, and R&D and production centers of operating and applications software.
  - Communications Equipment: digital program-control switches (annual 15 million lines by 2000), with priority given to China-developed HJD-04, EIM-601, C&C-08 and ZXJ10 models; fiber optic cables (3 million km per year by 2000); advanced digital mobile communications networks (e.g., 3G, GSM, and CDMA systems) and equipment; and satellite communications systems.[134]

---

[133] China has invested US$1.2 billion in "908-909" projects in Shanghai, in an attempt to fulfil this objective.

[134] China hopes that, after 2000, 50% or more of the communication equipment market share will be taken by domestically made communications products. And by then China may reach an annual production capacity of 2.5 million mobile exchanges, 2.6 million cellular and cordless phone sets, 100,000 base channels,

- Consumer Electronics: CATV and digital audio/video products, Internet related TV devices, digital broadcasting transmission equipment, traffic control and automobile electronic products, medical electronic devices, and advanced electronic systems and products for military uses.
- Networking technologies: network servers, interface development, office automation (OA), computer-integrated manufacturing (CIM), computer-aided design (CAD), and policy/management decision support systems (DSS).

- *Information Applications and Services:* As key to the national informatization, China has emphasized on the development of both information infrastructure and information applications and services. To push ahead for a better use of information, China is working to build up four layers of information systems to extensively promote information and communication applications as reflected by the nation's initiatives of e-government, e-enterprises, e-community and e-households:

  1. state information systems to meet national economic, political, administrative, educational, and military needs;[135]
  2. national sectorial information systems for different industry sectors such as finance and banking, aviation,

---

50 large and medium-sized satellite earth stations, 3000 VAST stations, and 400,000 sets of satellite TV receiving devices.

[135] China opened an online database system called *China Knowledge Infrastructure* (www.chinajournal.net.cn) in June 1999, which has about 6600 types of Chinese and foreign journals and periodicals, with millions of indexes, abstracts, and full texts, for public search. By 1998, 1,442 types of electronic media products were made available by about 100 electronic publishers in China, with market sales up to several thousand million Chinese yuan.

railways, taxation, commerce, power, agriculture, tourism, health care, and education;

3. business management systems and Internet based information systems for state-own and non-state-own enterprises;[136] and

4. regional and local information systems that offer services involving voice transmission, online data retrieval,[137] publishing, and multi-media to socio-economic institutions and the general public. China's Golden Projects and Internet-related initiatives are representative of these information application systems under construction. They are intended for a sharing of information resources and for provisions of basic and value-added/enhanced services.

In the early part of 1999, the Chinese government launched a campaign designated as "Government Online,"[138] which called for 60% of the government organizations at different levels to get online within the year. By the end of 1999, China reportedly had 2,479 "gov.cn" domain names in use; 68 central government organizations went online; about 800 government offices at different levels had their own WWW web servers for public services, or had already set up their own websites for online information exchange and distribution.

---

[136] For years, China's state own enterprises (SOEs) put a very small percentage of their capital in developing their computer systems. According to the Chinese State Economic and Trade Commission's statistics, China's top 300 SOEs in 1998 had only 0.3% of their annual fixed-assets investment allocated for the deployment of computer information systems. These firms invested only US$206 million in their internal computer network systems in 1999, but the figure represented an increase of 15.5% over 1998.

[137] In 1996, China had about 1200 databases. Most of these databases, however, are not networked and are fairly small in capacity -- larger than 100MB: 25%; 10-100MB: 42%; smaller than 10MB: 33%. These databases are concentrated in Beijing (34.6%), Guangdong (8.3%), Shanghai (7.2%), Sichuan (5.9%), and Tianjin (5.6%). In contrast, USA had approximately 5500 databases, many of which have a capacity of more than 1000MB.

[138] For details, check on www.gov.cn.

This "Government Online" campaign is endorsed by the State Council, funded by participating organizations and local governments, with the hope to have different government ministries, commissions, offices and information centers nationwide interconnected by an advanced network system, so that information can be effectively processed, transmitted, and shared. This way, government offices at different levels can raise their work and procurement efficiency, enhance their policy transparency, and provide better services to the general public.

Under the official mandate, China Telecom is the key implementer of this initiative,[139] while the State Economic and Trade Commission acts as a project coordinator. Thirteen Chinese media organizations such as People's Daily, Guangmin Daily, and Economic Daily have been involved in the project, and seven Chinese ISPs/ICPs have been selected to provide connection and data processing services. The project will deploy network hardware and software mainly supplied by IBM, Compaq, Microsoft, Huawei, Cisco, Ericsson, and Lucent. China Telecom agrees to provide Central government agencies with 128Kbps dedicated data networks, and provincial and city government offices with 64Kbps lines for connection with the national 163 and 169 backbones. China Telecom is requested to offer favorable terms for access to servers, database management, and service charges.

In April 2000, China's National Library in Beijing, endorsed by China's Ministry of Culture, officially launched an extensive digital library project, aiming at building up a digitized information network system in China that will fundamentally change the way conventional libraries store, index, process and present information. It will expand the volume of Chinese-language information resources on the Internet, propel the growth of China's knowledge-based economy, and revolutionize how China's libraries serve their customers. The project is jointly supported by other central government organizations and research and academic institutions. The huge database to be created through this project is expected to help with better conservation of

---

[139] In terms of the operating system for the Government Online project, China seems to be in favor of Linux, not Microsoft Windows.

China's historical and cultural heritages, and contribute to a faster development of China's science, technology, culture, education and publishing. Earlier, as a trial pilot sub-project for digital library, the National Library made 1,000-gigabytes of the information electronically available on its website (www.nlc.gov.cn), which generated 100 million page hits in 1999.

- *Policy and Regulatory Environment:*

In its informatization drives, the Chinese government seems to have reached some policy consensus that encompasses the following:

- Unified strategic planning and implementation under central and local governments
- Coordinated and concerted efforts among different players as a crucial factor for informatization
- Domestic forces perform the major role and receive favorable and protective treatment wherever appropriate
- Informatization goes hand in hand with industrialization, not one precedes or replaces the other
- Technology deployment and market demand as primary catalysts for development
- Development and sharing of information resources as one of the most important objectives
- Regulatory and legal framework as key to success

Regulatory and legal framework is the fundamental infrastructure of China's national informatization. It is recognized that China's informatization program involves multiple players and complex policy and regulatory issues and challenges. Among other things, a rational and effective regulatory and legal framework is urgently required. Such a framework should facilitate, support, and regulate the development of information infrastructure, network expansion, IT innovations and applications, and overall progress in information and communications.

To tackle the emerging policy and regulatory issues, China's State Council established an inter-ministerial body called the State Council

Informatization Leading Group in May 1996, with representations from 18 ministries and commissions. Ministry of Electronics Industry, MPT, State Planning Commission, State Economic and Trade Commission, State Science and Technology Commission, Ministry of Radio, Broadcast and Television, and People's Bank of China were among the principal members of this leading group. Under the Vice Premier Wu Bangguo's leadership, this State Council Leading Group has continued its mission in 2000. The State Council also called China's first senior-level national information policy conference in April 1998 in Shenzhen[140] to address critical issues such as China's information and communications legal framework, government administration, management of and interconnection between public and dedicated networks, network and information security and protection, intellectual property right, market competition, domestic industry development, resources allocation, capital investment, and international cooperation and foreign involvement.

---

[140] On the agenda of this national conference were informatization policy statements, SPC report on state informatization prospects for 2000 and 2010, MPT report on telecom development status, Ministry of Radio, Broadcast and TV report on development of broadcast and TV networks, Golden Projects, and ministerial and regional information exchange on initiatives of railways, education, Shanghai Infoport, Tianjin Infoport, Guangdong, Shenzhen, Hainan, Liaonin, Shangdong, Shanxi, Fujian, and Hunan.

Part Two: Policy and Regulatory Framework

Background Observation

The rapid development of China's communications and information takes place in a context of political and regulatory dynamics characterized by complex institutional interactions and conflicts. Economic, political, and technological forces are driving China's policy and regulatory authorities to rethink and restructure its conventional decision making processes and put forward new policies and regulations on communications and information. Rising market competition, as represented between MPT incumbents and emerging non-MPT players, growing availability of network-based advanced communication services and Internet applications, and foreign investment and involvement in China's vast communication and information market are three principal "yeasts" that stir up political and regulatory complexities and changes.

One of the spotlights that showcase institutional conflict of interest is Internet management and regulation. Officially, China's Internet related networks are regulated by MPT-MII, State Education Commission, State Administration of Radio, Films and Television (SARFT), and Chinese Academy of Sciences. MPT-MII is, in addition to offering Internet services on CHINANET, authorized to control the international gateways and issue licenses for Internet service providers (ISPs). However, each of these four organizations has, in principle, equal amount of political power to acquire control over Internet-linked networks and services. They all have their own plans and objectives which may go across borders and create tensions in terms of political and economic interest. Coordination and regulation for network access and interconnection, line leasing and service pricing, cost and revenue accounting, and network security and supervision have therefore become critical issues to the Chinese government.

There has been a strong urge that China makes its greatest effort to build a new policy and regulatory framework to provide rationalized leadership and effective regulation for the ever accelerated and very challenging development of communications and information industries. To date, this urge has largely been unmet, albeit China's State Council has created an ad hoc task force called the Leading Group for the National Informatization, and restructured MPT, MEI and MRFT into MII. China has not yet made formalized laws to regulate communications and information market, nor has it set up an independent and impartial authority to exercise regulatory power over communications and information sector.

The absence of a powerful regulatory framework seems to undercut the ability of the government to lead, oversee and regulate information and communications industry that is considered as a very sensitive and crucial sector. There has been a significant dilemma to the Chinese government on the development of information and communications. To implement the nation's modernization program, priority must be given to the application of information technologies, which suggests providing the general public with a wider and easier access to information, linking China's 1.2 billion people into a global communications network, and, to the government grave concern, creating a new environment that enables information to flow virtually beyond the government control.

The State Council represents China's central government in charge of the state administration and management, under which there is a complex and often overlapping hierarchy of players including commissions, ministries, special offices, and ad hoc task forces. Commissions are at a higher bureaucratic level than ministries. Within their respective spheres of competence, commissions in principle give instructions to ministries, help construct internal consensus, and strike balances among competing efforts. Commissions are supposed to take a more integrative view of the country's affairs than ministries that manage specific aspects of different sectors. In between commissions and line ministries are a few supra-ministerial entities, such as the Ministry of Finance and the People's Bank of China, which have comprehensive resources in jurisdiction and responsibilities. Special offices and ad hoc task forces are set up to handle special issues of the political or administrative areas. They may act as either short-term coordinating bodies, or long-range government entities. In many cases, top leaders sitting on the political bureau of the Party, the State Council, and the important commissions and ministries are the key drivers of policy making. Political power, in this context, is often vested more in individuals than in specific institutions. The elite influence initiates the policies, and relevant bureaucratic bodies configurate and implement them at both national and local levels.

The problems with this political structure came under attack by the new State Council leadership that launched a new wave of bureaucratic restructuring at the ninth National People's Congress held in March 1998,[141] with an objective to separate government functions from business operations, raise government efficiency, and curb bureaucracy and corruption. Previous 40 ministries and commissions were shrunk to 29,[142] with the State Economic and Trade

---

[141] Between 1980's and 1990's, China went through a number of campaigns aimed at downsizing or streamlining the number of ministries and commissions under the State Council, but government bodies ended being expanded or recurred under new names.

[142] Twelve ministries and three commissions were closed, lowered in rank, or merged into others; 3 commissions were renamed; and 22 ministries and commissions were kept unchanged. 3 new ministries and 1 new commission were established. The newly formed State Council then consists of four essential constituencies for (1) *state macro regulation and control* (*e.g.*, State Development and Planning Commission, State Economic and Trade Commission, Ministry of Finance, and People's Bank of China), (2) *specialized economic management* (*e.g.*, MII - formerly MPT, Ministry of Railways, MOFTEC, Ministry of Communications, Ministry of Construction, Ministry of Water Resources, and Ministry of Agriculture), (3) *administrative authorities for science, technology, education, culture, social security and resources* (*e.g.*,

Commission granted far more jurisdiction to oversee the nation's overall economy and industry sectors.

MPT, in this reshuffle, was renamed the Ministry of Information Industry (MII), while MEI and part of MRFT were merged into MII. MII's official mandate is proclaimed as including making plans, policies and regulations for information and communication industries, facilitating and overseeing R&D and manufacturing of telecom, IT and software products, and development and management of public backbone networks, radio broadcast and television networks, and dedicated networks. Officially, MII is also given the jurisdiction to administer the networks previously managed by MRFT and National Air and Space Aviation Industry Corporation. The former MPT's postal administration, now the State Postal Bureau, is under MII's management. All this change seems dramatic and resounding, making MPT's descendant MII a fresh-faced super-ministry, but the questions aroused include to what extent MII is truly different from MPT, whether MII is created only to reinforce MPT's existing monopolistic power, and what prospect is there for MII to practically become untied from China Telecom and local carriers in terms of separating government functions from business operations.

The crucial issues concerning China's communications and information development rest inherently on China's present political structure, policy making processes, and regulatory regime at both central and local levels. As the central party committee, the State Council, various commissions and ministries, ad hoc task forces, fractional elite contending power strife, and many other bureaucratic players are all involved in the decision making and enforcement

---

Ministry of Science and Technology, Ministry of Education, Ministry of Labor and Social Security, Ministry of Personnel, and Ministry of Land Resources), and (4) *state general affairs administration* (*e.g.,* Ministry of Foreign Affairs, Ministry of National Defense, Ministry of Culture, Ministry of Public Health, State Family Planning Commission, State Nationalities Affairs Commission, Ministry of Justice, Ministry of Public Security, Ministry of State Security, Ministry of Civil Affairs, Ministry of Supervision, and State Auditing Administration). This government restructuring, if thoroughly carried out, will in 3 years cut down the size of the government staff by 4 million nationwide.

processes for communication and information industries, institutional stakes are simply too high and too pervasive to be easily clarified. China's formal political structure seems to produce a unified, interactive, and hierarchical chain of governance, but in reality it is often divided, segmented, and stratified, generating interagency competition, power conflicts, and problems of coordination. Fragmentation of authority seems to be more of a core feature of the system than integration that is highly desired for. This political reality speaks for the high-profiled tensions and discord lingering among former MPT, MEI, and MRFT in China's information related policies and regulations, and explains why the State Council has established an ad hoc leading group and intensively engaged State Planning Commission and some other supra-ministerial authorities to link, buffer, and coordinate regulatory activities which concern the country's communication and information.

Cross-ministerial conflict of interest, overall leadership, and market regulation are among the most critical policy issues that the central government has to address. Apparently, the existing bureaucratic agencies can hardly provide the levers and resources of control and coordination needed to deal with the rapid expansion of information and communications. The State Council Leading Group for National Informatization has therefore evolved into horizon. This leading group, also named the State Council Steering Committee for National Information Infrastructure, was informally disclosed in early 1996[143] and then officially inaugurated in May of the same year, with representations from 18 different central government organizations such as MEI, MPT, the State Planning Commission, the State Economic and Trade Commission, and the State Science and Technology Commission.

The Leading Group was structured in three tiers. At the top were the interagency ministerial-level senior officials including MEI Minister Hu Qili, MPT Minister Wu Jichuan, and five other high-level officials.

---

[143] Chinese Premier Li Peng first mentioned the idea of having an informatization leading group at a State Council conference on January 23, 1996, in order for China to acquire economic and commercial competitiveness worldwide.

The second level was the Information Office (the Secretariat) that handles day-to-day operations. The office broke down into five departments: Planning, Network (Internet) Administration, Policy and Regulation, Key Project Coordination, and General Affairs. Lü Xinkui, MEI Vice Minister, acted as the director of the Information Office. At the third tier of the Leading Group structure was a 24-member experts group to provide technological advice.

The original mission and responsibility of the Leading Group is interpreted as that of coordination and administration among regulators and policymakers. Its primary functions are formally laid out as

- drafting polices and principles for national informatization, initiating and organizing the drafting of relevant laws and regulations;
- devising master plans and strategies to guide the development of the country's information infrastructure which covers plans for a national informatization infrastructure, the development of information resources, and personnel training;
- coordinating and overseeing cross-organization and trans-regional projects involving information technology, particularly those that impact the country's overall economic and social development;
- providing guidance on the planning, feasibility, and implementation of major information-related projects;
- coordinating and solving major problems related to large-scale computer information networks and connections with the global Internet; and
- organizing studies on emerging information technologies that could impact China's move toward informatization, and coordinating and assisting in setting state technology standards and application criteria.

The name "Leading Group," according to China's present bureaucratic structure, generally lacks a solid organizational ground and a statutory mandate. Leading groups are often established to address ad hoc short-term issues, and are dispersed eventually with their functions rolled into an existing government department. This is perhaps why the Informatization Leading Group's political power was at times eclipsed, and its ability to force policy changes overlooked. Besides, the Informatization Leading Group, due to its highly MEI-affiliated operational staff, was seen by some analysts as possibly acting as a vehicle for MEI in its rivalry with MPT, particularly in the dimension of the Leading Group's initiatives to oversee China's Internet-related networks[144] and to draft an information law that may counter-play MPT's effort in drafting China's telecommunications law.

For some time, speculations were spreading around that the Leading Group might become the core element of a new information commission to be chaired by a senior official from the State Planning Commission or MEI. The new information commission, if established, would enjoy a higher level of statutory authority and resources to exercise central control over the rapidly growing information industries while staying significantly independent of the commercial interests MPT, MEI, Ministry of Radio, Films, and TV (MRFT), and other component ministries held. Such a commission would possibly be formed as a result of the upgrading of the State Council Leading Group, or an institutional merger of MPT, MEI, and MRFT. In terms of the political hierarchy, it would be on par with the State Planning Commission and other supra-ministerial bodies. This widely speculated prospect, however, met strong resistance from the ministries involved, particularly from MPT and MRFT, who wanted to defend their own vested interest. What turned out in 1998 was the formation of a MPT-based ministry of information industry (MII), instead of an information commission. Although MII was officially given the jurisdiction to extensively regulate China's IT and telecom industries, which seems to have covered what the Leading Group was charged to do, the State Council Leading Group has never been officially dissolved.

---

[144] This was an area largely under MPT's control.

In the fall of 1999, the State Council announced its decision to establish a new leading group, the State Informatization Leading Group, with no mention of where the previous leading group is, or whether this new leading group is the direct successor or substitute of the old one. This leading group, mandated for IT and information related institutional coordination and cooperation, is headed by China's Vice Premier Wu Bangguo and MII Minister Wu Jichuan, with 15 members from various central government organizations. Under this leading group are four offices taking on different responsibilities: computer network and information security, state informatization promotion, Y2K resolution and contingency, and state informatization expert consultation group. The office of the expert consultation group is intertwined into the Computer Network and Information Security Management Center of the Chinese Academy of Sciences, and other offices are virtually housed within the MII departments of Informatization Promotion, IT Products Management, and Telecommunications Administration, with no assignment for additional staff.　In addition to the Leading Group and MPT-MII, key constituencies who significantly affected the previous directions of China's communications and information industries include, among others, State Radio Regulation Commission, State Planning Commission, State Science and Technology Commission, State Economic and Trade Commission, Ministry of Electronics Industry, Ministry of Foreign Trade and Economic Cooperation, Ministry of Railways, Ministry of Electric Power, and State Information Center.[145]

---

[145] Note the restructuring of some of these government organizations in March 1998.

The Ministry of Posts and Telecommunications (MPT)[146]

MPT is mandated by the State Council as the national regulatory and operating organization of telecommunications. In principle, MPT is responsible for the overall management and regulation of the country's telecom market, which means all the public networks should be controlled by MPT, and the private networks of various government organizations or industries should receive oversight and guidance from MPT. MPT issues telecom licenses and drafts telecom administrative orders and directives with consultation, if needed, from relevant ministries or commissions. The State Council Legal Affairs Bureau reviews the drafted documents, and State Council Standing Committee approves or disapproves them. Most of the telecom operational directives are first drafted by a specific MPT department, sent to the MPT Department of Policy and Regulation for reviews, and go through an approving process by MPT Minister and other senior officials.

As China's highest administrative power, the State Council makes major policy decisions concerning the overall development direction of information and communications. It oversees the workings of information related ministries and commissions, including that of MPT, develops overall strategies and plans for national projects and implementation structures, and provides coordination, arbitration, and support for nationally significant projects. All major telecom policies and documents proposed by MPT must go through the State Council's prior review. The relationships between MPT and central authorities and other government organizations reflect MPT's own position and how China's telecommunications are regulated and managed. MPT reports to and is responsible for the State Council that appoints MPT leadership. The rules and regulations on telecommunications and information involving important stakes of other ministries or commissions and local governments are usually proposed by MPT to the State Council for approval, and issued for implementation in the name of the State Council. One vice premier of

---

[146] Note the change in March 1998 of MPT to Ministry of Information Industry (MII).

the State Council is specifically assigned to take charge of communications and information industries. Currently, Vice Premier Wu Bangguo takes this role. MPT's development plans usually relate to the State Planning Commission's national industrial planning, while MPT's technology strategies may not be separated from the perspectives of the State Science and Technology Commission. Principal MPT decisions generally involve several rounds of ministerial interactions and balances.

State Radio Regulation Commission (SRRC)

SRRC, increasingly known to the public in recent years, operates like a cross-ministerial task force. It regulates and manages China's radio frequency spectrum resources for mobile, satellite, maritime, and aeronautic communications. Under the dual leadership of the State Council and the Central Military Commission, the SRRC is formed with one commissioner, three deputy commissioners, and twenty-two members who also hold leading positions in various ministries or commissions concerned with information and communications. (For more details on SRRC, see "Part Three: *Radio Spectrum Management* under Regulatory Issues, Strategic Implications")

State Planning Commission (SPC)[147]

Given the particular Chinese socio-economic and political environment, the State Planning Commission stands as an extremely powerful hand for the State Council in its planning and management of the country's economy. The commission is authorized by the State Council to undertake the responsibilities to formulate strategic and long-term goals for the national development, which is unveiled in China's ten-year, five-year and one-year development plans. The SPC initiates efforts in bringing the nation's finance, credits, interest rate, taxation, wages, materials, labor forces, investment, foreign

---

[147] SPC was renamed State Development Planning Commission in March 1998.

exchange, and domestic and foreign trade under the state macroeconomic control, and tries to put them on good balances. It facilitates the State Council in its process of making national policies concerning industrial structure, technology development, resources allocation, and foreign economic relations, and directs and coordinates the activities of different ministries in their developmental planning and implementation. SPC has the authority to review and approve (or reject) China's major telecom and information project proposals through its departments of long-term planning, industry policy, price regulation, and communications and energy.

State Economic and Trade Commission (SETC)[148]

In terms of the officially authorized functions and responsibilities, the State Economic and Trade Commission used to have the core task of overseeing and managing the implementation of the production plans made by SPC. SETC coordinates among ministries in the process of the state plan fulfillment. SETC was once acting as an internal trade commission, as opposed to the Ministry of Foreign Trade and Economic Cooperation (MOFTEC). To a certain degree, SETC's jurisdiction overlapped with that of the SPC. In March 1998, China's government restructuring campaign reinforced SETC's supra ministerial status. SETC became a new State Council powerhouse charged to oversee and manage a wide range of economic activities and industry sectors. SETC is granted authority to coordinates MPT and its competitors, and has taken over some of the important responsibilities from the MOFTEC, which extend across several ministries and organizations. SETC holds jurisdiction over both China Unicom and Ji Tong, a subsidiary of the former MEI. The specific role the SETC performs over these two telecoms companies is probably that of an equity watchdog. SETC also works with Ministry

---

[148] In the March 1998 NPC session, SETC was granted more jurisdiction over China's overall economy and industry sectors including machine-building, metallurgy, coal, textile, petrochemicals, electric power, light industry, and internal trade.

of Foreign Trade and Economic Cooperation on telecom-related WTO and APEC issues.

State Commission for Restructuring Economic Systems (SCRES)[149]

SCRES is mandated to work on the schemes of restructuring China's economic systems. It identifies the key problems, facilitates changes in China macroeconomic environment, and oversees large state-owned enterprises' reform. The SCRES's Department of Production and Administrative System has increasingly involved in the reform of the China communications and information sectors, and in supporting the growth of China Unicom and other non-MPT entities. The change in bureaucratic framework involving MPT, MEI, State Council Leading Group may have drawn on the organizational studies and policy proposals by SCRES.

State Science and Technology Commission (SSTC)[150]

As a national science and technology policymaking and advisory body, SSTC is charged with the responsibility to make guiding principles and policies for the nation's science and technology development. Two broad missions SSTC undertakes are (1) to illuminate the scientific and technological dimensions of the choices confronting China's leaders, and (2) to raise China's own science and technology standards to world levels. SSTC reviews and approves major technology oriented projects, draws up science and technology development plans based on the outline prepared by the SPC, and helps manage and allocate government funds for the SPC ratified projects. It also handles issues of international cooperation and

---

[149] SCRE was turned into a policy consulting board for the premier and other State Council senior officials in March 1998.

[150] SSTC was turned into the Ministry of Science and Technology in March 1998.

exchange in science and technology. Its key role in telecommunications modernization is to assess China's capacity and needs to absorb foreign technology. SSTC makes plans for tactics to disseminate foreign technology; and it promotes the diffusion of domestic innovations throughout the telecommunications R&D community. The SSTC attends to such strategic issues as the planning for the overall telecom technology framework, the selection and recommendation of the technology and standards, and the coordination for major technological programs across different industry sectors or regions.

Ministry of Electronics Industry (MEI)[151]

MEI represented a powerhouse for China's electronics technology based information and communications industry. Besides being mandated by the State Council to assume responsibility to make national policy, plans and strategy, MEI had under its leadership a wealth of nationwide resources and facilities engaged in electronics technology oriented manufacturing and R&D activities. The MEI's manufacturing and R&D bases focused on electronic components and equipment, computers (both hardware and software), and digital switching systems and components. MEI attached great importance to the advancement of electronic information systems and China's national Informatization.

Traditionally, the essential difference in responsibilities, defined by the State Council, between MEI and MPT, was that MEI acted as a manufacturer and developer of most telecommunications parts and systems while MPT was a telecommunications regulator and services provider. This different work distribution was getting blurred due to China's rapidly changing telecommunications environment in which technologies converge and the traditional telecommunications regulatory framework becomes outdated and ineffective. MEI tried to strengthen its manufacturing facilities and made significant moves to

---

[151] At the NPC 1998 conference, MEI was merged into MPT to form the new ministry of information industry. Part of MEI, according to some sources, has been made a national electronics corporation.

enter the telecommunications and information services market, as evidenced by the ministry's involvement in Ji Tong, Golden Projects, Internet services and China Unicom.

Ministry of Foreign Trade and Economic Cooperation (MOFTEC)

Compared with the SETC, the MOFTEC's responsibilities are focused on China's external economic and trade transactions and relations. The ministry works to ensure that the country's external trade, aid, and joint ventures serve the national interest. It formulates policies, regulations and strategies for China's foreign economic and trade activities in line with the domestic development goals set by the State Council. As a national regulator and mediator, the MOFTEC deals with issues of foreign trade, foreign economic cooperation, and foreign investment and loans. It regulates Chinese enterprises' investment overseas, approves foreign applications to set up business entities or agencies in China, coordinates inter-governmental, bilateral or multilateral economic cooperation programs, and administers trade shows and negotiations for China national corporations or government offices.

The most crucial role MOFTEC has with China's telecom and information industries is its negotiations at WTO and APEC regarding foreign equity ownership and service operations, for which the ministry has to consult MPT-MII and other government organizations for consensus. MOFTEC also has a stake in the areas of telecom equipment import and export, technology transfer, founding of joint ventures, and the use of foreign loans for telecom projects, due to the ministry's mandate to support or veto the submitted proposals. MOFTEC's judgements are based on its studies and analysis on whether particular information and communications technologies are worth importing, what capability China has to absorb the imported technologies, what sources of the technologies should be sought out, and whether the particular projects for communications and IT sectors are economically viable.

Ministry of Radio, Films, and Television (MRFT-SARFT)

MRFT performs the crucial media regulating functions for the China's central and local government organizations and the general public. It controls China's nationwide public media that deliver political ideology and official information. MRFT formulates policy and regulations for the country's mass media, and manages the programming and operation of films, broadcasting, and television. In addition, it builds and operates a large nationwide CATV system. Principal organizations administered by MRFT include China Central Television, China Radio International, China National Radio, China Film Administrative Bureau, China National Audio-Visual Corporation, Radio and TV Publishing House, the Design Institute of MRFT, Academy of Broadcasting Sciences and Technologies, China Broadcasting Arts Troupe, Beijing Film Academy, and Beijing Broadcasting Institute. To an important extent, MRFT is under the control of the Propaganda Department of the Chinese Communist Party Central Committee in terms of supervising and censoring the media content for press, radio, films and TV.

One critical challenge faced by MRFT is its CATV network construction and operation. MPT wants MRFT to employ its public telecom networks for CATV program transmissions, while MRFT has made ambitious plans to build its own long-distance and local cable systems to compete with MPT. The stake involved is both technological and financial. An independent cable system seems to benefit MRFT as regards its control of the broadband infrastructure and economic gains from China's enormous CATV, Internet, and data communications market. MPT strongly argues that all communication networks, including CATV and radio broadcasting networks, should fall within its jurisdiction. Duplicate network development and MRFT's network regulation cause a waste of resources and regulatory confusion. MPT favors the proposal to separate radio and TV content providers from their network ownership and operation, which will lead to the establishment of the radio and TV network operating companies subject to MPT's authority.

The government restructuring in March 1998 "downgraded" MRFT to a new regulating agency called the State Administration of Radio,

Film and Television (SARFT) which is officially brought under MPT's successor MII. However, it turns out that SARFT functions largely independent of MII, and its political power remains more or less that of a ministry.

Local Post and Telecommunications Administrations

China's economic reform and political dynamics have brought about a critical challenge to the power linkages between Beijing, the central government, and the locales, the regional, provincial, or city decision makers. The issue has always been what is the appropriate blend of national uniformity and local autonomy and how they are maintained in a good balance. Excessive centralization stifles local initiatives while too much decentralization may harm national interest. The leverage to maintain the balance is usually achieved through the center-local bargaining, on the basis of such local factors as strategic significance, economic resources, personal connection, and acumen of leaders. In this process, financial resources play a key role. With the trend of a more distributed budgetary structure, local governments in China have gained more control over their revenues and expenditures, hence, stronger power base in dealing with Beijing.

Similar situation applies to the telecom and information sector. As fundamental operation units, local post and telecommunication administrations (PTAs) are positioned to independently carry out both on-the-ground regulatory and implementation responsibilities. PTAs are under two sources of political and regulatory pressure, one from MPT and the other from the local governments. Local government involvement in PTAs is sometimes realized through ad hoc leading groups that exert cross-departmental forces over local PTAs' performance, or through the impact of local budgetary and other resources allocation. MPT, on the other hand, tries to retain its vertical control through such forces as development planning, technical standard, personnel appointment, and project review and approval. Under such a dualistic scheme, local PTAs can often have certain degrees of flexibility in their policies toward financing, investment arrangement, network operation, equipment purchase or manufacturing, and alliance with local or foreign players.

Local telecom laws and regulations are drafted by local PTAs, with consultation with relevant local organizations. The draft laws and regulations are submitted to the legal affairs offices of the local government for reviews, approved by local people's congress, and filed to the National People's Congress. Beijing, Shanghai, and 27 provinces in China have established their own local telecom laws. These local laws, however, can hardly be effectively enforced without a national telecom statutory framework.

Another area that has challenged the MPT-PTA relationship is capital investment. As PTAs are increasingly required to raise funds locally or from abroad, they have to work out ways to approach local or foreign entities, which may often go beyond the policy boundaries defined by MPT. Growing local market competition may also impose challenges to MPT's control, as PTAs go ahead with initiatives and innovations in their own interest. With the restructuring of MPT into MII, local PTAs are under immediate pressure of where to go in terms of their political relationships with the new ministry, and what bureaucratic structures they should adopt for themselves. The drive for a separation of regulation and operation may result in a structural change in the old MPT-PTA paradigm, which could mean new strategic alternatives for China's communications and information industries, such as the making of regional or local competing telecom operators,[152] or development of sectorial division of business into transmission, switching, and terminal service (*e.g.,* basic and value-added) providers.

---

[152] In May 1998, a MPT/MII delegation to Washington DC released that the AT&T 1984 split off into regional bell companies was being considered by the Chinese government as one of the alternatives for China Telecom's future restructuring. In response to the international view of MII as a super ministry, the delegation also claimed that MII's mission is to facilitate and coordinate, not to govern or control China's IT industries.

Part Three: Regulatory Issues, Strategic Implications

Brief Description

In a time of rapid changes propelled by communication networks, government leadership for information development is of vital importance. Policies, regulations, and legislation need to be made and enforced to address relevant issues and to create an information-friendly environment. Such an environment protects public interest, promotes investment and competition, and supports availability, diversity, high quality, and low cost of the information services and products. The role of the government also involves providing financing and incentives for development of information infrastructure and strategic projects, defining regulatory arrangements and institutional responsibilities, and establishing an effective regulatory regime to direct the course of the information industries and to resolve conflicting objectives and interests.

Accountability, transparency, agility, and efficiency of the government operations are required for governance of the information society. However, the Chinese government lags behind in fulfilling these requirements as China's IT policy and regulatory regime has long been besieged by many pragmatic contradictions between an entrenched, quasi-monopoly operator and an emerging set of well-powered competitors, between a strong desire to maintain central control and an increasing local autonomy, and between a bewildering array of advanced technologies on the ground and a highly rigid regulatory structure that is short of ability to manage and accommodate change.

China faces a full range of strategic issues and challenges in the process of achieving its ambitious goal of informatization, which, apparently, is underscored by the prospect of the technological convergence of communications, computing and media, plus the robust growth of the Internet and digital wireless services.[153] As technologies characterized by digitization, broad bandwidth, interactivity and multimedia keep transforming the way information, capital and concrete substances flow, conventional configuration of networks, industry, services and markets is being increasingly challenged.

The development strategy of China's information infrastructure, for example, is a good case in point. There have been two thoughtful but opposing views on the table:[154] (1) Critical communications infrastructure, including basic telecom networks, radio broadcasting, and cable TV systems should be separated from their service operations. The government should exclusively own, control, and manage this infrastructure. Whereas various information services on networks should be open for competition among different enterprises and companies who have access to network resources on a fair and level ground. (2) Telecom and cable TV sectors should both be encouraged to develop in the marketplace. Two network systems should be allowed to grow independently and compete with each

---

[153] This technological convergence is fostered by a number of technological innovations such as TCP/IP protocol for information transmission and processing, digitization of various information, advanced software that supports highly complex and intelligent applications and services, access technologies that make interconnection or interface of different networks possible and practical, and fiber-optic based broadband networks that facilitate multimedia, interactive, high-quality, and low-cost information transmission.

[154] Representative advocates of these views include Wang Xiaoqiang of MII Telecom Study Group, Fang Hongyi of SARFT Information Network Center, and Zhou Qiren of Beijing University's China Economic Research Center.

other. "Duplicate network construction" should be redefined with a serious account and calculation of the high economic costs generated by monopoly practices. The broadband and technologically converged infrastructure should gradually takeover the outdated telecom networks and replace the present HFC TV system to provide advanced and integrated services. The government role, in this context, is protecting competition and regulating the market behavior of different players.

China's notion of informatization is going through a constant process of upgrading. New issues emerge before old ones are solved, and new structures arise before old ones are put in place. Equipment-centric culture, technology superior mentality, and technocratic view on infrastructure development and information applications have been widespread among many of the China's policy makers and industry leaders, while contextual factors behind the use of technology and the interplay between technology and policy and regulations are often under-assessed or overlooked. Yet, this phenomenon is coming close to the verge of change.

The development of the advanced communication infrastructure, coupled with the application of the global Internet, has a potential that is extraordinary but at the same time contradictory to the Chinese government. On the one hand, the extensive wiring of China combined with intensive deployment of information technologies will promote economic and social development, help achieve higher productive efficiency and performance, and improve the country's ability to exercise political command and economic coordination. On the other hand, widespread applications of Internet-related technologies tend to create an environment in which political and economic activities are decentralized and fragmented, generating a serious government concern that China's political leadership and administrative oversight may therefore be weakened or downgraded when they need to be reinforced.

The prospect for China to enter the World Trade Organization (WTO) alerts the country that policy and strategic issues in a global setting will become much more critical and decisive in regard to China's strategic directions and alternatives. The most pressing policy and strategy questions China has to address immediately involve several important areas:

- *Infrastructure development*: What is the best option for China's national information infrastructure (NII) architecture? Where should the limited resources be allocated for infrastructure development? Should priority be given to much-needed basic services or to innovative therefore fast-changing services? How can the issue of technological convergence among telecom, computing, and media be addressed in the context of developing national backbone and local access networks? Can diversified investment structure be adopted for diversified network construction and operations?

- *Network management and control*: What is the most desirable way to manage and control long-distance and local networks deploying fiber optic, satellite, microwave, wireless mobile, and Internet technologies? Should the network structure be centralized or distributed? And how should the network operations be effectively regulated in a very dynamic market environment, by administrative measures or by formalized legal procedures?

- *Industry restructuring*: How should China restructure and transform its IT and communication industries to best allocate investment and productive resources when technological and industry convergence collectively heralds a massive shift in the scope, scale, cost, and delivery of information services, as well as in the enterprises that provide information services? To what degree and how fast should China further open its door for foreign investment and external involvement in communications and information sector? What should the industry players do to prepare themselves with stronger capability to compete effectively in both domestic and international marketplace, given the perspective of global economic integration and China's admission into the World Trade Organization?

- *Institutional synergy*: What can and should be done to secure interconnectivity, coordination, and balanced development between monopoly public network carriers and dedicated and emerging network operators? How can China achieve a higher degree of consensus and interoperability among different government organizations that have crucial stakes in information and communications?
- *Risk concern*:[155] What technological, security, economic, and political risks and vulnerability will China be exposed to, as the country continuously becomes part of the global community which is increasingly networked and influenced by advanced information technologies? What strategic measures should be adopted to manage and minimize information risks, in the face of potential threat from the network world, while not strangling the healthy growth of the information applications?
- *Legal Framework*: What legal mechanism should be established to address the very crucial issues pertinent to technology and network convergence, online intellectual property rights, information and network security, Internet democracy and crimes, dispute resolution for electronic business and communications, and privacy and confidentiality in cyberspace?

Unlike the development in many countries, privatization of the state-own enterprises is not a driving force in China's telecom sector, even though diverse government functions and entities at all levels have been making efforts towards structural and functional reforms to encourage corporatization of telecom enterprises. A more open, free, and competitive telecom and information market could attract more investment, improve efficiency, and further stimulate China's development. It would also work to undercut the central

---

[155] This concern is emphatically raised by the Chinese government after the Asian financial crisis, as regards how advanced IT will affect the stability and development of China's financial and banking sectors.

government's power of surveillance and control. The concepts of market forces and overall development balance, not just investment and technology, are gaining important footholds, but the Chinese leadership is laboring to carefully manage the introduction of market forces that may, slowly or rapidly, erode the country's fundamental political structure. While telecom privatization continues as the pet rock of Wall Street, the World Bank, and policy makers of the developed nations across the globe, there is little economic and no political incentive for the Chinese government to follow this direction. This partially explains why the particular sensitivities of direct foreign ownership in China's telecom sector.

The absence of a clear and independent regulatory mechanism to facilitate market-based competition remains the most daunting handicap for China's new information highway riders. Albeit many countries have restructured their telecom and IT sectors and created independent or quasi-independent regulators, China remains at the earliest stages of this process. The good news, however, is that a broad consensus has been reached within the Chinese government that a legal and regulatory framework for telecom and IT industries is badly required. The concept of globalization is making inroads in China, and Chinese telecom and IT businesses have began to prepare themselves for roles on the international stage. This will have strategic impact on both China's and the world's telecom and IT arena. As China's policies in relationship with major trading partners take on higher priority, new constituencies beyond the traditional telecom and IT dimensions will become more attentive. China's past promises leave room for cynicism, but its serious offer to apply WTO rules for performance under internationally recognized rules is encouraging, and its commitment to gradually allow foreign investment in the country's basic and value-added telecom services upon gaining WTO membership should be looked as a significant step forward.

In March 1998, with Zhu Rongji's replacement of Li Peng as the Chinese Premier, China pushed for a new bureaucratic restructuring campaign, aiming at streamlining the government organizations, cutting down expenses, and raising efficiency. The process at the central government level involved a cut of 25% of the State Council bureaus and offices, which affected 515 leading officials and 47.5% of staff in 82 departments and institutions, of whom only 36% remain in their former positions, while 48.2% get transferred to new posts, and 15.7% have to either retire or find jobs outside the State Council. The fundamental drive behind this restructuring is to break from the previous government structure that was shaped in the context of state command economy, and redefine government functions and power configuration, as required by the new economic and political environment, through separation of administrative and regulatory functions from business operations and commercial activities.

Telecommunications and information regulatory and policy regime, apparently, felt the strongest impact. Three conflicting organizations, the Ministry of Post and Telecommunications (MPT), the Ministry of Electronics Industry (MEI), and the Ministry of Radio, Film and Television (MRFT) were revamped into a new ministry named the Ministry of Information Industry (MII). The official objective is to set up a centralized and unified leading mechanism for communication and information policy making and development planning.

The significance of MII seems to be threefold. First, it is in compliance with the general trend of technological convergence of telecom, computing, and media. Second, the fierce institutional conflicts among MPT, MEI, and MRFT could be weakened or eclipsed. And third, if MII does split its government functions from direct control over business operations, a new market environment may emerge, in which China Telecom, China Unicom, JiTong, China Netcom, local PTAs and other industry players become corporatized and compete with one another on a level ground.

The challenges and issues faced by this attempted three-ministry merger are formidable. Politically, MII looks like a three-party bureaucratic compromise imposed by the new State Council top leadership. It could prove to be exceedingly difficult and complex to strike a good balance among the battling power groups involved in terms of the organizational structure and personnel arrangement.[156] Operationally, as MII is ambitiously mandated to tackle such pervasive regulation and management issues regarding post and telecom, equipment and appliances manufacturing, computer hardware and software, radio broadcast and TV transmission, and overall national informatization, how the ministry can be constructed into an organization that is structurally efficient and functionally effective remains a crucial question. In addition, under the MPT-MEI-MRFT reform, provincial and local entities of these Beijing parents are put to an awkward position: will they remain the same administrative structure as before or change to business enterprises operated without MPT/MII's direct intervention or managerial control?

Because of its expanded power base and jurisdiction proclaimed by the State Council, MII is widely looked on as a super ministry. However, with its principal leadership, staff, departments, and offices deriving from MPT, there is plenty of ground for suspicion that MII's road ahead is rugged and fitful and that the new ministry may operate very much under the shadow of the old MPT, MEI, and MRFT. Concerns have also grown that China's IT related industries at large might be governed by a newly named regime MII that carries forward the legacies of MPT and operates as MPT, except that it is more concentrated in power and more monopolistic in the market.

The performance of MII since its formation has, to some extent, reinforced these concerns. But on the other hand, MII has also demonstrated that it is struggling to become different from the old MPT.

Specifically, there are ten major regulatory and strategic issues that are intrinsic with many years of China's telecommunications and information industry legacies:

---

[156] Sources indicated that resistance from mid-level officials to job reassignment and relocation was fairly strong.

MPT-MII:[157] *Power and Practice*

MPT has been playing multiple and monopolistic roles as a policy maker, an industry regulator, and a network operator. MPT is at the same time a player and a judge in telecom playing field, as put in an athletic metaphor by former China Unicom president, who criticized MPT's practices as most unfair and unequitable. MPT dominates China's telecom market through its stiff control over traffic, pricing, technical standard, service outlets, and network interconnection. Official rationales for MPT monopoly included:

- As an investment and technology intensive industry for infrastructure, telecommunications needs to be planned, developed, managed, and operated by a centrally controlled organization, so as to benefit from economies of scale and scope, and avoid duplicate construction and waste of resources;
- The obligation of universal service can only be met by a government-controlled entity, not by profit-seeking businesses;
- A strong belief that network ownership and network services should be bundled together, not separated.
- As telecommunications involve state security and safety, telecom networks should be operated with high protection and low vulnerability. Therefore, it is sensible to maintain control and minimize the number of players.

MPT's monopoly in China telecommunications has brought about six major consequences:

---

[157] Although MPT is renamed the Ministry of Information Industry, discussion and analysis of MPT remains valid and important, as China's telecom and information industry and regulatory framework has been shaped over the past decades by MPT, as well as by several other institutions discussed in this book. Their influence and legacy will not be easily removed, at least for quite some time ahead.

1. Uncompetitive prices and installation charges
2. Price discrimination (*e.g.,* interconnection fees for MPT and non-MPT entities)
3. Cross-subsidization to gain sectorial advantages in market competition.
4. Barriers to effective competition, such as the lack of unbundled local access to China Telecom's networks and monopoly practice in telecom resources allocation
5. Poor service quality, low productivity, and
6. Slow technology innovation, limited service choice, and weak customer protection

MPT's long-held position, however, is being confronted by fledgling competition from non-MPT entities such as Unicom, Jitong, PLA, and foreign players. MPT admits that an organizational reform is necessary, which essentially means "three separations" between telecom regulation and operation, between administration and management functions, and between postal and telecom services. MPT claims that the public networks it runs do not belong to MPT but to the state.[158]   The ministry is responsible for network construction, maintenance, operations, and regulation. MPT insists that since the ministry is given such official mandates as operation and maintenance of the national networks, policy and technical standards setting, and telecom market regulation, there is no need to create a new independent regulatory body.[159]

MPT constantly makes it an important objective and a reiterated pledge that its regulatory and operational functions should be split off into two parts, one regulatory body that makes and implements policies and regulations, and one commercial organization that responds to market forces and operates complex telecom services.

---

[158] It is obvious, however, that MPT counts these networks as part of its fixed assets.

[159] See MPT minister's interview with China Business Review, Telecommunications, *South China Morning Post*, August 1997.

The road to a successful reform has proven to be rough and tough. Lack of expertise and policy framework in making a smooth transition for the targeted separations may have been part of the pragmatic reasons. But resistance to change also stems from many other conceptual and pragmatic factors.

In 1994, MPT's telecom operating arm, the Directorate General of Telecommunications (DGT), was given a corporate name, "China Telecom," in reaction to the rise of China Unicom. However, China Telecom is not yet a genuinely corporatized entity. The terms DGT and China Telecom are often used interchangeably by MPT on different occasions. China Telecom, though officially designated as a national business operator for public telecom services, is not yet fully independent of MPT, as its major decisions regarding finance, investment, planning, and personnel are still under MPT's control. Overlap and mixture of functions between MPT and China Telecom are seen in many areas. For instance, China Telecom acts as MPT in regulating public radio frequencies and civil satellite communications used or operated by MPT enterprises. It is only in developing key national projects and in operating the country's wireless mobile roaming networks and international long-distance networks where China Telecom looks somehow like an independent corporation.

Another interesting phenomenon is that China Telecom, except for providing some technical guidance and operating coordination, does not have operational or managerial leadership for provincial and local telecom carriers (PTAs). PTAs act as provincial and local "MPTs" in making local policies and regulations, and in operating local telecom and postal services. They are under a dual control of provincial authorities and MPT. MPT's political power over PTAs rest mainly in the following aspects:

- PTAs are not registered as legal entities with absolute business management autonomies. In principle, provincial and local P&T assets belong to the state (or MPT), therefore, cannot be transferred or liquidated at PTAs' discretion.
- PTA leading figures are appointed by MPT, and

- PTAs' budget and revenue plans are guided by MPT. MPT collects revenues generated by international, inter-provincial long-distance calls, and by some other businesses from PTAs, hands part of them to the state as income taxes or contributions (except local sales tax which is paid by PTAs), and redistributes a share of funds back to PTAs based on predetermined formula, or through a profit sharing scheme between MPT and PTAs.

However, the internal structure of the MPT affords its provincial and local offshoots with a certain degree of autonomy. Existing regulations allow PTAs to approve and issue required licenses to operate telecom businesses within their own regions. While MPT's power is primarily exercised in national or cross-provincial projects and operations, provincial and local PTAs enjoy a reasonable degree of autonomy. In recent years, this autonomy has been growing as a result of the weakened MPT-PTA interface and the increased policy incentives for decentralization. PTAs regard themselves as rightfully and practically more autonomous, thus caring less and less about what MPT in Beijing thinks. PTAs keep revenues generated from cellular mobile services; they are positioned to finance a bulk of the network constructions and operations and to select equipment suppliers. In addition, PTAs seem to be more liberal and flexible with foreign investment and with projects involving international players.

China Unicom

With powerful allies at the top and activist leadership from the former Ministry of Electronics Industry that had long-term ambitions for telecom equipment and service applications, and the ministries of railways and power, China Unicom, or *Lian Tong* in Chinese, emerged in 1994 as China's second national telecom operator to develop competitive telecom networks and services outside the MPT. Shareholders of this new company included the three ministries and 13 large Chinese state-owned corporations, with RMB one billion yuan (US$120 million) registered for the startup capital.

Unicom had an ambitious plan to develop its extensive business in local, long-distance, wireless mobile, data communication, and value-added services for the Chinese public, which deviated from the government's initial intent to entrust the company with a mission to undertake the following responsibilities:

- Interconnect various dedicated networks to provide public telephone services (10% local and long-distance service,[160] 30% wireless mobile services by 2000) and data and value-added services to MPT unserved and underserved areas
- Initiate competition against MPT, so as to achieve better economic efficiency in the use of telecom resources and to speed up telecom infrastructure and services development
- Stimulate and enhance investment in telecom industry from domestic and international sources

Despite being touted as the platform for duopolistic competition with MPT-China Telecom, Unicom was seriously hampered by MPT's continued oversight and interconnection controls. MPT acted as a judge (regulator) who set and enforced rules and supported rival teammate. In contrast, Unicom was only an unprotected player with limited stamina to do any broken field running. Earlier, MPT fiercely opposed the idea of setting up Unicom by arguing that telecommunications is a natural monopoly involving national and strategic security considerations. MPT used cross-country reference and pointed to other countries that did not permit competition before having their nationwide telecom networks and services well set in place.

In principle, Unicom was expected to abide by the rules and regulations set by MPT in terms of service provision, network construction, and technical standards. Unicom helped till the ground for competition in China's telecom network environment, but it did

---

[160] Interpretation of "long distance service" for Unicom was different between MPT and Unicom: MPT insisted that it was domestic, not international, while Unicom said it was both.

not lived up to its plans, projections, or timetables. One of the weapons MPT wielded to combat Unicom was interconnection between Unicom access networks and MPT backbone and local networks. Without interconnection, Unicom could not offer its planned services on its completed local access networks. Access charges, revenue-sharing scheme, and technical accommodation were most apparent issues that held back Unicom's network interconnection.[161] MPT also required that Unicom keep only a small proportion of the revenue no matter whether calls originate or terminate on Unicom's side.[162]

As a new national telecom operator, Unicom was inexperienced in making good business plans and strategies. Instead of concentrating its limited resources on priority projects for specific market segments that have large market demand and good potential for return on investment, the company spread out its ambitious hands to virtually all areas of telecom services, resulting in inefficiency, waste, retarded development, and small scale of economies. In network planning and construction, Unicom adopted a decentralized approach, i.e., assigning the job responsibility to separate regional shareholders and relying on them to build network systems for service operation. The consequences of this approach led to inefficient use of resources, delay in network and facility installation, and increased difficulty in network operation and management.

---

[161] Delay in network interconnection was a way MPT used to hold back Unicom's progress. Unicom claimed that its completed networks had to wait 6-15 months before interconnection could be made with MPT networks. MPT's delay, however, had a backfire effect on itself, as MPT would lose potential airtime revenues and monthly fees from Unicom service operations. Some observers commented by saying that MPT may considers this loss a drop in the ocean compared with the need to slow down Unicom's development in the market.

[162] The pricing mechanism for interconnection heavily favors MPT-China Telecom. For a call generated by Unicom user and terminated on the MPT's network, Unicom paid MPT 80% of a local call charge of RMB 0.12 yuan per three-minute block. When the call was made in reverse direction, MPT enjoyed the similar dominance over the revenues by paying just 10% of the RMB 0.12 yuan to Unicom.

Since Unicom was a complex of three powerful ministries and thirteen large state-owned companies as shareholders, each of which has their own vested interest. Besides the problem with the top management, lack of coordination and the competing and sometimes conflicting political and economic interests among these shareholders have plagued Unicom from its earliest days. While some progress has been made, shareholders continue to complain about lack of transparency in its management and operations. Unicom has not had a formalized charter based on the China's corporate law to regulate and standardize its organizational structure and business operations. As Unicom's branches and subsidiaries in different cities were rushed into existence, their inter-relationships with the headquarters and with one another were not clearly defined. Their local operations lacked good interface with the Beijing headquarters and with local governments.

On the front of policy and regulations, Unicom and MPT had serious debates centering on many important issues.

Unicom contended that the networks it builds should be regarded as China's second public network. Therefore, it should receive the identical policy treatment as MPT's China Telecom does. Unicom says it is in a position to provide virtually all kinds of communication services, and the notion of long-distance service should embrace international telephony. MPT, on the other hand, attempted to restrict Unicom's service scopes to local wireless mobile and it argues that international telephony should not be part of Unicom's long-distance package. MPT contended that to make best use of resources, China should have a unified single network system operated by MPT. Thus, instead of developing a second public network system, Unicom's role and the networks it builds should be supplementary to the MPT's, not parallel to them.

Unicom appealed to the State Council for amendment of the State Council Document No.178 (1993) to lift the government restrictions that Unicom could only offer local and long-distance telephone services in underserved or unserved areas. Unicom wanted official authorization to compete with MPT in local, long-distance, and international services on an equal basis. MPT insisted that its networks already covered almost all the areas and cities, there was no need for Unicom to build duplicate networks to offer services. MPT argued that international services should be operated by MPT alone, because the MPT control would (1) ensure a high degree of communication security; (2) raise China's leverage for telecom negotiations with foreign countries (e.g., in international accounting rates); and (3) make best use of China's international circuits and information gateways that have sufficient capacity to meet the present cross-border traffic demand.

Unicom regarded telephone numbers as resources that belong to the people. MPT should allow Unicom to use this resource free of charge. MPT argued that telephone codes and numbers should be assigned by ITU and allocated by specific network operators according to specific standards, not used by Unicom at its will. Unicom believed that telecom tariff policy decisions should be made by the central government organizations responsible for national economics and market regulation, not by the parochial MPT. As a new fledgling player, Unicom wanted significant flexibility in its rate decisions so as to be competitive, while MPT insisted that it should have exclusive right and power to set telecom rates for all operators.

Unicom and MPT had conflicting views on network access and interconnection. MPT asserted that in order to insure good operating and capacity conditions for MPT's public networks, network interconnection with Unicom should be made in the mode of tandem-to-tandem exchange connection (i.e. one MPT tandem exchange connects with one Unicom tandem exchange). MPT also insisted that its (or local PTAs') approval and technical verification for Unicom's network projects were necessary before the interconnection could be made, while Unicom held that it did not need to go through a lengthy process of the project-specific approval by MPT and that tandem-to-tandem interconnection scheme cost too much in time and money. In addition, MPT said it should determine points of interconnection, and the costs incurred for the linkage between the point of interconnection and Unicom networks should be fully borne by Unicom. MPT cited the traditional incumbent carrier argument that this was necessary because of its obligations for universal service and subsidization of loss-making postal services.

Unicom syndrome created serious concerns. The State Council formed a special task force (with members from SPC, SCER and SETC) to review and examine the issues. In May 1997, the task force concluded that, for the company to survive and grow, Unicom should be given rights to provide not only wireless mobile services but also fixed-line voice and data services. The official document thus formulated urged MPT to support and cooperate with Unicom in network interconnection, number allocation, and tariff setting. It clarified Unicom's legitimacy to go ahead with its projects in Tianjin, Shanghai, Sichuan province, and Chongqing municipality[163] on the development of wireline telecom services. The committee recommended that Unicom's request to provide international services be put on hold.

Compared with MPT-controlled China Telecom, Unicom in fact had some intrinsic advantages as listed below, but the company, unfortunately, failed to transfer these advantages to its best interest. The advantages Unicom had included

- Higher efficiency and cost-effectiveness due to its much smaller staffing, as opposed to MPT's 1.2 million employees nationwide
- More flexibility in investment, corporate structure, and resource allocation
- More opportunities and privilege to focus its development on particular technologies (*e.g.,* ATM, SDH, CDMA, WLL, xDSL, and other advanced systems), selected geographic areas, and specific customer segments
- Better channels for utilizing foreign capital and technology

---

[163] The venture is being funded by US Sprint and Japan's Sumitomo Corp, with an initial investment of US$30 million in the first phase. Trunk cabling work began on a fixed-line network connecting Chengdu and Chongqing, which was backed by US company Asian-American Telecommunications Corp, part of Metromedia.

- No obligation that China Telecom undertakes for universal service, or cross-subsidies for different telecom sectors and postal services

Public expectation was that Unicom would soon bring competition, lower prices, and better services to China's telecom market. Unicom's performance turned out well below this expectation. Unicom was dwarfed by China Telecom in many aspects. In the middle of 1999, Unicom's fixed line exchange capacity was a bit more than 200,000 lines, with approximately 30,000 subscribers, as opposed to China Telecom's 140 million lines and 100 million plus subscribers. Meanwhile, Unicom had about 15,000 km of fiber optic cable installed while China Telecom's long-distance fiber-optic cable system reached more than 200,000 km in length. On the wireless mobile side, Unicom was also nowhere close to China Telecom. By June 1999, Unicom installed more than 3 million lines of its GSM mobile capacity with over 2000 base stations and had about 2.5 million subscribers for its GSM services and 3.4 million for paging services, while China Telecom installed approximately 45 million lines of mobile network capacity with more than 32,000 base stations. China Telecom's mobile subscription reached 32 million and 42 million for cellular and paging services.

Battling on two fronts, Unicom had a hard time growing. Externally, it confronted with enormous barriers set by MPT; internally, it had severe bickering and twisting both inside its core and among its major shareholders. Unicom suffered mainly from

- *Weak structural and organizational integrity* Unicom was hit by its seeming blessings of a complex combination of stakeholders and penetrating local branches. Lack of coordination and conflicts of political and economic interest among different parties appeared as undermining forces, while expected deployment of excessive capacity and spare facilities of dedicated networks operated by Unicom's major shareholders proved costly and problematic. Interface between Unicom headquarters in Beijing and its local branches was weak, or, in some cases, mismanaged. Unicom's integrity issue was partially evidenced by its frequent top management reshuffles.[164]

- *Political impact* Policy decisions by the top leadership concerning Unicom were often influenced by individual officials and various government organizations, which may have had little sense in economic and financial terms. Vague and often contradictory regulatory framework dictated that Unicom and MPT had to approach policy issues through the channels of lobbying, bargaining, and negotiating, not through formalized administrative or legal procedures.
- *Management team* Unicom's management team consisted primarily of former government officials and electronic engineers, with no solid background or capability in telecommunications. They were short of expertise and experience in network development and operations. This leadership defect created management problems and flaws in business plans and strategies.
- *Resources scarcity* Unlike what it anticipated, Unicom was short of financial, technical, managerial, and human resources. The company was operating with its hands tied on the back by limited resources, particularly, funding and working capital. Unicom was not prepared about the importance of these resources in running advanced communications business as a fully-fledged telecom operator.
- *Distribution and sales channel* MPT-China Telecom had an extensive network of distribution and sales across China, while Unicom had very limited and separated distribution and sales outlets to meet its ambitious plan for various services and a broad geographic coverage.

---

[164] Unicom had five major top management replacements over the past few years: Zhao Weichen of State Economic and Trade Commission; Yang Changji of the same commission; Li Huifen of Tianjin Municipal Government; Liu Jianfeng of Ministry of Electronics Industry; and Yang Xianzu of MPT-MII.

As a new and ambitious player, Unicom needed billions of dollars for startup and development. Because of its shortage of funding, Unicom relied heavily on foreign investment through an innovative China-China-Foreign (CCF) scheme. That is, Unicom formed a joint venture (investment company) with one or more Chinese domestic entities, this JV would then negotiate a contract for Unicom project investment with one or more foreign firms. Under this arrangement, 70-80% of the operation revenues (including installation fees, equipment depreciation, and after-tax profits) should go back to the CCF for investment payoffs. The terms of benefits, on a case-to-case basis, were generally extended over a period of 12-15 years.[165] Foreign partners, dependent on their shares of the investment, were promised a return of 15-18 or higher percent if revenues were generated from service provisions or other operations. The CCF scheme worked to some extent, as Unicom raised almost 70% of its capital from foreign sources based on this scheme.

There were two critical issues with this scheme: first, the CCF joint-venture had to involve a very complex mechanism to hold different parties together, and second, foreign investors had little access to the information about network management and operation - something essential to their financial stakes. Unicom expected that the company could significantly benefit from this fund-raising arrangement because it did not seem to violate the Chinese policy of not allowing foreign direct investment in network equity ownership, and it distributed the investment into smaller amounts that can be more efficiently approved by local governments.[166] However, delays

---

[165] Deals with foreign investors were structured slightly differently around this scheme based on specific project conditions and how liberal the officials involved were. Some deals fell in grey policy areas where legality could be questioned. In these cases, foreign companies would look for greater rates of return to offset larger potential risks.

[166] The Chinese regulation said that foreign investment below US$30 million in size could be reviewed and approved by local governments, while the projects beyond US$30 million in investment must go to the central government for approval.

in project construction, low managerial efficiency, and unclear prospects for profitability hurt both Unicom and foreign investors. In 1998, Unicom started to seriously consider raising money through stock listing and bond issuance at home and abroad,[167] using other investment models such as BOT, BTO, or initiating direct and innovative partnerships with foreign firms.

Because of the issues and problems Unicom faced, the company's growth was slow and minimal. By 1999, Unicom's telecom revenue was about US$2 billion, 6% of the China's total. Its mobile market share was around 10% in China. Unicom's ambitious plan to offer large-scale wired local and long-distance phone services remained pretty much a dream. Many counted the emergence of MII as a good and new phase for Unicom, for the new ministry may give Unicom a more level playing field to compete with China Telecom. Opposing views, however, regarded the new regulatory situation as negative to Unicom, as the company might easily be acquired or squeezed out of the market by MII-backed China Telecom.

In May 1999, the positive count seemed to have won an upper hand. The State Council issued a document voicing a stronger support for Unicom through a variety of policy measures. MII, the offspring of MPT, also signaled a change towards Unicom. The officially announced measures include:

1. Guo Xin, China Telecom's national paging company is transferred to Unicom. Guo Xin takes 60% of the paging market in China. The company had 40 million subscribers and US$180 million of profits in 1998. The company's 1999 assets totaled almost US$1.6 billion, a very significant amount to Unicom, once the transfer is completed.

2. Unicom is granted the exclusive rights to build and operate a nationwide CDMA network. The four-city CDMA trial operations (with a combined capacity of 140,000 lines and

---

[167] Unicom President Li Huifen said in April 1998 that proposal had been sent to the State Council for approval for domestic bond issuance, A-share listing in Shanghai and Shenzhen, and H-share listing in Hong Kong.

over ---60,000 subscribers) and the assets of China Great Wall Mobile Communications (a China Telecom-Military joint venture) are officially turned over to Unicom. Unicom is reported to have earmarked US$845 million for initial CDMA network development with a capacity of 2 million lines that will be expanded to 10 million lines for 160 cities later. Unicom plans to take 30% of the wireless mobile market by 2003.[168] In February 2000, Unicom signed a framework agreement with US Qualcomm, which allows Unicom to deploy narrow-band IS-95 CDMA technology through paying Qualcomm royalties for its intellectual property rights (IPR). The agreement also gives authorization to the licensed Chinese equipment manufacturers to make CDMA equipment.[169]

3.   Unicom, jointly with other three Chinese operators (China Telecom, JiTong, and China Netcom), is given official authorization to invest US$300-400 million for IP-base telephony services development. Unicom has been permitted to expand its services to virtually all possible areas, including local, long-distance and international telephony, radio paging, GSM and CDMA wireless mobile, IP-telephony, and data communications. Currently, the Chinese government allows Unicom to discount its rates for telephony services by as much as 10% and requires no Unicom obligation to provide universal services in rural and remote areas.

4.   In addition to the current four Internet network and service operators, Unicom is endorsed to become the fifth national

---

[168] Problems in 1999 Sino-US relations delayed Unicom's roll-out of CDMA. In December 1999, Unicom announced it would soon launch it initial CDMA network development. The project was bidden by twelve domestic and international CDMA vendors. Unicom said the four foreign vendors (Lucent, Nortel, Motorola, and Samsung) would be given priority because they had provided equipment for China's CDMA trials. Unicom also said it may need five or six vendors. China's domestic manufacturers Da Tang, Huawei, Great Dragon, ZTE, Jinpeng, and Zhong Xin were reportedly on the list of bidders.

[169] However, this Unicom-Qualcomm agreement was held back from implementation, due to economic, political, and technology reasons.

operator (UNINET) to offer Internet related (private line) access and data services.

5. Management support: a number of MPT/MII key officials are relocated to Unicom to take leading positions. They include former MPT Vice Minister Yang Xianzu, MPT Data Communications Bureau Director Liu Yunjie, MPT Planning Department Director Wang Jianzhou, and Shi Cuiming, Head of China Telecom (HK). This new management team has pushed for the corporate management restructuring which includes acquisition of previously dispersed subsidiaries for a higher degree of centralized and effective management, stock options for company employees, and hiring of three external board members who are consulted for important decision making and are charged to chair corporate auditing and staff compensation matters.

6. (6) Under the State Council's approval, Unicom went for initial public offering (IPO) in Hong Kong and New York. Unicom's share listing raised more than US$6 billion for the company's much-needed capital for development. The central government also allocated RMB 5 billion in cash (US$620 million) to support Unicom. Furthermore, China Development Bank[170] has signed a lending agreement with Unicom to provide long-term commercial loans amounting up to RMB10 billion yuan (US$1.2 billion).[171]

7. All these measures are important, because they indicate the Chinese government's intended efforts to restructure the country's telecommunications industry into a more competitive, more corporatized, and more market-driven sector. In this process, Unicom may enjoy some unique and favorable opportunities to grow into a real competitor. The

[170] China Development Bank is China's largest state bank that makes policy loans to support large state-own enterprises, or large state projects.

[171] In 2000-2002, Unicom needs approximately RMB 100 billion (US$12.5 billion) in capital for development. Unicom's plan is to raise funds from three sources: international capital market (US$6 billion), Unicom's operating cash flow (US$5 billion), and commercial loans (US$1.5 billion).

road for Unicom, however, will by no means be smooth. Speculation has been around that Unicom may have to, in one way or another, make strategic alliances with other communication operators, such as railway or cable network operators, in order to gain competitiveness against China Telecom and other rivals. Unicom's future relies on many variables that can either turn the company up or push it down.

Telecommunications Law

Telecommunications in China has been operated with a vacancy of effective legal framework.[172] Policy decisions are made by ministerial or administrative processes. Industry and market regulations are based on MPT or State Council directives and orders which tend to change frequently. That is, no codified legal mechanism is available yet to regulate communications and information forces, the most dynamic part of the Chinese economy, or to arbitrate and settle disputes among conflicting stakeholders. Instead, senior official's personal influence is often called in for coordination and negotiations aimed at compromises, not problem solutions.

Since 1980, hundreds of MPT and State Council administrative rules, regulations, and directives have been issued concerning tariff control, installation fees, licensing, terminal equipment, technical standards, radio frequency, satellite services, market discipline, and ban on network involvement by foreign firms, many of which are made to justify MPT's monopolistic position and protect MPT's vested interest.

---

[172] Telecom legal framework should encompass telecom laws, rules and regulations at national and local levels, and the mechanism to enforce and interpret the laws and regulations.

MPT has, for the past two decades, drafted several versions of China Telecommunications Law,[173] but none of them obtained widespread consensus and was made ready for the National People's Congress for final consideration. The process has proved to be slow, painful, and complicated, apparently on account of the conflicts of interest among different players involved, and because each draft made tends to reflect MPT's predisposition and its desire to preserve its ministerial primacy. MPT's limited transparency and limited interactions with other government organizations have also aroused widespread suspicions about the impartiality and fairness of the draft. The former MEI, on the other hand, set up a special telecom law drafting team around 1995 in an attempt to propose a draft law in opposition to that of MPT's, but its effort was of little avail.

In the late 1997, a MPT's version of the draft law was submitted to the State Council Legal Affairs Bureau, and distributed to the hands of relevant government organizations for reviews and comments.[174] MII claimed in the early 1999 that a new version of China's telecom law was being drafted for reviews. One year later, MII officials said again that a draft telecom law would be ready by the end of 2000. According to the MII minister, the passing of China's telecom law is listed on the priority agenda of the National People's Congress (NPC),[175] but when exactly it will finally be approved and made ready

---

[173] Telecom law drafting in China was first initiated in 1980's. The State Council brought the telecom law drafting into agenda in 1985, and the National People's Congress did the same in 1993.

[174] Major reviewers included MEI, Ministry of Broadcast, Movies and TV, State Planning Commission, State Council (i.e., Leading Group, Legal Affairs Bureau, and Standing Committee), NPC Legislative Committee and some other government organizations.

[175] According to the Chinese Constitution, China's supreme law making and interpreting body is the National People's Congress and its Standing Committee, meanwhile, the State Council and a wide range of government organizations can get involved in proposing, drafting, reviewing, and amending laws. The State Council, central government organizations, as well as the people's congress and government agencies at local levels, are entitled to issue directives, orders, and local laws, provided they do not violate the Constitution and national laws. The

for enforcement remains uncertain. In interim, MII indicated that a provisional directive may have to be proclaimed as an interim regulation on China's telecom and information market prior to the establishment of the national telecom law to regulate China's telecom and Internet services market.

In August 2000, MII's draft versions of the Regulation for the Administration of Telecommunications (RAT) and the Regulation for Foreign Invested Telecommunications Enterprises (RFITE) were reported as being submitted to the State Council and circulated among the relevant government organizations for reviews and approval. RAT attempts to categorise China's telecom service carriers into proprietary network operators (e.g., domestic and international telecom services, mobile, satellite and data services, and Internet and multimedia services) and non-proprietary network operators (e.g., telecom resalers, value-added and wireless paging services, innovative and information services). RAT also tries to specify related licensing rules and procedures. The new regulation indicates that all telecom service providers in China must get the government approvals and licenses. Basic service providers must acquire official authorization and licenses from MII while value-added service providers must have approvals and licenses from provincial and municipal governments or from MII if the services cover more than one province or municipality. Share structures of basic and value-added services have different degrees of restrictions. RFITE proposes new rules to regulate officially allowed emerging Sino-foreign equity joint ventures, and drafted out discretionary approval procedures and mandatory qualification criteria for both Chinese and foreign investors who will get involved in telecom joint ventures operating in China.

Critiques of the MPT-MII draft laws focus on their failure or inadequacy to appropriately and clearly address the most crucial

---

State Council is in a position to (a) issue administrative orders and directives; (b) make proposals to the People's Congress for establishing new laws and amending the laws being enforced; (3) draft new laws upon the request from the People's Congress; and (4) revise or revoke administrative rules set by ministries or local governments if they are considered as inappropriate.

issues facing China telecommunications and information industries, including

- Separation of regulatory and operational functions
- Regulatory framework: its structure, mission, authority, operations, and checks and balance of power
- Anti-monopoly and market regulation in favor of competition
- Network interconnection among different service providers
- Tariff and rate management and regulation
- Monopoly and multi-carrier market competition
- Telecom industry and corporate structures
- New regulatory environment in the face of rapid technology innovation and convergence
- Regulation on Internet-related network development and provision of services
- International cooperation and foreign investment

To minimize the involvement of institutional bias and self-interest, many in China have proposed that a special committee, led by the State Council Legal Affairs Office and composed of qualified members and experts from all telecom related ministries and commissions, be formed to draft the law, or setting up an independent ad hoc task force led by the NPC Legislative Committee to do the drafting. In addition, recommendations have been put forward to establish an independent policy and regulatory regime, *e.g.*, State Information Commission, in place of the previous MPT, MEI, State Council Informatization Leading Group, or any others, to assume full regulatory responsibilities for China's communications and information development.[176]

---

[176] Part of the commission's jurisdiction is proposed to cover such dimensions as regulation of telecom charges; resources (radio frequency, numbering, satellite orbits, and public networks) allocation based on fairness, efficiency, and public welfare; setting of technical standards; ruling and coordination for interconnection; and arbitration of institutional disputes.

Foreign Participation and Market Liberalization

Since 1949 when the People's Republic of China was born, China's telecommunications network ownership and operation have been under strict control. Direct foreign investment in telecom service sector or network operation has been explicitly prohibited. MPT reiterated on many occasions that the government is unlikely to relax this policy, at least for a foreseeable future.

Increasing demand for telecom services and the need to provide adequate infrastructure, however, are driving Chinese authorities to rethink this policy of retaining control over telecom networks and services in a context where foreign funds, management expertise, and the state-of-the-art technologies are becoming more critical to China's further development.

In principle, China has drawn a distinction between infrastructure and services investment. Foreign firms are legitimately positioned to supply equipment and technologies, conduct telecom and IT R&D projects, as well as collaborate with Chinese partners in officially approved ventures for information infrastructure development, provided they have no role in network ownership or operations. Specifically, the roles foreign companies can play include

1. Providing loans
2. Leasing arrangement
3. Build-Transfer-Operate (BTO) projects
4. Joint venture projects in which foreign investors benefit, upfront or within a mutually agreed timeframe, from a fixed amount or through revenue/profit sharing scheme
5. Joining hands with MPT's overseas companies, such as Hong Kong based Tianbo Co., to launch investment ventures for China's telecom projects
6. Investing in securities issued by MPT-MII and other Chinese organization or enterprises (with the State Council's approval) in overseas capital markets

7. Cooperating with Chinese partners in ways mutually accepted[177]

Facing the strict ban on direct foreign investment, some foreign companies appeared more courageous and innovative than others in deploying China's policy gray areas. Xin De Telecom International Ventures Co., a joint venture set up in 1996 between Siemens AG and China International Trust and Investment Co (CITIC) offers a good example. Xin De provided US$180 million to China Unicom to lease mobile phone equipment from Siemens and to expand services in four Chinese cities. Xin De bypassed China's ban and avoided the so-called Chinese-Chinese-Foreign (CCF) investment fate by structuring itself not as a joint venture but as a leasing company. Xin De's investment in China's telecom sector falls in leasing arrangement that is legal and pragmatic. Xin De gets the equity-like returns from Unicom. What is different from a typical lease is that Xin De provides support and training to make sure the new equipment is put to good use and returns are maximized. Besides, the loan involved is unsecured and repayment is tied to a quarterly assessment of the project's financial performance and number of new subscribers. The leasing contract works like an equity investment without ownership. It generally involves an interrelationship among the investors/lenders, strategic players, equipment and service suppliers, and telecom operators. The advantages for the investors/lenders include good risk-return profile, stable legal endorsement, and feasible exit strategies. To the operators, this scheme offers business independence, funding for equipment leasing, flexible arrangement for repayment, and access to technical and management support. Benefits also extend to strategic players and equipment suppliers. Financed leasing conforms to Chinese official regulations set by MII, MOFTEC and SPC. It has the special support

---

[177] These policy innovations, particularly item 7, leave room for policy elasticity or speculations on change.

from the article 243 of China's new contract law, and enjoys transparent tax and accounting treatment.[178]

In spite of the official position preventing foreign involvement in network ownership and service provision, Chinese authorities have never explicitly stated that the door is absolutely closed. Instead, what has been repeatedly denoted is that "the conditions and the time are not yet ripe," and that when China has achieved a certain level of telecom services and market status, current policies will become invalid. The most distant deadline for this policy change suggested by the Chinese government was for 2020, as put in China's document submitted to APEC. But it could be 2010, or even sooner, if the said conditions change faster than expected.[179] The "conditions" talked about by MPT generally refer to the situation in which China's telecom sector must cross-subsidize loss-making postal services;[180] there is no legal framework to regulate telecom market behavior; and MPT enjoys favorable government policies as incentives for universal service and overall national telecom development, which cannot be rendered to foreign firms who operate for profit gains.

More specifically, China's officially raised arguments for not opening telecom services and network ownership to foreign firms include

---

[178] Since 1981, China has had more than 41 Sino-foreign leasing companies under MOFTEC, with over US$7 billion capital raised.

[179] MPT Minister made these comments in an interview with China Business Review, Telecommunications, *South China Morning Post* in August 1997.

[180] China's postal industry lost US$723 million and US$843 million in 1996 and 1997 respectively. Besides, the sector needs up to US$1.08 billion of capital investment yearly to maintain the necessary growth. Telecom has been subsidizing postal services for years. The State Postal Bureau under MII has proposed to restructure its 2000 service sites into 239 independent mail handling centers across the country to lower the costs and raise efficiency. Proposed options of funding for postal services include continued telecom subsidies, capital allocation from the state budget, deployment of postal savings deposits (US$35 billion in total in 1997), and higher per-letter mailing rate, from US$0.06 to US$0.12, to cover the current per-letter mailing cost of US$0.09 and fund postal development.

- Telecom network operation concerns China's national security, integrity, and sovereignty. Fear of foreign control over telecom facilities and information, especially in time of emergency and military confrontation or war.
- China's immature telecom market conditions: incomplete market regulatory framework and lack of national telecom law; low teledensity and services penetration; disparity in regional development.
- Existing issues of tariff structure, network interconnection, and universal service. MPT has to undertake the obligation to subsidize loss-making postal services and to provide non-profit telecom services in poor and rural regions while foreign investors will not have such an obligation, and thus are at a better competitive position in the marketplace.
- At present, China cannot compete with foreign players on an equal footing, because of its current disadvantages relative to capital, technology, and management expertise.
- Unclear status of assets ownership among the Chinese telecom enterprises which may lead to asset drain or invisible privatization if foreign firms become involved in equity ownership and network operations

Under increased pressure from different sources, China has initiated limited competition. Telecom equipment supplies have been liberalized, with international vendors and Chinese domestic firms competing severely with one another. In 1993, the government proclaimed nine areas of information and communications open for operation by state-owned or collectively-owned enterprises through a process of official licensing or administrative approval by MPT or its subsidiaries (PTAs). These include radio paging, 800MHz dispatch service, 450MHz mobile communications service, VSAT, telephone information service, computer information service, e-mail, EDI and Videotext service.

In exchange for financing equipment purchases and network deployment, foreign investors have been allowed to negotiate repayment through a fixed share of network operating revenues. However, the formula for this revenue sharing is quite problematic, because foreign investors are detached from network operation and they have no access to financial data and management processes. Non-standardized accounting system in Chinese corporations is also an important concern. China's State Council in May 1997 issued a document that provided a framework for closer cooperative joint ventures between foreign and Chinese partners in telecom market. To a confined extent, China has experimented with joint investment, co-operative construction, and profit-sharing based on the proportionate investment for telecom projects, but the official position to ban foreign and private involvement in telecom network ownership and operations has remained unchanged.

The 1998 listing of China Telecom (Hong Kong) in the international capital markets apparently contradicted the country's long-held telecom policy. Assuming this financing vehicle does contain China Telecom (Guangdong and Zhejiang cellular facilities) assets, the question arises as to where the line can be drawn with regard to foreign ownership and operation, and whether international investors are investing in the equipment or in the services of the China Telecom business. In another word, will China's absorption of foreign capital from international security markets entail or lead to a breakup of the current Chinese telecom policy on foreign equity ownership? Or should China's policy statement on foreign involvement be redefined and re-interpreted?

China sent an informal message to the world in the early 1997 that value-added services, such as electronic and voice mail, electronic data interchange (EDI), on-line database retrieval and processing, would likely be opened to foreign firms or Sino-foreign joint ventures for operation in "test cities" before 2000 under the condition that only a maximum of one-third of the stake could be taken by the foreign partner.[181] In March 1999, two years later, nothing seemed to have

---

[181] Early 1998, Chinese policy makers also indicated that telecommunications will be one of the industries to be opened to foreign investors in the test cities of the middle and western regions to boost the economic development there.

happened in regard to foreign investment, except the signing of a framework agreement between China Telecom and AT&T to jointly provide value-added services in Shanghai Pudong. The agreement, however, could not be implemented until the Chinese government gives a final approval. It was not until November 15, 1999 when China and the United States, after a series of painstaking negotiation, reached a bilateral WTO agreement, that China's "ice-burg" on foreign investment in telecom services began to melt. China, reportedly, made the promise that, upon the country's formal accession into WTO, U.S. companies will be allowed to take as much as 49% of the equity shares in China's telecom businesses, and the figure will go up to 50% two years afterwards. The details of how this promise would materialize were not released, but one has to always bear in mind: "the devil is in details."

Initial Public Offering: China Telecom (HK) Deal

China Telecom (HK) listing on Hong Kong and New York Stock Exchanges and its high profiled equity deal with Cable&Wireless (C&W)-Hong Kong Telecom (HKT) occurred to the world as unique cases of significance. They prompted a widespread contemplation about whether China's MPT was testing its water by offering foreign investors a stake in so-called trial areas of data communications and mobile phone services, whether foreign investors would be provided with a telecom proxy in China by investing in China Telecom (HK), and what may happen to China's telecom market and regulatory structure short term and beyond. International business community looked at China Telecom (HK)'s initial public offering (IPO) as the beginning of China's telecom industry's privatization, but the Chinese government regarded it primarily as an effective way to raise capital for development. The implications of this IPO on China's telecom industry point specifically to the sector's

- Growing demand for funds from international capital market
- Propensity to implement corporate governance and state enterprise restructuring[182]
- Policy adjustment and regulatory complexity toward sensitive investment schemes and foreign involvement[183]
- New initiatives to integrate with Hong Kong and the rest of the world by opening new channels for China telecom industry to gain access abroad and for foreign investors to make potential inroads into China's telecom market.

On June 6, 1997, Chinese MPT Minister Wu Jichuan[184] and C&W CEO Richard Brown signed an agreement in Beijing about stock purchases of HK Telecom and China Telecom (HK) by both sides. The deal was obviously driven by both political and commercial considerations.

Politically, China is inclined to acquire control of the strategic industries like telecommunications in HK, use HK's position as a telecom hub, and reach out into international telecom market through having a stake in HKT that has points of presence in over 80 countries. Commercially, China needs to tap into HKT who has the most advanced communications infrastructure and who is among the most profitable revenue earners in Asia.[185]

---

[182] For example, organization merger and asset acquisition.

[183] The most apparent regulatory issue is how the Chinese government treats Hong Kong businesses like HKT: is HKT a foreign entity or a domestic one? Different treatment will have different policy consequences.

[184] Minister Wu declared that China Telecom (HK)'s public listing in Hong Kong is a capital-raising exercise, not a way to allow foreign involvement in China telecom's management or operations. He also emphasized that it is the sole vehicle for foreign investment in China's fast growing telecom sector.

[185] HKT's 1997 fiscal year-end (ended March 31, 1997) turnover up 10.8% to HK$32.58 billion (US$4.24 billion). (cf. China Telecom's 1996 revenue was about US$15 billion,) HKT has the lion's share of the region's US$1 billion telecom hubbing market, with 500 of the region's 900 multinational hubbing customers operating out of HK. Though small in area, HK ranks alongside full-sized nations as the world's tenth largest international telephone traffic hub.

As indicated by the initial agreement, China Telecom (HK)[186] would, in the first stage, purchase 640 million shares of HKT stock at the price of 14.25 HK dollar per share,[187] amounting to a total of 9.177 billion HK dollar (US$1.2 billion), 5.51% of the HKT's current market value. In February 1998, China Telecom (HK) accelerated its efforts for a larger HKT ownership (12-13%) by striking a deal with China Everbright Holdings[188] which will sell its 7.8% (904.69 million shares) stake of HKT at the per-share price of HK$14.20 for HK$12.85 billion (US$1.66 billion). MPT indicated that the HKT shares it obtained would be held as long-term investment and thus would not be injected into its HK-listed subsidiary China Telecom (HK).

In the second stage, C&W would, as planned, sell more HKT shares to China Telecom (HK) until the shares of HKT become equally spread between C&W and China Telecom (HK) (from about 59.44% by C&W to approximately 30% by both C&W and China Telecom).[189] China Telecom may eventually acquire more than half of the shares to achieve control of HKT. This way, China Telecom will not only gain commercial interest from HKT but also have the right to participate in the corporate decision making process by nominating its members to HKT's Board of Directors. This planned second stage, however, remained unrealized until the Spring of 2000 when Pacific Century CyberWorks acquired HKT's 54% share from C&W.[190]

---

[186] China Telecom (HK) reportedly had a total revenue of HK$14.47 billion (US$1.86 billion) and after-tax profit of HK$4.63 billion (US$593.5 million) for 1997, up 10% over the previous year.

[187] Close to the end of 1999, per share price rose to HK$43, 300% higher than its initial price.

[188] Like CITIC, China Everbright Holdings is the investment arm of the Chinese State Council. CITIC sold its entire 7.8% HKT stakes to Everbright Holdings just several months earlier.

[189] Up to the early 2000, this second-phase plan did not seem to have been implemented.

[190] By that time HKT was 54% owned by C&W, 12% by China Telecom (HK), 8% by Hong Kong government, and 26% by smaller share holders.

In exchange, MPT was expected to sell a significant amount of China Telecom (HK) shares to C&W,[191] making a further exception to the Chinese rule that no foreign company can hold equity ownership of the Chinese telecom entities. C&W, according to the agreement, would become a major foreign investor of China Telecom (HK). It turned out, however, when China Telecom (HK)'s one quarter enlarged share capital was initially floated in Hong Kong Stock Exchange in October 1997, C&W had a setback, as it was not invited to take part in the floatation. What the British telecom player claimed about the situation was that China Telecom (HK) did not satisfy its strategic objectives as the assets of the Chinese company only included two mobile phone networks which did not involve C&W's expertise and capabilities.[192]

It was not clear, though, if the deal C&W agreed to go for was a result of the Chinese government pressure for the British company to relinquish its controlling interest in HKT after HK's return to China, or a business strategy willfully pursued by C&W to exchange for an inside track to future mainland China's telecom business. But it was conspicuous that C&W's stake in HKT was of vital importance, since the 54% HKT share held by C&W accounted for 65% of the company's worldwide operating profit. By approaching MPT, C&W may have intended to secure a distinct and combined presence in HK and mainland China, which would enable C&W to get an advantageous position over its competitors in Asia.

China Telecom (HK) reportedly raised US$4.225 billion[193] as the net proceeds from its global offering of a total of 2.771 billion shares, an implied value for China Telecom (HK) on listing of US$17.96

---

[191] Reports said C&W was tipped to take up to 25% stake of China Telecom (HK) around April 1998.

[192] Both C&W and HKT CEO stated that the purchase of HK Telecom by China Telecom was to be an admission for the three partners to join hands and invest in future mainland ventures, when they talked about C&W's perspective for a significant stake in China Telecom (HK).

[193] MPT has a vague statement on whether the capital raised will be used for China Telecom (HK) or for China Telecom elsewhere.

billion.[194] Of this amount, about 280 million shares were made available in the United States and Canada as American Depository shares, 370.59 million shares arranged for international placement outside the US, Canada and Asia, and the remaining 2120.41 million shares for institutional investors in Hong Kong and Asia.[195] Approximately US$3.4 billion raised would be used for capital expenditure in 1997-2000, i.e., for network capacity expansion, new billing and clearing systems, and the introduction of DCS/GSM 1800 etc.

China Telecom (HK)'s assets were first injected from cellular networks and facilities of the Guangdong and Zhejian PTAs, with 3.45 million subscribers (97.5% of the total in these two provinces) by 1997. Mobile phone subscribers in these two provinces together accounted for about one third of the China's mobile market at that time.[196] China Telecom (HK) later acquired more mobile network assets (GSM and TACS) from Jiangsu, Fujian, Henen and Hainan provinces,[197] which boosted its nationwide market share to 36% and after-tax income to US$1.25 billion in 1999.[198] The payment to the parent company China Telecom for this acquisition amounted to US$6.4 billion, of which US$3.4 billion would be in new shares,

---

[194] Of the total US$17.96 billion, it was estimated that a premium of up to US$9 billion for future cheap asset injections was included, which gave a figure of about US$9 billion for core operations.

[195] Source: *China Daily* (Oct. 1997) and *China Telecom Update* (Jan. 1998).

[196] China Telecom (HK) planned to invest US$843 million in Guangdong and US$481 million in Zhejiang for their mobile network development in 1998.

[197] Total 1999 annual revenue of Fujian, Henen and Hainan networks was more than US$670 million, with an estimated combined profit of US$300 million.

[198] China Telecom (HK)'s 1998 acquisition of Jiangsu mobile networks involved a payment of HK$22.47 billion (US$2.9 billion). This price offered was 19.2 times the Jiangsu mobile network's projected earnings for 1998, or 7.3 times its 1998 Ebitda multiples - earnings after adjusting for interest income and expense, non-operating income, and costs and depreciation. Jiansu Mobile had more than 99.5% of the local market share in Jiansu Province, which had a population of 71 million and US$1,100 for per capita GDP.

US$2.45 billion in cash,[199] and the remainder from bank borrowings and internal resources.[200] China Telecom (HK) claimed that it plans to invest a total of US$10.4 billion in these six mobile networks between 2000 and 2002, specifically, US$3.4 billion in 2000, US$3.6 billion in 2001 and US$3.4 billion in 2002, for network expansion and upgrade. Because of its strong market position, China Telecom (HK) has gained the third highest weighting in Hong Kong's Heng Sheng Index, accounting for 10.5% of the benchmark measure.

The lead underwriters involved in China Telecom (HK)'s initial deal (IPO) and subsequent share listing included China Development Finance, Goldman Sachs (Asia) L.L.C., China International Capital Corp Ltd., Bear Stearns Asia Ltd., Morgan Stanley Dean Witter, Credit Lyonnais Securities (Asia) Ltd., Donaldson, Lufkin & Jenrette Asia Ltd., HSBC Investment Bank Asia Ltd., Jardine Fleming Securities Ltd., and Merrill Lynch Far East Ltd. Joint underwriters for its bond sale were Chase Securities Inc., Merrill Lynch and Bank of China International Capital Ltd.

Capital Investment and Financing

MPT's global IPO indicates that funding for a sustainable development of China's telecom sector is by no means sufficient and tapping into international sources is increasingly important. Over the past decades, the Chinese central government budget for telecom industry declined sharply from 90% of the total investment in 1978 to

---

[199] Of this amount, US$1.65 was planned to draw from a share placement, and US$500 million from 5-year bonds. China Telecom (HK) deliberately had only about 20% of its total debt from foreign bonds as a preventive measure to lower the company's risk from devaluation of the Chinese currency. In this deal, China Telecom (HK) paid about US$1900 per subscriber to acquire the networks, while it paid about US$2800 per subscriber to acquire Jiangsu's network in 1998.

[200] China Telecom (HK) had about US$2 billion net cash in hand.

virtually zero[201] in 1997 while the demand for capital has enormously increased. MPT's marked achievement, to a significant degree, relied on the policy advantages that allowed for the influx of funds through low taxation, high equipment depreciation, and high installation and service charges.

During the past five years or so, capital investment for China telecom development was roughly broken down into three major sources:

1. Telecom installation fees[202] and services surcharges permitted by government policy made up over one third of the total.
2. High depreciation on telecom fixed assets,[203] which accounted for another one third of the investment.
3. The last one-third came from reinvestment from the after-tax profit[204] earned from telecom services, loans from domestic

---

[201] MPT got only about RMB100 million yuan a year in the form of grants from the government to pay for medical and other institutional expenses.

[202] Beijing, for instance, the installation fee in the 1980s was 400 yuan per line. With the special government policy to help fund development, the installation fee was raised to 1,500 yuan and then it mounted to 5,000 yuan. In poorer areas installation rates are lower - about 2,000-3000 yuan. In 1999, this fee dropped to between 1,000-500 yuan. China's telephone users complained about the high installation fees by saying that they were unfairly charged for both the "hen" (networks) and the "egg" (the services), when they only needed to purchase the latter.

[203] By 1998 China had an accumulated total of about RMB 580 billion (US$72 billion) worth of telecom and postal assets, of which telecom sector had RMB 547.3 billion (US$66 billion). According to MPT Minister Wu Jichuan when he visited Washington in December 1997, a 16% comprehensive rate applies to China's telecom equipment depreciation. Another MPT official indicated that telecom equipment is depreciated to almost a write-off value within 3-5 years and, in 1997 alone, China's telecom equipment depreciation was amounted up to US$6 billion.

[204] MPT's 1997 net profit was RMB12 billion (US$1.5 billion), of which about RMB4 billion (US$0.5 billion) was used to finance telecom development.

commercial banks, equipment suppliers' credits, foreign loans from the World Bank, Asia Development Bank, foreign governments (e.g., Japanese, European, and Canadian), and foreign commercial banks.[205]

As a major source of funding, installation fees and service revenues were crucial to China's telecom investment. The strong demand for services may help keep the high level of these charges for some time to come. In addition, high sales price of mobile communication handsets plus registration fees and service charges provided the sector a substantial cash pool for reinvestment. However, installation fees and service charges[206] can hardly maintain their current untenable level without challenge. They will face a declining curve once market competition grows and demand for basic services saturates. Besides, MPT and PTAs are now obliged to pay an equal rate of taxes[207] as other industry sectors. All these may soon factor into a situation in which MPT will lose its previous funding advantages and will have to explore new vehicles for investment to sustain development.

To address the critical issue of funding, Chinese central government and MPT have since 1993 brought forth new policies and strategies. They called for domestic investment diversification and attempted more aggressively to reach out for foreign investment and financing. Domestic diversification means (a) PTAs, government organizations, and business companies at both national and local levels are all

---

[205] China utilized a total of about US$6.6 billion in international loans between 1978 and 1996 for telecom equipment purchases, accounting for only a very small proportion of the total investment. An OECD agreement in 1993 significantly cut government soft loans to China's telecom projects. The World Bank and Asian Development Bank also announced later that they would gradually eliminate loans to China's telecom projects.

[206] Average installation fees have dropped in 1997 from previous 4000-5000 yuan to 2000-3000 yuan, service rates have also fallen, particularly for long-distance and international services.

[207] Preferential tax policy for telecom sector was terminated in 1996. MPT, in 1997, paid about RMB 150 million yuan for income tax, of which RMB 40-50 million yuan was paid as local sales tax.

encouraged to raise funds for telecom development; (b) expanded forms of funding are permitted, which include commercial and policy loans and credits, local government allocation of capital, revenue reinvestment, and securities issuance. Overseas, financial aid from international organizations and governments, international commercial loans and credits, foreign supplier financing, project financing and other innovative mechanisms are officially supported channels to procure investment. MPT and China's telecom operators have also been looking toward raising money through public stock and bond offering in international capital markets. They anticipate that international capital markets could be potentially the largest and most important sources of funds for China's long-term telecom development.

The proclaimed policies and regulations to stimulate funding from different sources including the use of foreign currency have, in effect, opened up China's telecom equipment supplies market to both domestic and overseas manufacturers in terms of equipment production and marketing. MPT has given green lights for domestic manufacturers to raise foreign capital by way of acquiring various credits and loans or listing on domestic stock exchanges.

Between 1996 and 2000, a minimum of US$65 billion is required for the planned telecom growth.[208] MPT estimated that out of this amount at least 15% needs to be raised overseas. The concern is that if MPT sources of investment dry up as a result of the change in policy incentives (such as favorable pricing and tax benefits[209] etc.) and of shrinking installation and other surcharges[210] previously obtainable, will sufficient funding be available to meet the capital requirement for further development. Besides, because China telecom sector has been doing well, soft and concessionary loans from the multilateral

---

[208] In April 1998, *China Daily* estimated that between 1998 and 2000, US$54.2 billion is needed for China telecom development.

[209] MPT-China Telecom has to pay to the central government an income tax at the rate of 33%. PTAs have to pay local sales tax at the rate of 3.2%. Previous tax breaks or incentives are terminated.

[210] These surcharges are seeing a continued decline due to the growing market competition and saturation of subscription for basic services in big cities.

institutions have been largely cut, innovation of policies to open up new funding sources will have to be put on the government agenda. Domestic commercial loans may, to some extent, help solve the problem, but China will be in a disadvantaged position if it loses access to a vast pool of various foreign capital abroad. Current Chinese telecom industry structure and regulations concerning foreign investment, however, stand as important hurdles to both foreign direct investment (FDI) and international capital markets. Foreign firms are prohibited from holding equity stakes or operating wired and wireless networks, Chinese telecom companies do not have rights to make their assets marketable to foreign investors. This constrains China's hand to apply new technologies and management skills, and refrains the country from raising large sums of foreign capital for faster development. The good news is that the Chinese government is reportedly rethinking its investment strategies and may consider, on a trial basis initially, getting foreign investment via Build-Transfer-Operate (BTO),[211] not BOT,[212] and Build-Lease-Operate (BLO) schemes.

WTO Accession and Telecommunications Liberalization

China's efforts to gain the World Trade Organization (WTO) accession have been a complex, conflicting, lengthy, and multi-

---

[211] For instance, in May 1997, Sprint and Metromedia, two US communications firms, got permission in principle from the State Council to work with Unicom to build fixed-line networks in Tianjin and Chongqing. The arrangement seems to be that of BTO.

[212] Since 1997, BOT has been tried for several power plant projects in Guangdong, Guangxi, Shanghai, Hunan, and Sichuan on a limited recourse basis. To attract foreign lenders, China's experimental BOT program is set to include such features as a fair and transparent bidding process, State Planning Commission supervision, 100% foreign ownership, credit support for offtake payments, government compensation for early termination of the concession, convertibility and transferability of foreign currency for debt service and equity returns, and fast track of contract negotiation and approval process.

faceted process affected by many political, economic, and international factors. WTO to China is described by many as a long-term gain at the price of short-term pain. Despite various debates and controversies on pros and cons, WTO membership will generate opportunities and challenges, benefits and risks, to the Chinese economy.

China's economic research institutions estimated that, in approximately five years' time after China's entry, WTO membership will help China increase its annual GDP by 3-5 percentage points, double the country's foreign trade volume from 1998's US$320 billion to US$600 billion in 2005, and create millions of new jobs. According to a study by China's State Council Development and Research Center, if China enters WTO in 2000, in five years' time, the country's GDP and social welfare income will be approximately US$25 billion and US$20 billion (based on 1995 price level) higher than if China remains outside WTO, representing 1.5% and 1.2% of the nation's estimated GDP in 2005. This projected macroeconomic gain is primarily based on a presumption of a higher economic efficiency that can be derived from the reallocation of resources resulting from China's greater integration into the global economy.

Major strategic benefits for China as a full WTO member may include:

- a greater inflow of foreign investment, a higher volume of export, and a larger pool of private domestic capital as a result of the improved investment environment;
- better opportunities for Chinese enterprises to obtain capital, technology, management expertise and market access outside China;
- introduction of an equitable and non-discriminatory trading mechanism based on WTO rules and multilateral dispute resolution processes;
- lower operation costs for Chinese enterprises to access foreign market, and greater international pressure to expedite China's industry restructuring and enterprise reform to obtain better competitiveness and efficiency; and

- legitimization of China's role in establishing and enforcing global trading regulations.

From an international perspective, benefits overweigh costs if China joins the WTO. In strategic and political terms, a developing China that gradually accepts international norms and integrates its economy with the rest of the world should be much better than an isolated and possibly unstable China. WTO admission will formally commit China to substantially reduce its tariff and non-tariff barriers to imports of foreign-made goods and services. The U.S., for instance, is estimated to benefit from increasing its immediate exports to China by US$3.1 billion, and, if foreign direct investment that could follow liberalization is taken into consideration, the U.S. could see additional US$13 billion worth of exports to China by the year 2005.[213] WTO accession could help deepen and accelerate China's market liberalization and reform of state-own enterprises. Formalizing the commitments in WTO would keep Chinese liberalization on track as resistance inevitably arises from China's affected industry sectors. WTO membership would also provide international investors and trading partners with more confidence and greater predictability about China's market environment.

The challenges China faces, however, are tough and immediate. Although the WTO may give a grace period for the protection of China's fledgling industries, the country's high-cost and poorly-managed economic sectors are liable to suffer from fierce international competition. Like many countries, China is concerned about the potential loss of sovereignty and the prospects of economic damage, such as weakened government control of China's key industries, large-scale structural unemployment, and social dislocation that may result from foreign competition. WTO membership will require major changes on several fronts: more market access must be provided to international companies; the legal and regulatory environment must be improved with higher international standards and

---

[213] These estimates are made by Institute for International Economics and Goldman Sachs.

greater transparency; tariff and non-tariff barriers to trade must be removed; foreign exchange control must be relaxed; issues of intellectual property rights, subsidies and product safeguards must be adequately addressed; and current Chinese demand on foreign companies to export products and provide technology transfer in return for market access must be eliminated.

WTO membership tends to have greater impact on China's service industries and technology and capital intensive sectors, including telecommunications, financial services, insurance, automobile, airlines, agriculture, and pharmaceuticals, as these sectors have a higher degree of vulnerability, given their present government protection and limited competitiveness in capital, managerial, and R&D resources. The impact WTO membership makes on China's economic forces may vary. For businesses whose operations are internationally competitive, WTO membership may offer more benefits than pressure. However, for enterprises that dominate China's domestic market at present but are not efficient enough to compete internationally, WTO membership may cause many of them to suffer from increased foreign competition and from decreased financial resources that may switch to more competitive firms. China's local economic entities, that have flourished because of the country's economic liberalization and political decentralization, but that are smaller in economies of scale and are weaker in the marketplace, may be exposed to a serious threat from China's WTO accession even if local officials try to subsidize and protect these entities.

To comply with the WTO requirements and to provide adequate legal protection to foreign businesses, China's administrative and legal environment must be further developed toward internal consistency, completeness, transparency, and enforceability. China's economic and institutional systems will have to go through a significant transition aimed at bringing the country closer to widely accepted international trade and investment practices. China will need to revise or change its current laws and regulations concerning import and export, investment, dumping, subsidy, foreign exchange, business operations, and electronic commerce. The Chinese government has openly admitted that there is considerable inconsistency or even conflicts in

China's pre-WTO policies and regulations. These policies and regulations mainly include China's Contract Law, Corporate Law, Foreign Trade Law, Sino-Foreign Jointly Funded Enterprise Law, Sino-Foreign Cooperative Enterprise Law, and Foreign-Invested Enterprise Law. Reform of these laws will be difficult and time consuming, but crucial if China makes a serious WTO commitment.[214]

Despite the challenges, China recognizes that trade and investment liberalization under the WTO regime is two important engines driving economic development. The Chinese government looks at the WTO as the "economic United Nations" that may lead to a "second economic reform" in China. As a member of the WTO, China will benefit not only from comprehensive and tangible economic gains, but also from the establishment of an internationally recognized legal framework that pushes forward China's economic reform and open up, helps separate government from businesses, tackles the issue of China's gray economy and corruption, facilitates Chinese enterprises' reshaping in terms of organizational structure, resources allocation and business practices, and grants Chinese businesses a broader access to the world marketplace.

In its negotiations for WTO admission, Beijing appeared to accept WTO principles on market liberalization, insisted on a pursuit of balance between rights and obligations, and accepted that China would seriously consider different options and proposals. China's official position on WTO accession has adhered to five points:

1. The Chinese government takes a realistic, flexible, and active approach in seeking its WTO membership.
2. The WTO is significantly deficient without China's participation.

---

[214] In this process, China's policy analysts suggested that China, deleting non-binding clauses and provisions, integrate laws dealing respectively with JVs, Sino-foreign cooperative companies, and sole foreign-funded firms into a new corporate law which abides by the general principles of market economy.

3. China is a developing, not developed, country. The obligations imposed on China should match the country's current economic strength. It is unreasonable to demand too high an entrance fee from China. China will not seek WTO entry at the expense of its fundamental interests and rights.[215]

4. China must be given a transitional grace period to gradually meet the WTO requirements, such as phasing out of tariffs, cutting of import quotas, and elimination of non- tariff trade barriers.

5. The Chinese government accepts the principle of "standstill," namely China will not, in the process of negotiation, promulgate new policies or laws that are inconsistent with the WTO rules.

Since 1998, China has shown greater flexibility and increased willingness to make substantial concessions to meet the WTO criteria. In early 1999, China intensified its efforts to enter the WTO. The country's Central Bank Governor and MOFTEC Minister announced that further concessions would be made in banking, commerce, and trade areas.[216] China apparently hoped to wrap up its 13-year negotiations prior to the end of 1999 to prevent the country from being charged higher entrance fees if new rules were added at the November WTO talks in Seattle.

Failure to join WTO soon would mean another long waiting period, during which the country would lose the opportunity to enjoy many immediate benefits, such as extended preferential low export tariffs, protection from unilateral trade sanctions and anti-dumping actions through the WTO dispute settlement mechanism;[217] closure of the

---

[215] Wu Yi, State Councilor, and Shi Guangsheng, Minister of MOFTEC, both reiterated this stance in April 1998 and May 1999.

[216] Telecom industry, however, was not mentioned for concession.

[217] In the WTO, trade disputes or complaints are submitted to Panels of Experts, who are empowered to issue rulings and recommendations. If a Member fails to comply with a ruling, WTO will authorize powerful trade sanctions in a timely and decisive way. In contrast, bilateral agreements and unilateral sanctions are generally far less effective in enforcement.

annual U.S. Congress debate over NTR ("normal trade relations," formerly, "most favored nation" treatment) status that casts a harsh light on US-China political and economic issues;[218] acquisition of a seat for China in making new WTO rules; a larger inflow of foreign investment due to improved investment environment and higher investor confidence; and incentives to drive China's sheltered state enterprises to reform faster and become more competitive internationally.

China's path towards WTO membership has not been smooth. In April 1999, when the Chinese premier visited the U.S., China offered to make significant market-opening concessions in industries that had largely been off limits to foreign competition. The concessions cover tariff reduction, trading protocols, and market access concerning products and services in telecommunications, information, agriculture, insurance, and banking. In telecommunications, restrictions on imports of radio pagers and mobile phones would be eliminated six years after China's WTO entry, foreign investors would be allowed to take 25% equity stakes in basic service joint ventures four years after the entry, and they may take up to 35% stakes in mobile and value-added communications ventures three years after China joins WTO. China's earlier offer in this area to foreign investors was 25%, with

---

[218] China has enjoyed MFN-NTR status since 1980 on an annual renewal basis. The U.S. must grant China a permanent NTR status in order to implement the US-China WTO agreement reached in November 1999. Otherwise, China would have a right to withhold its WTO commitments from the U.S. and the two countries would invoke the so-called "non-application" clause of WTO Article XIII, which would permit U.S. and China , as an incoming member, to not apply WTO trade liberalizing commitments and obligations to each other, and the two countries would base their trade relations on a 1979 U.S.-China trade agreement and other bilateral agreements, not on WTO rules. That is, China would become a WTO member and extend its rights and benefits specified by WTO to all of its trading partners who are WTO members, but not to the U.S. Normal Trade Relations (NTR) status is presently denied by the U.S. for political reasons to only a few nations such as Afghanistan, Cambodia, Cuba, Laos, North Korea, and Yugoslavia.

five years required after the WTO admission.[219] The April offer was comprehensive and consistent with WTO principles. It reflected the Chinese government's serious willingness to incur domestic political costs for the sake of obtaining an international agreement in China's long-term interest.

However, this new move experienced a vigorous backlash after the U.S. allegations of the Chinese espionage and the bombing by U.S.-led NATO of the Chinese embassy in Belgrade in May 1999. Tension in U.S.-China relations triggered a new wave of political conflict that cast doubts over China's WTO entry. Domestically, WTO issue was raised from a difficult policy arena to a realm of elite politics involving conflicting political constituencies. The Chinese hard-line resistance to U.S. and WTO accession grew to its height. Whether or not China should open its telecom and other "sensitive" markets to foreign companies again aroused an intense policy debate and a serious bureaucratic review. In June, China's State Councilor Wu Yi and MOFTEC officials declared that China could withdraw its offers for WTO entry if Chinese enterprises and government believed the terms on the negotiation table to be unacceptable, or if the U.S. and the West demands went beyond the level of China's tolerance. In July, however, Chinese premier Zhu Rongji softened the tone by saying that China would not withdraw the market-opening concessions that were offered to the U.S. in April as a part of the bid to join the WTO.

The WTO Basic Telecommunications Agreement[220] reached in Geneva in February 1997 by 69 countries to liberalize their telecom service markets for competition poses an increased pressure on

---

[219] US official report said that China would allow up to 49% of the foreign shares for all telecom services, and 51% for value-added and paging services four years after China's WTO accession.

[220] The negotiations toward this agreement were based on the General Agreement on Trade in Services (GATS) which provides a body of legally binding multilateral concepts, principles, and rules for progressive liberalization of trade and investment in services. GATS also provides a potential to raise the economic efficiency of members' service industries through improvements in domestic resource allocation and improved access to lower-cost and higher-quality services.

China. The WTO telecom agreement sets a new benchmark on which new WTO membership application may be evaluated.[221] This adds difficulties to negotiations between China and other countries as telecommunications has long been controlled by the Chinese government and the industry is considered to be one of the last frontiers for liberalization. The pressure on China specifically derives from the regulatory principles and requirements for opening telecom services market on both domestic and multilateral dimensions, as concerning

- pro-competitive environment of policies and regulations,
- network interconnection and licensing criteria,
- independent and transparent regulatory regime,
- cost-based pricing structure,
- foreign equity ownership and management control of network and communication facilities,
- market access for competing players in telecom services and equipment supplies, and
- national (non-discriminatory) treatment for foreign firms.[222]

Market access to communications and financial services has been a primary source of concern and objection from the international community regarding China's WTO entry. These two industry sectors are considered by China as among the most sensitive, therefore,

---

[221] Telecom market access commitments made by WTO members cover both cross-border supply of telecommunications and services provided through the establishment of foreign firms, and these countries' commercial presence, including the ability to own and operate independent telecom network infrastructure. Services concerned include voice telephony, data transmission, telex, telegraph, facsimile, private leased circuit services (i.e., the sale or lease of transmission capacity), fixed and mobile satellite systems and services, cellular telephony, mobile data services, paging, and personal communications systems.

[222] A Chinese government official in charge of WTO negotiation in early 2000 stressed on the importance of the national treatment for foreign firms. He stated that China's previous preferential treatment for some foreign firms discriminated against other foreign companies and Chinese firms. It should be eliminated.

should be opened last and with adequate precautions. China sees its WTO accession as beneficial mainly to the country's external trade and several other economic sectors, while WTO admission may threaten the country's telecom services sector which is least prepared for competition.

For years, China's policy makers have been very cautious about information and communication. They have held a notion that telecommunications concerns the nation's security and sovereignty, therefore, it cannot be opened to the outside world. Since 1998, this long-held position seems to have been increasingly challenged. China's policy debate on foreign investment in telecommunications has shifted from a strict ban to considerations of what degree and how soon foreign network equity ownership and telecom service operation can be allowed without subverting China's national interest.[223] The Chinese central government has been trying hard to measure the overall strategic costs and benefits WTO may bring if China's telecommunications and information industries are liberalized to the outside world.

China's telecommunications regulator, MII, believes that market liberalization forced by China's WTO membership will bring more disadvantages and risks than benefits to the country's fledgling telecommunications and information services, even though it may provide more incentives for China's information technology sector to grow. China's telecommunications equipment market, the MII argues, is already fully competitive with almost all international players and several rising Chinese firms competing against one another. The most prominent Chinese companies include Julong, Datang, Zhongxin, Huawei and Jinpeng, which have developed and marketed their own brand-name products such as digital SPC switch (ZX10, C&CO), switch model 04, and CDMA-based switch and M30 mobile systems.

MII and China's IT industry predict that there will be two important advantages WTO membership can bring to the Chinese

---

[223] This is a significant change from MPT's previous position. For many years, telecommunications in China was regarded as a sector different from other commercial industries, therefore, it must be controlled by the government.

telecommunications equipment manufacturers: (1) the current tariff of 12% on imported components and parts, on which the Chinese firms depend for production, will be lowered to 3% or less, thus resulting in significantly lower equipment cost and sales prices.[224] (2) WTO accession will remove some of the foreign obstacles that have prevented the Chinese firms from marketing their products outside China.

However, these predicted advantages may soon disappear if China implements its commitment to the WTO requirement that import tariffs on telecommunications and IT equipment be eliminated by the year 2005, and that telecommunications equipment purchases be based on technology-neutral and non-discriminatory terms. China's telecom equipment manufacturers will face a difficult situation, as their price advantage and policy support will be undercut and network service carriers will select equipment vendors based more on economic and technology factors which may favor foreign competitors.

Until July 1999, China continued to disfavor radical ideas of trading telecommunications network and services for WTO accession, albeit the government had decided to significantly lower trade tariffs and reduce non-tariff barriers, and had worked out new packages of concessions in previously prohibited industry sectors to meet the

---

[224] During the 1997 Clinton-Jiang Summit, the Chinese government made a decision to join the Information Technology Agreement of WTO to gradually cut tariffs on computers, telecom equipment, semiconductor, and other IT products from about 35%[224] to zero by the year 2005. Since then, substantial tariff reduction has been implemented on computer products, including CPUs, POSs, ATMs, UPSs, keyboards, mice, monitors, printers, stylus, voltage stabilizers, and database processing units, from approximately 20% in 1997 to 12% in 1999. This move has given Chinese IT producers who rely on foreign components a cost advantage, but it also has created a more level playing field for international firms to compete in China, at the same time, it has imposed a pressure on China's domestic IT component producers to become more competitive.

WTO criteria.[225] By then, China's 1997 Geneva proposal to allow 25% foreign investment in ventures of telecommunications value-added services in Shanghai and Guangzhou had not been materialized. The Chinese Premier's 1999 tentative offer of 35% foreign investment in telecommunications sector had not yet been granted final bureaucratic approval. MII's position that opening telecom market should not be treated as a prerequisite for China's WTO entry was apparently upheld. MII, in fact, tried to ward off foreign involvement by making new policy statements between September and October that China's Internet business was not allowed to acquire any foreign investment.

On November 15, 1999, a landmark breakthrough emerged. After six extraordinary days of painstaking negotiations in Beijing, U.S. and China, with critical top-level political interventions, reached a framework agreement that puts China significantly closer to its WTO accession.[226] China's overall offer in this bilateral agreement does not contrast much from its April accord when Chinese premier Zhu visited the U.S., but it goes further in a number of areas including import surge mechanisms, anti-dumping protocols, import of movies, auto-financing, securities, capital market access, and telecommunications. According to the U.S. government official summary, China's concession for telecommunications in regard to foreign equity shares (%) reads as follows:[227]

---

[225] China is reported to be opening more industry sectors for international competition, such as financial and insurance services, tourism, transportation, railways, retailing, and power supplies.

[226] After the US-China agreement, China still needs to negotiate with more than 20 countries or regions on terms of trade of products and services, obtain legislative endorsement of WTO member countries and to win two thirds of the WTO ministerial votes before the country can officially become a member of WTO.

[227] Upon China's WTO accession, foreign investment in value-added and mobile services is allowed in Beijing, Shanghai and Guangzhou only. The same restriction applies to the third-year investment by foreign firms in China's domestic and international long distance services.

	Upon Accession	01	02	Year 03	04	05	06
Value-added Services (including Internet and Paging)	30	49	50				
Mobile Voice and Data	25	35	49				
Domestic Long-distance				25		35	49
International Long-distance				25		35	49

China's commitments mark its first agreement to open its telecommunications sector, both to the scope of services and to direct investment in telecommunications businesses. Through these commitments, China will become a member of the Basic Telecommunications Agreement. Tariffs on IT products, such as computers, semiconductors and all Internet-related equipment will fall from the current average of 13.5% to 0% by the year 2005.

Upon its accession to the WTO, China will phase out all geographic restrictions for paging and value-added services in 2 years, mobile cellular in 5 years and domestic wireline services in 6 years. China's key telecommunications services corridors in Beijing, Shanghai, and Guangzhou, which represents approximately 75% of all domestic traffic, will open immediately on accession in all telecommunications services. China will allow 50% foreign ownership for value added and paging services in two years, 49% foreign stake in mobile and data services in 5 years; and 49% foreign equity share in international and domestic telecom services in 6 years.

Internet services will be liberalized at the same rate as other key telecommunications services and foreign investment will be allowed. China has agreed that it will ensure that state-owned and state-invested enterprises will make purchases and sales based solely on commercial considerations, such as price, quality, availability and marketability, and provide U.S. firms with the opportunity to compete for sales and purchases on non-discriminatory terms and conditions.

China has also agreed that the government will not influence these commercial decisions (either directly or indirectly) except in a WTO consistent manner. In terms of regulatory principles, China has agreed to implement the pro-competitive regulatory principles embodied in the Basic Telecommunications Agreement (including cost-based pricing, interconnection rights and an independent regulatory authority), and agreed to technology-neutral scheduling, which means foreign suppliers can use any technology they choose to provide telecommunications services.

This concession on telecommunications market should be looked on as a dramatic development, given China's stiff position on telecommunications during many years of the U.S.- China WTO negotiation. The change in the government position also reveals China's increased enthusiasm to enter the WTO. In May 2000 when China and European Union reached the bilateral agreement on China's WTO accession, the terms on telecom liberalization appeared to have been pushed one step further: the waiting time for wireless mobile services to open for international competition is shortened from 5 years to 3 years, with 25% of the equity share allowed for foreign investors right after China's WTO accession, 35% one year afterwards, and up to 49% in 3 years. China also committed to open its domestic network leasing market to foreign firms in conjunction with the WTO membership.

Chinese media reports and official commentaries, however, presented plenty of room for discrepancy. Chinese policy makers have attempted to clarify the deal by stating that the opening of the country's telecom market will go through a regulated and step-by-step process. They indicated that China will have to open, in two years after the country's WTO accession, its value-added telecom services, which include Internet-related network services, e-commerce, data transport and processing, intelligent networks, and telephone messaging services. Within three years, radio paging will be liberalized for competition. Wireless mobile and satellite communication services will only be partially opened for managed competition within five to six years. Foreign investors in these service sectors will be permitted to initially hold 30% and then 50% of the shares, not controlling stakes.

Foreign participation in China's basic wireline telecom services will be permitted last. Foreign stakes in basic telecom services will be allowed from 25% to 49% in about six years after China's WTO entry, while geographic restrictions on different telecom services will be phased out within five or six years. Chinese sources also have made it clear that a strict licensing mechanism and effective legal and administrative regulations will be enforced in the process of the telecom market liberalization to regulate foreign equity ownership and business operations. In addition, the Chinese government has implied that it will continue to reserve leverage over foreign involvement when specific projects or ventures are negotiated.

The pressure to enter the WTO has pushed forward the reform of China's telecom sector, which was earlier cruising along its "set course." Countermeasures have been proposed to meet these challenges. MII and State Development Planning Commission officials have recommended special policies to direct initial foreign investment toward China's northwest regions where telecom infrastructure and services are underdeveloped. Other policy recommendations include improving service quality and rationalizing telecom and Internet service charges, formulating internationally compatible rules and regulations to regulate market behaviors of both domestic and foreign players, and preparing domestic telecom and IT enterprises with better competitiveness by speeding up their organizational restructuring and by strengthening their management practices. Strategically, proposals have been made for China to consider giving priority to cross-region alliances with strong overseas Chinese-related multinational corporations for absorption of capital and managerial resources. Hong Kong, for instance, may receive a strategic preference because of its well-established position in technology and network advancement, in international telecom linkage and management expertise, and in natural affinity and coherence with mainland China in terms of culture, language, and territory.

Institutional Conflict of Interests

Institutional frictions or conflicts of interest among MPT, MEI, MRFT, MOR, MEP, PLA,[228] and several others have increased over the past few years. Most of these institutions have their own dedicated network capacities or technology expertise available, and intend to exercise their muscles in developing their own public services to enter the country's lucrative and vast communications and information market. Coupled with this economic interest, the reshaping of the political powers in a context of rapid socio-economic structural changes and the fast-paced technological innovations are all impetus for institutional conflicts. MPT's legitimacy as a monopoly is, never before, severely challenged as the traditional lines between telecommunications, computer networking, and information media become continually blurred, and as the competing players grow stronger. Conflict of interest among these players frequently stimulates the issue of resource allocation and industry regulation and management. Emerging Internet applications in China is also an important factor that increasingly complicates China's structure of the institutional stakes.

Compared with its competitors, MPT had a weak image in history. But over the past decade MPT has risen as more powerful, partially due to its important financial contribution to the central government,[229] and partially due to the official development priority given to telecommunications and information. MEI, MOR, and MOP, three of the MPT's rival ministries, were looked on as enjoying strong

---

[228] They are: Ministry of Electronics Industry; Ministry of Radio, Films and Television; Ministry of Railways; Ministry of Electric Power; People's Liberation Army. In fact, friction between MPT and other organizations began at least two decades ago when institutional users of communications found themselves frustrated by the sporadic and sluggish performance of MPT in providing telecom services, which triggered the launching of "private" networks. Note: MPT, MEI, MRFT, and MEP were restructured in March 1998.

[229] MPT claimed in 1998 that telecom sector's financial contribution to the Chinese government was number two, next only to the country's tobacco industry.

power bases under the State Council. They allied in 1994 to become key shareholders of China Unicom in an attempt to combat MPT by offering telecom and computer-based information services.

Unicom's rise is a political move that indicates an explicit overrule of MPT by the State Council in the name of reducing monopoly and boosting development. In addition to Unicom, MEI also set up a communications operator named Jitong Corporation to implement its strategy of entering China's telecom market. MRFT, China's mass media regulator and operator, used to define its business as Party (CCP) and government ideological functions, but it is now aggressively engaged to utilize its nationwide system of TV and broadcast networks and services to compete with MPT. MPT, on the other hand, has been pulling its strength of existing monopoly incumbents to hold back the advancement of its fledgling rivals.

The conflicts between MPT and MRFT focus on how CATV programs should be transmitted to the end users. MPT says its network capacities are sufficient and economical to meet this need, while MRFT insists on building its own fiber-optic cable networks to make CATV services more flexible, more controllable, and less expensive. In addition, MRFT may have a future-oriented perspective of offering voice, data, and video services on its own networks as emerging digital technology promises to do so. MRFT currently has not acquired the statutory right to provide public data and voice services, but it is actively involved in network development and in adopting new technologies with an ambition to eventually attain capabilities and official permission to provide such services. MPT, or MII as later renamed, has put on its agenda to bring CATV networks under its control. The ministry has pushed to separate cable network operations from cable programming functions so as to win the power to regulate cable networks and make MRFT a mere content regulator, or an "ideological gatekeeper." In March 1999, MRFT, after being reformed into the State Administration of Radio, Film and TV (SARFT), launched a serious challenge to China Telecom's monopoly by stating that China CATV industry is to be restructured into a national CATV network corporation (group), with provincial and local branches, to develop and offer public CATV, data broadcasting,

Internet access, and a variety of value-added information services. The initial project undertaken by this corporation is designated as China High-speed Internet Demonstration Project, which involves a joint participation of SARFT, Chinese Academy of Sciences, the Ministry of Railways, and Shanghai IT sector. The mission of this project is to apply IP-based high-speed routering and compress multiplexing technologies to CATV and railway fiber optic cables already widely available,[230] so as to offer advanced integrated information services in 15 Chinese cities. Once successful, the project will be expanded to other provinces and cities.

In September 1999, MRFT-SARFT's vision seemed to have moved a substantive step forward. China Network Communications Corporation (China Netcom or CNC) was officially established, with a startup capital of US$50.6 million from government funds and bank loans. CNC's initial funding sources also include capital investment from the four key shareholders and the potential issuance of the 10-year T-bonds.[231] The Chinese Academy of Sciences (CAS), SARFT, the Ministry of Railways, and Shanghai Municipal Government each hold 25% of the company's share. China Netcom, chaired by a CAS

---

[230] In 1999, China had 320 million TV sets and 40 million VCDs in use. China's CATV trunk networks, roughly 250,000 km long (more than 100,000 km of which was SDH fiber optic cable, the rest was microwave or satellite networks), and local access networks (more than 3.5 million km, about 10% of which was 2-way HFC by 1999) had covered most of the Chinese cities and towns, 70% of the villages, and 50% of the total landmass, with more than 85 million CATV program viewers. Provincial and city CATV networks were in 1999 estimated at over RMB 200 billion yuan (US$25 billion) in value. China's CATV networks (hybrid fiber coax – HFC, 450-750MHz) are operated by several hundred provincial and local TV stations. China's CATV experts estimated that with an investment of one billion yuan (US$125 million), current provincial and city long-distance CATV networks could be connected.

[231] CNC Chairman Yan Yiyun said in December 1999 that CNC's registered capital was about US$43 million. The initial project would need US$60 million, which would consist of US$20 million from the Chinese government, US$20 from bank loans, and the rest from 4 equal-amount capital input by the four major shareholders.

vice president and managed by Edward Tian, former CEO of a U.S.-based networking firm AsiaInfo,[232] emerges as a strong potential competitor to China Telecom and China Unicom. Its strategic objective is, in line with China's state designated demonstration project, to deploy advanced fiber optic technology, build a high-speed (20Gbps) IP-over-DWDM backbone, and interconnect regional and local CATV and railway cable networks for provision of broadband data communication, multimedia, Internet access, voice telephony, and video-on-demand services to business enterprises, government offices, telecom carriers, ISPs/ICPs, and the country's 85 million CATV subscribers.

China Netcom is widely viewed as an alternative source of backbone connectivity. If it works out, ChinaNet may create a different landscape in China's communications market. ChinaNet is competitive in financial, technological, and political terms.[233] Presently, the network capacity of China's TV and railway industries is smaller than that of China Telecom's, yet, the network covers 70% of the Chinese cities and 50% of the country's territory. Its bandwidth is many times higher than China Telecom's, which may translate into lower transmission costs and higher competitiveness in the market. This appeals to the consumers who will benefit from the network superiority in speed, quality and expenses. CNC's initiative, however, also serves as a case in point where political concerns and commercial conflicts surface. While the Chinese State Council turned on the green light for CNC, in September 1999, the leadership released a self-contradictory document No.82 (1999), saying that radio and CATV networks should be maintained for dedicated use, they cannot go public unless permitted, and there should be a division of services between television and telecom sectors, no cross road or overlap

---

[232] According to Reuters, Edward Tian founded AsiaInfo Computer Network Co. Ltd. in 1993 and turned it into a US$87 million Internet company within six years.

[233] Four of the CNC's shareholders all have strong political support from the top leadership. Chinese President Jiang's son is one of the key players for this venture. He oversees the Shanghai stake in CNC, and holds the vice presidency of the Chinese Academy of Sciences (CAS).

endorsed.[234] The State Council's message may have been directly prompted by the violent confrontations between telecom and cable TV operators in Hunan Province and other localities involving their high financial interest. What the message really meant is not clear, because it could have been a message of the government dilemma as a result of the telecom-TV clashes. In such circumstance, market risks, policy inconsistency, and institutional management and coordination are clearly the toughest issues that CNC has to deal with strenuously.

Among some 70 Chinese government and business organizations that operate their own dedicated networks, the Ministry of Railways and its incumbent enterprises have an extensive communications network system with the total comprehensive capacity next to that of China Telecom. This system runs through all the Chinese cities except Lhasa and Haikou. By 1998, the railway networks had a total 120,000 km (66,000 km long distance lines) of communication lines, with a switching capacity of 1.5 million lines. Besides, the railway industry has built 42,242 km of fiber optic backbone networks, 4,593 km of digital microwave networks, and a satellite communication system covering more than seventy large and medium-sized Chinese cities. These railway communication networks currently have about 60% of their capacity unused. They can be made available for public telecom services that compete with China Telecom. Railway industry's extensive communications infrastructure and its spare network capacity have been targeted by Unicom for years, Netcom, and railway operators for lucrative deployment. In May 1999, the Ministry of Railways announced it would set up a new national communications entity, China Railway Communications and Information Corporation (Group), to provide comprehensive communication services to the general public, alongside China Telecom and Unicom. The implementation of this plan requires the official approval from the State Council[235] and a upgrade of the

---

[234] Shanghai is designated as an exception: the city is allowed to experiment in integrating cable and telecom networks for different services.

[235] Railway Ministry official Peng Peng said in May 1999 that "we should have no problem getting permission from the State Council. We can start to provide

networks by the railway industry from an internally focused and operated system into an open, public service oriented, and well connected and managed communication system.

China Telecom has another potential competitor, the People's Liberation Army (PLA). PLA has been active in China telecom market for some time by leasing MPT trunk lines and using PLA's spare frequencies and excess capacity to offer trunk radio, AMPS cellular, and paging services. In general, PLA service carriers are not explicitly authorized or highly profiled. They usually involve themselves in gray-area and small-scale operations where the State Council and MPT regulations are not exactly clear. Despite the debates within PLA on whether commercial operations of telecom services should be conducted, some divisions of PLA have made plans to deploy code division multiple access (IS-95 CDMA),[236] a US-developed technology, to offer mobile services which are potentially better in terms of capacity and efficiency than existing analog and digital GSM systems. Shanghai, Beijing, Guangdong, and Xi'an have been selected by PLA as initial trial cities, and 35 other cities across 20 provinces will be the next-phase targets.[237]

PLA's move has achieved blessings from the State Council which proposed in 1995 harnessing the PLA controlled radio spectrum and MPT's public networks to offer public services. PLA has formed a 50-50 joint venture with MPT, namely, China Great Wall Mobile

---

comprehensive telecom services within six to eight months after the State Council approval and network improvement."

[236] PLA (Great Wall Co.) completed the installation of China's first CDMA network in Beijing in 1997 with an initial capacity for 43,000 subscribers.

[237] Motorola supplies the technology for Beijing trial, with 30 base stations covering most of the city area within the third ring road. Samsung, Nortel, and Lucent Technologies provide technologies for Shanghai, Xi'an, and Guangdong (CDMA-AMPS) respectively. In 1999, the estimated number of subscribers were 50,000 (Beijing), 50,000 (Shanghai), 20,000 (Guangzhou), and 13,000 (Xi'an). Qualcomm will provide Beijing site with the handsets. In February 2000, it was reported by "Virtual China" that Motorola and Compaq would supply CDMA equipment and solutions to the Great Wall, Beijing, for roaming and fraud detection.

Communications Corporation,[238] to materialize its ambitions. PLA's commercial vehicle for this venture is the telecoms department of China Electronic System Engineering Co (CESEC), which has local branches in many of the Chinese cities. If successful with the initial trials, the Great Wall will likely become the first operator in China to provide CDMA mobile services (800MHz).

MPT has a mixed stake in this joint venture. On one hand, the Great Wall can be used as a way to deploy more advanced technologies and to hedge its current reliance on TACS and GSM technologies. On the other hand, MPT may have concerns over this venture, as CESEC may sooner or later impose a strong challenge to MPT's existing market dominance by initiating important commercial presence.[239] Structurally, 50-50 share does not give MPT any superiority in the venture's management control. Instead, PLA regional setups may have a greater influence upon decision-making processes.[240] The situation of the Great Wall Communications has become much more complicated and uncertain because three new factors have set in: a) MPT's restructure into MII; b) China's official announcement that Unicom is granted special rights to adopt CDMA technology; and c) the Chinese government's decision to pull the military off commercial activities. When Unicom was granted the "exclusive" right to deploy CDMA technology in 1999, MII decided to turn the Great Wall to Unicom for operation. What happened by February 2000 was that China Telecom pulled out of the Great Wall, whereas the military maintained its stake in the company and began crafting new partnerships in order to expand its CDMA networks for public

---

[238] Some foreign players and European banks have been reportedly involved in the Great Wall business to provide capital or technology. PLA joined hands with Hutchison Whampoa Ltd. of Hong Kong for finance (US$388 million) and construction of CDMA networks in major Chinese cities. Motorola, Samsung, Nortel, and Lucent Technologies are major equipment suppliers while Qualcomm and others are to provide handsets.

[239] In its interest, MPT may want to hold up the project to give time to its own cellular operations for a larger customer base for competition.

[240] This PLA initiative, however, has been complicated by the Chinese government's decision to segregate the military from commercial operations.

services.[241] The Great Wall's CDMA networks got connected in February with the network of Hebei Century Mobile Communications Corp. Unicom's ambition to takeover the Great Wall remained in the air.[242]

Technical Standards

The strategic issue of technical standards is provoked by (1) China's large investment in purchasing telecom equipment and advanced systems from different sources; (2) decentralized pattern of local equipment procurement and vendor selection; (3) accelerated technology innovation and competing technology alternatives that complicate the environment in which technical standards are made. In general, China's practices relating to technical standards have not been sufficiently coordinated, even under MPT's seemingly strict regulations. Lack of an effective mechanism for establishing technical standards and product testing and certification has often led to confusions in equipment marketing and an incompatibility of telecom systems, which apparently obstructs China's efforts to create an integrated national information infrastructure.

Currently, the majority of the equipment and facilities installed in China for telecom switching, transmission, and network management are imported from or supplied by various foreign related companies from Europe, USA, and Asia. Alcatel,[243] Motorola, Lucent, Ericsson,

---

[241] In February 2000, a MII official who declined to be identified, said "the military has permission to build local CDMA joint ventures." China Satellite Telecom Broadcast Corp., Legend, Founder, and Beijing ZhongGuancun Technology Development Ltd. have expressed their interest in taking equity positions in the Century Mobile.

[242] Wu Duhua, Unicom's official in charge of CDMA, talked about the Great Wall's move by saying "the demand is huge and duplicating infrastructure won't be a problem," "we are stronger than them, we are more capable, and we'll definitely do it better."

[243] Shanghai Bell Telecom Equipment Corporation of Alcatel is reported to have taken 25-30% of China's program controlled exchange market.

Nokia, Siemens, Nortel and NEC have taken large shares of China's telecom technology market, while Chinese firms, *e.g.,* Datang, Zhongxin, Huawei, Great Dragon, Eastern Communications and Xiamen Xiaxin Electronics, are struggling to increase the applications of such digital program control systems as HJD-04, C&C-08, EIM-601, DS-30, C&C08, DS200A/B, CNC1000, LXJ-10, ZXJ10, JSN-IB and SP30 that are domestically developed and marketed. In October 1998, M30-G mobile switching system and GSM900/1800 base station system designed and manufactured by China's Datang Telecom Group passed the MII test and were recognized as the country's first self-developed state-of-the-art mobile technology, which marked China's growing ability to compete with foreign countries.

As a result, China has become a testbed or battlefield for many different technical standards and network systems.[244] The complexity of the technology applications is figuratively described as "eight countries, nine systems," i.e., nine technical systems from eight countries are in operation,[245] not to mention the systems developed by Chinese firms. Systems deploying analog and digital technologies such as TACS, AMPS, GSM, CDMA, PCN, PCS, DECT and FPLMTS are being experimented and applied by the Chinese operators affiliated with different political organizations or in different regions. System coordination and management have largely lagged behind these trials and implementations, resulting in higher development cost, greater subscriber concerns, more misuse of spectrum resources, and heavier burdens on technology integration and network interconnection.

China's battle for specific standards is not only linked to technologies, but also to economic and political considerations. A best noted and ongoing case is the battle between Global System for

---

[244] In 1996, MPT was reported to be carrying out compatibility tests for 22 different Stored Program Control switching systems.

[245] For example, these systems are in use by Chinese operators: Japan's F150 of Fujitsu and Neat61 of NEC; Sweden's AXE10 of Ericsson; Belgium's S1240 of Alcatel; France's E10B; Germany's EWSD of Siemens; USA's 5ESS of Lucent; Canada's DMS of Nortel; and the system developed by Nokia of Finland.

Mobile Communications (GSM-TDMA) developed by European telecom industries (*e.g.,* Ericsson) and Code Division Multiple Access (CDMA-"Spread Spectrum") developed by American telecom players (*e.g.,* Qualcomm).[246] GSM is a set of ETSI standards specifying the infrastructure for digital cellular service, including radio interface (900MHz/1800MHz), switching, signaling, and intelligent network. GSM has gained widespread acceptance with deployment in more than 100 countries. CDMA is reportedly featured as offering a much larger capacity, more efficient use of bandwidth, and superior voice quality. To gain an upper hand in China for official acceptance of either of these standards, Ericsson, Qualcomm and many other telecom players have fought head to head and spared no efforts in lobbying the Chinese government.

U.S. push for CDMA800 led to the trials in four Chinese cities (Beijing, Shanghai, Xi'an, and Panyu-Guangdong) while the relative maturity and wide applications of GSM resulted in China's enthusiastic adoption of the system. By 1999, majority of the Chinese wireless mobile services was operated on GSM platforms. GSM took about 95% of the digital mobile service market share in China. In spite of its smaller capacity, radio interference, unstable voice quality and spectrum issues, as compared with CDMA, GSM appears to have been favored by China,[247] and the debate among government officials and industry experts on GSM and CDMA resulted in a one-year suspension of the CDMA network development.

Three speculative reasons behind China's GSM preference are: (1) China has invested a large sum of capital (approximately US$30 billion by the middle of 2000) for GSM network development. Majority of the Chinese cities have been connected by GSM networks (e.g., China

---

[246] In February 2000, GSM had about 250 million users while CDMA had about 50 million worldwide.

[247] It was reported in February 1999 that MPT/MII decided to hold back its initiatives in CDMA trials and deployment. China would, by sticking to GSM, preserve the nation's backbone networks for W-CDMA. CDMA presented two application problems in China: (1) lack of UIM (user interface module) in the market to let service subscribers to change handsets or easily use prepaid cards; (2) dual-mode handsets sold in China cannot transfer from GSM to CDMA.

Telecom's 138 and 139 networks, Unicom's 130 network) for widespread public services and, internationally, over 100 countries offer GSM network services, which takes more than 60% of the world digital mobile market. China's GSM investment should get its returns. It would make no sense to reinvest heavily to replace a system that is just readily available for services.[248] (2) With a view to the technology upgrading, China believes 2G mobile services should be in operation for another 5-6 years before 3G can be massively rolled out in the market. China seems to look more to W-CDMA, a system developed by the GSM alliance for the next generation of cellular platform, as W-CDMA is compatible with the current GSM system, it should be economically and technologically more viable than US developed CDMA-2000. (3) As MPT is officially placed to perform the role of setting telecom standards, other institutional forces that promote non-MPT liked standards tend to have less influence. In terms of the standards for the third generation mobile (3G, or ITU proposed IMT-2000 series),[249]

China is seriously involved in studies of W-CDMA,[250] CDMA-2000, and patented Chinese TD-SCDMA[251] systems for the country's 3G

---

[248] David Crowe, Editor of *Cellular Networking Perspectives*, commented by saying that " W-CDMA is so far in the future that China will have to spend sizable sums on an upgrade, even if the country stays with GSM networks. China would easily spend as much money upgrading to W-CDMA from GSM as it would spend switching to a CDMA standard."

[249] Three generations of mobile systems refer to analog (1G), digital GSM-TDMA (2G), and IMT-2000 series (3G).

[250] W-CDMA is developed by European companies and is said to be GSM compatible. Apart from MII research institutes, several Chinese companies are also involved in the assessment of W-CDMA and TD-SCDMA. These companies include Datang, Huawei, Zhongxin, and Jin Peng.

[251] A Chinese company named Xin Wei Telecom has developed a system called TD-S (Synchronous) CDMA, which is China patented and compatible with GSM. This China developed TD-SCDMA system has been submitted to ITU for one of the standard options for the next generation mobile communications. ITU has reportedly reviewed TD-SCDMA and accepted it as one of the alternative standards for the third-generation wireless mobile communications.

mobile communications options. In 1999, MII and the State Development Planning Commission launched a major 3G-focused R&D project with an initial co-investment of RMB300 million (US$37 million). Eight Chinese enterprises were involved in this project, including Great Dragon, Datang, Zhongxing, and Huawei. As TD-SCDMA is China developed, it seems to have been favored by some Chinese officials and industry leaders, but how this Chinese system will work out remains uncertain, because the acceptance of it will depend not only on the Chinese government, but also on whether or not a consensus can be reached among the equipment manufacturers, the service carriers, and other market forces. It is possible that the three said systems may prevail for China's 3G, each with a different market share and user segment.

In March 1999, however, shortly before the Chinese premier's state visit to the U.S., the battle between GSM and CDMA saw a sharp turn. China sent out the signal that the country would widely adopt CDMA for its wireless mobile services and that China Unicom would be the beneficiary to receive official license for the deployment of CDMA. This Chinese policy change towards CDMA, if true, may have had four justifications behind. One, it could have been part of the Chinese government efforts to strengthen China Unicom to compete against China Telecom.[252] Two, CDMA adoption could have been a concession to the U.S. that may help China's bid to join the World Trade Organization. Three, as Ericsson and Qualcomm had reached an agreement in the early 1999 that Ericsson would purchase Qualcomm's CDMA division, and Qualcomm would have rights to market Ericsson's GSM system in America, there seemed to be no more ground to fight over these two standards that may ultimately become compatible with each other. Four, China's CDMA applications would lead to purchases worth billions of dollars from big U.S. high-

---

[252] Unicom was reported as having submitted a plan to the State Council for CDMA deployment to help compete with China Telecom. Unicom plans to roll out CDMA and recruit 10 million subscribers by the year 2000, and 40 million subscribers by 2005.

tech companies such as Motorola, Lucent, and Qualcomm. This, to some extent, would generate pressure on the U.S. government to relax its high-tech export control to China and improve the balance of trade between the two countries.

Radio Spectrum Management

The spectrum of radio frequencies is a strategic and scarce resource for wireless and mobile communications. Strategic, because electromagnetic frequencies are used for voice, data, and video communications for social, economic, political, security, and military purposes. Scarce, because only a limited range of frequencies is practically applicable.[253] In today's marketplace, tensions often arise between those who manage or have control over spectrum and those who do not, but acquire availability of it. The strategic issues derived from radio spectrum management involve a set of complex areas regarding frequency allocation, licensing or assignment, economic efficiency of spectrum utilization, harmonization of different frequency deployments, and overall regulatory mechanism.[254]

China's spectrum regulatory regime is the State Radio Regulation Commission (SRRC).[255] It is not well known but well powered. SRRC operates like a cross-ministry/commission task force, regulating and managing China's radio frequency spectrum resources for mobile, satellite, maritime, and aeronautic communications. Under the dual jurisdiction of the State Council and the Central Military Commission, the core of SRRC consists of one commissioner, three deputy commissioners, and twenty-two members who also hold

---

[253] Technically, however, radio frequencies are infinite in band: they have no low or high limit.

[254] These specifically involve frequency allocation and reallocation, coordination and shared use, geographic coverage, number and method of allocation or assignment, user eligibility, structure, functions, and authority of the regulatory regime.

[255] SRRC is physically located within the MPT-MII, but it functions independently.

leading positions in various ministries or commissions. The significance of the SRRC is self-evident: a vice premier of the State Council chairs the commission, while the Minister of MPT-MII, the Assistant to Chief of the General Staff of the Central Military Commission, and the Deputy Secretary General of the State Council jointly take the seats of the SRRC Deputy Commissioners.[256]

SRRC is mandated to provide supreme leadership over the national allocation and management of radio frequency spectrum, and regulate and coordinate different forces that acquire the use of radio frequency in China. SRRC also has provincial offices across the country, which are linked to relevant technical and overseeing facilities. One specific problem facing the SRRC in recent years is frequency congestion and interference caused by the soaring demand and service provision for mobile and wireless communications.[257] In addition, rapid expansion of telecom services and growing market competition have increasingly challenged SRRC: the long-held way of administratively assigning frequencies to different operators seems to be under question, whereas to what extent and how spectrum management should be rationalized based on the market principles of equality and fairness remains largely unclear.[258]

Unlike many western countries where allocation of radio frequency spectrum is now implemented through such market mechanisms as competitive bidding and auctioning, China still relies on SRRC's

---

[256] Even though these political figures may play symbolic roles for SRRC, the central government's motive to keep radio frequency under its control is reflected in this SRRC formation.

[257] During 1998 and 1999, the status of China's spectrum utilization for public communications was as follows: the frequencies 1.7-2.7GHz range was widely used and almost fully loaded. Major adjustment was needed for this range to help further develop mobile communications. 3-28GHz range was mainly used for microwave and satellite communications. The 16 plus GHz range was under-used, with adequate room for more utilization. Above 28 GHz, the spectrum was largely unused.

[258] China has begun the practice of charging a small fee for the use of spectrum by telecom service providers, but fee-based licensing, or competitive bidding, lottery, and auctioning is not yet implemented.

administrative hand in spectrum allocation. To maintain a supreme control and to alleviate the already emerging frequency conflict among MPT, the military (PLA), non-MPT ministries, and enterprises that struggle for certain frequency bandwidth, SRRC firmly holds that radio frequency spectrum is a state resource, it should be centrally allocated, rationally developed, and economically utilized. One change, however, SRRC has made by deploying the economic leverage is that besides administrative assignment, market auction is getting recognized for spectrum allocation. Telecom operators assigned with specific radio frequencies need to pay a certain amount of fees.[259] The intended objective of this policy change seems merely to curtail the inefficient use or waste of the assigned spectrum, not to set a more liberal regulatory framework for spectrum management.

With the emerging battle among different players for radio frequency spectrum.[260] Who gets what and how much often becomes an issue important in both political and commercial dimensions, as control and allocation of the radio frequencies often reflect a conflict of political power and economic interests. The stakes involved in spectrum assignment are high and complex, as radio spectrum is contingent with both MPT public network carriers and non-MPT private network operators who strive for larger market penetration, quicker network development, and exclusive technical standards.[261]

---

[259] In 1989 China instituted a national plan to charge fees for use of radio frequencies. China's plan is modeled on the Canadian Plan, which charges radio frequency users different rates based on frequency band, type of services, time needed, and geographic region.

[260] According to Yang Chungqing, Director of China National Radio Monitoring Center, by mid-1995, bands below 1000 MHz were quite crowed in China mobile telecommunications.

[261] In 1980's, SRRC segregated spectrum for private and public mobile communications and ruled that TACS system (European cellular standard) using the 900 MHz frequency be reserved for public cellular applications, the AMPS system (North American cellular standard) using 800 MHz band for private networks, (450 MHz was also designated for private networks and certain remote applications), and 150 MHz for all paging networks. But practices inconsistent with SRRC rules have occurred. For instance, some PTAs have

A case in point is the MPT-Unicom competition, which has pushed SRRC to allot 905-915 MHz (for mobile station transmission) and 950-954 MHz (for base station transmission) to the MPT networks, while 909-915 MHz (for mobile station transmission) and 954-960 MHz (for base station transmission) to Unicom networks. In addition, SRRC also allocated 835-839 MHz and 880-884 MHz to Unicom as transmitting frequencies from mobile and base stations respectively. SRRC indicated that if any dispute occurs in public cellular applications involving the use of 900 MHz frequency band, tri-literal consultations should first be sought among MPT, Unicom, and the equipment users.

To reaffirm its centralized control, SRRC has issued a series of new regulations since 1994, which essentially require:

- The use of radio frequency must, in the first place, go through a formal process of application and authorization or licensing.
- Leasing or transfer of the SRRC assigned or allocated frequency should be prohibited.
- Radio transmitting or receiving equipment in use must meet the technical standards approved by the SRRC.
- Assigned or allocated frequencies can be used only for SRRC-approved services.
- No frequencies assigned for the military can be used for public wireless services.

The PLA's position to control 800 MHz spectrum was reaffirmed by a document (Order 128) issued jointly by the SRRC and the Central Military Commission in September 1993. The document reinforced the SRRC's role to allocate radio frequencies for commercial use, and reassured the PLA of its authority over much of

---

adopted NMT 450 MHz Nordic Systems and analogue AMPS systems for public networks, while the Ministry of Petroleum is operating a private 900 MHz network.

the 800 MHz frequency range for its own use.[262] However, increased market liberalization and competition in certain public telecom services such as paging and radio dispatch services have created problematic frequency interference to the military communications, particularly to the military flight control systems.

---

[262] MPT, in its course of developing the international standard spectrum 860-880 MHz for its CT2 and AMPS mobile cellular services, may have been upset with SRRC's decision to give the PLA control over 825–845 MHz and 870–890 MHz for its own exploitation.

Part Four: Foreign Involvement

Why is China Strategically Important?

China's development in communications and information has been of particular attraction to many foreign firms who view China as a country with strategic importance to their global competitiveness and business expansions. The key factor that underlies this attraction is market potential. In 1997, for instance, with a teledensity of 93%, US telecom service revenue was more than US$180 billion.[263] China, in the same year, reached a nationwide teledensity of 7.2% and had a total telecom revenue of only US$17 billion, less than 10% of the US market turnover. If China's teledensity increases by 13 times to reach the US 1997 level,[264] plus the growth of data, Internet, cable, satellite, and other forms of enhanced communication services, China's market size could become no less than US$200 billion. To this end, billions of communication lines and various facilities will need to be added, and an enormous amount of equipment and facilities installed.[265]

---

[263] US traditional telecom market is estimated to grow from US$171 billion in 1996 to US$246 billion in 2001, while datacom market will grow from US$8 billion in 1996 to US$60 billion in the same timeframe.

[264] Note: one percentage growth in China's teledensity will mean over 12 million new subscribers.

[265] It is estimated that China will install 25 million mobile lines with 1.5 million channels and 30,000 – 40,000 base stations in the year 2000. 20 – 22 million mobile handsets will be purchased in the same year. China's mobile equipment

China's market potential in communications and information sector is based on a realistic projection, not on an optimistic illusion. Market potential dictates that China is a land of opportunities appealing to persistent foreign telecom and information players. Unlike the Gold Rush in California and Alaska more than one hundred years ago, international investors have come to agree that China represents a substantive and concrete opportunity. They know, from a strategic viewpoint, they cannot afford not to get themselves involved. What matters is the strategy, tactics and timing of their investment. China's large landmass, 1.25 billion potential consumers, high economic growth momentum, relatively low labor cost, and rather undeveloped telecom and information infrastructure and services are all apparent stimulus to foreign investors. More specific catalysts for foreign involvement include China's ambitious communications and information expansion plans, the weakened central control over provincial and local telecom operations, the increased access to market, and the industry's arduous campaign to seek foreign investment and cooperation for a portfolio of benefits such as capital inflow, industrial restructuring and upgrading, transfer of technology and management expertise, and tax revenues and job creation.[266]

The bottom-line inducement, however, is the expectation of huge profits to be generated from the lucrative Chinese market. As China implements its ambitious plans to replace aging equipment, upgrade the technology, expand telecom networks to vast unserved areas nationwide, and develop electronic-based commerce, it will presumably make large purchases worth tens of billions of dollars from overseas vendors in switching, transmission, and terminal systems.[267] China telecom and information market, by 2000, may

---

market is then estimated to be over US$12 billion, which is segmented into US$8 billion for networks and US$4 billion for handsets.

[266] According to the *People's Daily*, there were already more than 17 million Chinese working at foreign related businesses in 1997. 14% of the country's tax was collected from foreign related firms, and 45% of China's exports were affiliated with foreign related firms' production in the same year.

[267] Lucent estimated that by 2000 it may earn as much revenue from the China equipment market as from the U.S. domestic one.

grow to over US$60 billion, and by 2010 it may reach US$80-100 billion. This profit-making prospect will create a huge market demand for a broad range of foreign technology and equipment, which covers both basic and advanced dimensions such as digital switching equipment, lower-speed fiber-optic cable, wireless networks and terminal equipment, satellite communications equipment, high-speed fiber-optic cable, digital data communications networks, value-added services networks, mobile communication facilities, and network management and support systems.[268]

By sheer weight of its huge population, high economic growth, and fast growing consumption, China in the 21st century is expected to have more telephones, more cellular phones, more pagers, more transmission lines -- more everything in telecommunications -- than any other country. China's 1999 IT market size, however, was only 2-3 percent that of the United States. The country's IT spending as a percentage of GDP remained below one percent. By the world standard, China's current telecom market is rather small. Even if it expands by 2003 to the estimated US$45 billion, it will only be 6% of the world's estimated US$815 billion market.[269] This means both a tremendous room for growth and a small pie at present that crowds of foreign vendors have to compete for. Apparently, it is still years before China's IT market matures to a state where many firms can achieve adequate sales volumes to cover costs and pay back investment. The risk factor to smaller firms is that it may take 10-15 years before they can harvest returns on their investment when their business or products no longer survive. Besides, China remains an elusive and difficult market for foreign companies hoping to connect and collect. High start-up and operation costs, perpetual human resources issues, distribution channel development, transparency and enforcement of laws, policy and regulatory instability, and

---

[268] Foreign investors believe the biggest opportunities for revenues lie in the operating of the complex systems needed to back a large phone network, particularly in areas of service, customer care and billing.

[269] Lucent Technologies estimated that by 2003 telecom market in Asia-Pacific will be US$ 165 billion; Latin America, US$55 billion; Europe, US$210 billion; and North America, US$340 billion.

bureaucratic obstacles to repatriation of funds have often discouraged or even frustrated many international companies that have set steps in China.[270]

The emergence of the MII to regulate and oversee IT and communications industries may have a significant impact on foreign firms that operate or plan to operate in China. Positively, MII could be a regulatory regime that is integrated, more transparent, and less politically confusing. Foreign investors may no longer need to go through competing government bodies that had different priorities for project approvals. On the other hand, MII could decrease the opportunities for foreign investors to play one ministry off against another. That is, they may lose much of the room, available when MPT, MEI etc. were in place, for ministerial leveraging and bypassing. A condensed ministry with multiple ministries' mandates might result in a super-monopoly with the shadow of the old MPT, and therefore detrimental to market access and competition by foreign companies.

MII's impact on foreign players have specifically shown in two occurrences:

One, with the consolidated power, MII re-asserted its control over China Unicom by trying to restrict the company to wireless mobile network services and to bond Unicom's outreaching hands with foreign investors. In September 1998, MII proposed to the State Council that CCF[271] - Chinese-Chinese-Foreign model of investment created by Unicom should be prohibited as it violates, in a

---

[270] In February 1998, Fiducia, a China-based management consultancy, did a survey of 96 managers of European firms and reported that among the European firms operating in China, 54% performed worse than forecast, 21% just met their target, and only 25% did better than their plans. Many surveyed said they over-estimated China's market demand, and local corruption was one of the factors affecting their operations.

[271] This model involves three parties, China Unicom, a Chinese business entity, and foreign investors. Unicom forms a JV with a Chinese entity and this JV acts as an investment clearing house for foreign investors. Foreign investment is injected into Unicom projects via the JV and returns are made to foreign investors through this investment company.

sophisticated way, China's regulation of not allowing foreign investment in network construction.[272] MII's proposal turned to be a policy that bans all Unicom's 43 projects (worth more than US$1 billion) involving some twenty five international companies including Sprint, McCaw International, Metromedia, AmTec, Bell Canada, Telesystems, NTT, Deutsche Telekom, France Telecom, Siemens, and Sumitomo, who invested significant amounts in Unicom's GSM mobile, paging, and fixed line projects.

MII proposed three alternative solutions to end CCF projects. One of them was to place all the received foreign investment in a "fund" or "loan" that will be repaid, plus interest, for continual support of Unicom's projects. The other was to buy out the shares from the foreign investors, with a suggested return of 10-15%. This second approach, however, was costly to the Chinese government and may earn China further opposition to its effort for WTO admission. It may also create a feeding frenzy on the part of the foreign companies who believe compensation should also account for the market value of the investment, or, in another word, treat for the lost opportunities. The third option suggested that foreign investors be given the equivalent of their investment in proposed Unicom overseas IPO shares and thus their direct investment becomes stocks.[273]

MII's move caused deep concerns among the international players who, in a collective effort, delivered a confidential letter to the Chinese premier in February 1999 to urge against discouraging foreign investment[274] in China and to call for a change from CCF to normal

---

[272] MII minister stated that some of the CCF ventures have broken China's regulation by allowing foreign companies to derive revenue from installation fees, not from operations, but he used the term "irregular", not "illegal" on many occasions to describe Unicom's CCF financing strategy.

[273] Unicom held a differential policy for CCF settlement. That is, in addition to the principal payment, better-performing projects receive a return of current commercial rate plus 3-5 percentage points, added by some stock options; average-performing projects receive a return of the current commercial loan rate; and poorly-performing or loss-making projects only receive a return of deposit rate.

[274] Particularly strategic and portfolio investment.

equity participation. While MII pushed hard and set the deadline for October 1, 1999, and Unicom, anxious to clear the way for an overseas IPO, wanted to force a quick settlement by paying off foreign investors through a loan-like schedule, the see-saw dispute dragged on and no significant deal was reached until December 1999 when U.S. Metromedia International Group announced that it would receive US$90 million in loan repayment and additional US$6 million after the termination of its joint projects with Unicom.[275] Foreign companies confronted with Unicom on CCF settlement terms, as they insisted that compensation should be based on real market valuation, which involves sum total of all cash flow received by Unicom, and potential returns from network services over the life of the signed contract, not based on a simple loan repayment scheme. They threatened litigation against Unicom if a fair balance of interest could not be reached. Foreign investors also hoped to rely on China's WTO accession for protection by grandfathering provisions.[276]   In early June 2000, the CCF issue finally seemed to be reaching a compromised solution: Unicom would pay back RMB9.8 billion (US$1.18 billion) to foreign investors as their investment principal and RMB4 billion (US$483 million) as compensation. Some of the foreign investors also received some RMB5.2 billion (US$628 million) worth of share options as compensation.

Two, MII in early November 1998 announced, as an official policy, that Chinese telecom companies, for their development projects, should purchase domestically made mobile equipment and facilities wherever possible. Chinese-foreign joint ventures that produce telecom equipment in China were urged to buy "made-in-China" raw materials. MII estimated that, in the area of mobile telecom equipment market, Chinese manufacturers had less than 10% of the market share in 1998. It should rise to about 40% by 2001, and about 70% by 2003. In the fall of 1999, media reported that MII was making plans

---

[275] This payment is reported as 28% higher than Metromedia's original investment.

[276] The issue of CCF lingered on from October 1998 to June 2000 when Unicom continued negotiations with several foreign firms about settling their deals.

to impose production quotas and import restrictions on foreign mobile phones in China's market, in order to foster the growth and market share of nine Chinese domestic companies that manufacture mobile phones. These companies include Eastern Communications, Xiamen Electronics, Zhong Xin Telecom, TCL Communications, Shenzhen Kejian, Haier Group, Shenzhen Konka Group, Southern High Technology, and Fenghua Bodao. This plan, if implemented, may carry a significant weight because MII has a strong influence over principal procurement decisions of the Chinese telecom carriers in the country's US$7.5 billion mobile equipment market, despite that the ministry cannot have much to say about individual consumer's choices. Foreign players, Ericsson, Nokia, and Motorola, for instance, may face a tougher challenge and come under greater pressure to localize their operations to win sales contracts or they may have to further slash their profit margin to compete for customers.[277] The regulatory ambiguity, however, is in how to distinguish "foreign made" from "China made" in the first place, since Sino-foreign joint ventures and sole Chinese firms are not easily classified.

Who Are Most Actively Involved?

To date, foreign involvement in China's telecom and information is largely in the field of equipment supplies, technical consultancy and assistance, and provision of loans. Since the early 1980's, China's telecom equipment market has been made wide open to foreign companies, advanced network systems, facilities, and equipment have been introduced in; about US$6.6 billion worth of international loans have been deployed mainly for equipment purchase financing. In contrast, network operation and equity ownership by foreign firms remain prohibited by the current Chinese rules and regulations.

Foreign companies that have made profits out of the China's telecom and IT boom are primarily equipment manufacturers and

---

[277] These three foreign companies take more than 80% of the China's mobile equipment market share in 1999.

computer suppliers. Those having set a good market position in China are large multinational corporations from USA, France, Germany, Sweden, Japan, Canada, Finland, and South Korea. They include Alcatel, Motorola, Ericsson, NEC, Siemens, Nokia, Lucent, Nortel, Cisco, 3Com, Hughes, Globalstar, IBM, Hewlett Packard, Intel,[278] Compaq, AMD, Microsoft,[279] UTStarcom, Matsushita, Acer, Samsung, and AST. They provide equipment, systems, and solutions in transmission, switching, data communications, network access, and mobile facilities and handsets.

More than seventy overseas telecom or information business entities have, in one way or another, approached or involved themselves in China in a vast array of activities, such as forming manufacturing joint ventures with the MPT, local PTAs, and non-MPT enterprises, establishing representative offices or operating branches, or participating in various trade, consulting, and technology related events. Their business scope ranges from manufacturing fiber-optic cable and electronic switching equipment, and producing cellular phones and paging systems, supplying various kinds of communications devices and components, to providing technological support and consulting services for systems integration and network construction and management.

Foreign-Chinese joint ventures are gradually entering into a reinvestment cycle, looking to raise expansion capital or debt offshore. International telecom and information service providers, on the other hand, are equally active despite the current policy barriers that hold foreign firms from direct involvement in network operation and management. They believe that China's telecom market will continue to grow, policy and regulatory regime will change with the passage of time, and new ground will be open bit by bit for foreign investors and operators. In addition, the risk profile in China will continue to change for different types of business involvement, as the

---

[278] Intel in May 1998 announced it would invest US$50 million over the coming 5 years to build a IT R&D center in Shanghai.

[279] Microsoft in early 1998 signed a framework agreement with China Telecom on joint development of Internet and Intranet applications in China.

demand for telecom and information services will, on a constant basis, expand and develop well into the 21st century. AT&T, Sprint, MCI, Cable and Wireless, Hong Kong Telecom, British Telecom, GlobalOne, Singapore Telecom, Deutsche Telekom, and Telstra are among the most prominent and aggressive international operators who watch closely and patiently, and try hard for progress in accessing the China market.

Because of this international eagerness for entry, competition among foreign players is stiff and vigorous. Competitive pressure has created a fragmented market and is squeezing margins to the point where foreign vendors find it increasingly hard to make substantial profits. Prices of equipment, both wireless and fixed-line, have fallen by 20 to 30 per cent in the past two years[280] because international vendors are keen on their business strategy of achieving a strong market position by initially offering lower rates and charging a premium later. According to a 1998 survey by A.T. Kearney Inc., only 41% of the seventy foreign operations were profitable. Sole foreign owned firms seemed to do better than joint ventures. Competition is also reflected in non-pricing areas in which Chinese partners request favorable vendor arrangements such as supplier financing, training programs, and technology transfer.

To gain the first-mover advantages, Alcatel, Siemens, Nortel, Ericsson, and NEC, among some others, have acted quickly. Their early arrivals in China have assisted them in acquiring better strategic competitive positions as reflected by market share, profitability, and technological dominance. The advantages of early or timely entry also include economies of scale, higher productivity at lower costs - opportunity cost too - due to learning and experience effects, brand preference and customer recognition, lower-cost access to financial capital, raw materials, and distribution channels. Intangible but more important advantages, however, rest on the establishment of barriers to lock out rivals and a close relationship with Chinese government organizations, business partners, and end-users.

---

[280] The prices of many telecom equipment sold to China by foreign vendors are lower than the prices they offer in South America and Africa.

Large international corporations seem to understand that in a rapidly changing industry, stagnation means death, and expanding business opportunities in China is crucial to their long-term success. With a vision on China's great market potential, they tend to move quickly in pushing ahead for implementation of long-term investment strategies, despite the fact that they often have to invest time, money and effort for no immediate gains.

Small- and mid-sized entrepreneurial foreign companies are part of the wave to do business in China's telecom and IT market, albeit their names do not appear as frequently in the press. The shares of some of these companies are affected significantly or dramatically by how their China business goes. Apart from equipment supplies, Internet and electronic commerce related services have been the areas they strategize and target for. The most noted of these companies include CMGI, New Tel Ltd., China Digital Group, Pacific Century Cyberworks, iAdvantage of Sun Hung Kai Property Ltd., Cheung Kong, eVision USA, ChinaMallOnline, eCommerce.com, Entrust, Tradelink, TradeCard, Zi Corporation, Graphon Corporation, Global Crossing, Xin Net, and GRIC Communications Inc. They have either launched business ventures in China or are enthusiastically taking initiatives to enter that market. The business activities of these companies range from provisions of software for Internet access by TV, cellular phones and other digital devices, web server co-location, venture capital, technology support and network integration, Internet development and applications, broadband Internet access and connectivity, Internet portal operation, search engine and free e-mail services, and innovative e-finance, e-banking, and e-commerce related solutions.

What Are the Trends?

Foreign involvement in China telecom and information market has in recent years been going through transformation from conventional equipment and components sales by direct distribution channels or intermediary agents[281] to a far more diversified range of activities. Many foreign firms seem to have understood that, to establish a stronghold in China, they should adopt new business strategies based on considerations of a much wider variety of strategically relevant variables rather than a single factor of immediate profitability.

To secure a solid competitive position in a marketplace significantly different from that of the developed countries, foreign players need to rethink how corporate resources can be better channelled and allocated, and how business objectives can be matched with, or accommodated to, China's regulatory and market requirements for telecommunications development.

Unlike the market environment in the mid-1980s, China's telecom and information sector is emerging substantially as a consumer market, with a higher level of user sophistication and diversity of needs for infrastructure and applications. Broadband network capacity and wireless mobile access to data and Internet, for example, are getting more targeted by Chinese users. Foreign firms are increasingly faced with new competitive forces such as the threat of entry by both international and China domestic players, the fast-paced technological innovation and obsolescence, the consumer's growing access to new product and service alternatives, and the increased bargaining power and economic leverage Chinese government and enterprises have in negotiating with overseas companies. Under such circumstances, foreign companies seem to have become more sophisticated in their approach to China, and have grown more knowledgeable, through trial and error, about the market they operate in. Their business strategies and tactics appear to have adapted more to China's market environment, and their business activities are readjusted on a frequent basis to achieve corporate missions and to meet China's changing consumer demand. The following summarizes what the trends are in regard to foreign companies' operations in China.

---

[281] Supplying telecoms equipment and components through exports has proved disadvantageous in costs, prices, market information, and development. Exporting is often affected by bilateral political relations and corresponding trade policies.

Localization

Joint Ventures:

These are business alliances[282] with Chinese partners to gain competitive advantages of (*i*) wide access to China's domestic market, (*ii*) economies of scale for lower costs, (*iii*) use of local resources such as marketing expertise, distribution networks, tax incentives, and financing support, and (*iv*) timely business adjustment to respond to market and policy changes. Joint ventures help foreign firms establish close relationships with the Chinese government and various organizations, which is essentially important to business success in China. Partners of foreign alliance are being extended from the MPT controlled departments or its local PTAs to non-MPT forces including government ministries, China Unicom, Jitong, local enterprises or government agencies, and the military. Cross alliances involving different foreign firms and Chinese entities have also emerged.

Localized Manufacture:[283]

"Localized" here refers to the type of products, site of production, use of a local work force and materials, and corporate culture and

---

[282] In the western world, strategic alliance relationships in a broad sense include second sourcing, cooperative marketing, distribution ties, licensing, subcontracting, product development agreement, teaming agreement, technology exchange, financial participation, equity purchase (buy-out), merger and acquisition, hostile takeover, and joint venture.

[283] Major sources of SPC switching equipment for China were: (*i*) home-made products such as HJD-04, more than 700,000 lines in service, and DS-30, 50,000 in service—home-production capacity is estimated as 3 million lines in 1995 (about 300 domestic manufacturers in operation); (*ii*) imported products, mainly from Alcatel, NEC, Fujitsu, Ericsson, Nortel, Siemens, and Lucent; (*iii*) products made locally by joint ventures with Alcatel, Siemens, NEC, Nortel, and Lucent (*CTC News* **1**, 18, Oct. 5, 1995, 1-2).

management style, plus specific-marketing strategies suited to the conditions of the China domestic market. Examples include Motorola that decided to design and manufacture a series of radio products specially to meet the needs of Chinese users and Lucent that made an important shift from simple assembly to full-fledged local manufacture of the 5ESS (R)-2000 switching systems. Motorola, Siemens, Nortel, Alcatel, NEC, Ericsson, Philips, Panasonic, and Mitsubishi are among many foreign companies that have committed considerable amounts of financial and technological resources to set up localized manufacture facilities in China. The business structure of the localized manufacture may include Sino-foreign joint ventures, cooperative ventures, wholly foreign-funded ventures, and licensing agreements. Recently, joint ventures involving multiple or cross players have come into existence. The MPT Beijing Wire Communications Plant,[284] for instance, has set up eight joint ventures with different foreign companies, most notably, NCR of USA[285], Ericsson of Sweden, and C&W of UK, which have joint venture relations with other Chinese or foreign firms.

Equipment manufacturing joint ventures tend to help foreign partners in policy and regulatory areas because loopholes may exist in policies dealing with component import, taxation, and other domestic company related issues. Localized manufacture receives a great deal of Chinese official support, because it tends to be one of the most effective means for technology transfer. Currently, localized manufacture of 900 MHz digital cellular communications equipment, synchronous optic fiber, and microwave communications systems and instruments, ATM and SDH transmission systems, as well as DXC and NM equipment, and satellite earth stations (Telephony Earth Stations [TES]) and data stations (Personal Earth Stations [PES]) are strongly recommended and encouraged by the Chinese government.

---

[284] Beijing Wire Communications Plant is a Chinese company that developed the first telephone switchboard and the first electronic computer in China in the late 1950's.

[285] NCR was the world largest automated teller machine (ATM) maker. It had 40% of the ATM market share in China.

Localized Marketing and Penetration:

In addition to localized manufacture, foreign firms have been paying close attention to the ways they deploy in marketing their products, services, and corporate image and reputations in China. In terms of distribution channels, foreign companies are trying to contract with both foreign distributors operating in China, and/or Chinese distributors that have hands-on local market knowhow and experience. Nokia, for example, has distribution agreements with Brightpoint and Cellstar, which operate many local retail outlets in Chinese cities via wholesale and franchise arrangements. Localized marketing and penetration also reflect the approaches taken by foreign companies in associating their business tactics with the Chinese domestic cultural values, consumer tastes, and socio-political preferences. To make the messages of corporate creditability, advanced technology, and superb product/service quality most convincing and receptive to the Chinese public, AT&T, Motorola, and Ericsson have been doing exceptional jobs in exploiting Chinese cultural values for their promotional purposes, as represented in their ingenious design of the advertising messages incarnated in the themes of human relationships, family ties, behavioral norms, technology at one's fingertips, Chinese chess playing, and long-standing faith, trust, and respect.

Localized penetration has been an important business strategy for many foreign players who have become aware of the opportunities emerging from China's regional and provincial economic dynamics, power decentralization, and competing development agendas. Direct business relationships with local PTAs or non-MPT partners in the form of equipment and system supplies or joint venture arrangements for manufacture or network construction give foreign firms the advantages of getting around some bureaucratic and regulatory hurdles, staying directly in touch with the changing marketplace, and effectively targeting and serving specific customer needs.

Donation of funds or facilities is another way employed for establishing foreign corporate image and recognition in China, because the giveaway effects to build in the Chinese government and people a positive attitude toward the donor who cares about helping China in technology development and public well-being. Good instances of this trend are AT&T's donation of US$150,000 to the Hope Foundation, a health care and educational organization in China, for the construction of a children's medical center in Shanghai; Intel's donation of US$250,000 worth of computer workstations to Jiaotong and Fudan universities in Shanghai; and the donation by the Advanced Micro Devices Company (AMD) of a communications lab to Qinghua University in Beijing.

Localized Human Resources:

Localization of human resources performs several functions: it helps cut down the high salary expenses and various benefits required for expatriates who are sent from home countries to work in China; it demonstrates foreign firms' long-term commitment to China; it benefits foreign firms because local employees, through training, can become highly skilled and capable workforce. In addition, local staff possess a special mix of social connections, language and culture competence. They also have local knowledge about the market, the customers, and the government operation. Michael Ricks, President of Ericsson China, claimed in December 1999 that 90% of the company's 4000 employees in China were local Chinese working for its 23 representative offices and 8 joint ventures. Multinational corporation's localization efforts are also expanding to managerial positions. In Beijing alone, more than 100 out of 20,000 Chinese staff working at 5,000 foreign entities in 1998 were appointed general managers or deputy managers. International IT companies, such as Nortel, Hewlett Packard, Sprint International, Cisco, Compaq, Lucent and Microsoft, have favored Chinese nationals for CEO and department director positions in charge of their China operations.

Common recognition by foreign companies is that identifying, recruiting, and retaining qualified local personnel for management positions has become crucial to their business success in China. However, as more and more international firms enter into China, the demand for managerial personnel and skilled workers has intensified.

Besides, job switch by local Chinese to search for better career opportunities has made the problem of employee turnover worse in foreign invested firms.[286] Job switch among foreign expatriates to other foreign firms is also becoming more common than before.[287] Research indicates that principal factors for high employment turnover include job satisfaction, career planning and growth, work environment, interpersonal relationships, way of supervision, and salary and compensation packages.

In addition to day-to-day operations and manufacturing, localization of human resources is increasingly reflected in multinational corporations' campaign to establish R&D centers in China. To foreign companies, the benefit of this move should be manifold. By having localized R&D centers, foreign companies attempt to polish their image for technology transfer; they may raise their public reputation as facilitators for China's technology innovation; they can take the advantage of a vast pool of locally educated talent and well-trained personnel to upgrade or renew their products and technologies at relatively lower costs. Furthermore, localized R&D activities may get foreign companies better positioned in terms of their economic and strategic competitiveness both within China and internationally. Microsoft, Motorola, IBM, Intel, Nortel, Lucent, Cisco, Ericsson, Fujitsu and NEC are among the most aggressive multinationals in investing financial resources and in joining forces with China's universities and research institutions to set up local R&D centers. These companies have also reached out to utilize many of the returned Chinese students who were trained and educated abroad.

---

[286] A study shows that, in Shanghai, personnel turnover in some foreign invested firms is as high as 30%. Some well-qualified local staff is like "frequent flyers": they switch jobs 2 or 3 times every five years.

[287] A *China Daily* report in May 10, 1998, said that among the expatriates working in China, two out of five left before their contracts expired, and one out of five left within six months.

Growing Competition

With the entry of increasing number of players, competition in China's telecom and IT market is being intensified and extended. Domestically, the MPT-MII incumbent China Telecom and local PTAs are involved in the battle with the non-MPT players represented or backed by different government ministries, China Unicom, Jitong, China Netcom, the military, and other state or non-state enterprises for financial resources, market share, technological advantage, and overseas collaboration. Pressure on foreign companies to compete with one another and with Chinese counterparts has also become increasingly fierce.[288] Foreign players are faced with increasing competitive forces created by both Chinese domestic firms' and international rival firms' strategic moves to jockey for market positions and gain competitive edges, as reflected in product manufacture, marketing, price cut, technology standard and specification-related issues, and the heated contest to establish joint ventures and other forms of alliances with various Chinese partners situated in different political and geographic territories. In business negotiations, foreign firms often have to offer some favorable terms in order to beat down competition. The ability to provide preferable financial and credit terms seems more and more important as a deciding factor for winning or losing a business contract. Capital, technology, management, corporate structure and culture, products and services, as well as business strategies and tactics that adapt to China's political and market changes have all become very crucial in acquiring and maintaining a competitive position.

In some areas of telecom equipment manufacturing, China is moving towards self-sufficiency. China's manufacture of switching equipment reached 15 million lines in 1997, and approximately 20 million in 1998, accounting for 90% and 97% of the total capacity installed. The country's most notable domestic players include Datang,

---

[288] For instance, Ericsson, Nokia, Motorola, Siemens and Alcatel are five giant competitors in China's mobile system and handset market.

Huawei,[289] Giant Dragon, Zhongxing, Jin Peng, TCL, PTIC of MPT, and Wuhan Research Institute. They manufacture telecom switches, fiber optic cable, and terminal devices. Some of them have developed China-licensed GSM systems for Chinese carriers, which competes in the market and drives the prices of GSM equipment down by an average of 25%. Several provinces, such as Liaonin and Fujian, have benefited from deploying China-made GSM equipment, as they cut project investment by 20-30%. In addition, some 20 joint venture manufacturers – many majority-Chinese owned – have been able to supply a complete array of equipment and systems, covering dual GSM switch, base station, mobile intelligence system, common channel system signaling, calling center operation, IP gateway, network power supervision, and advanced digital system. These emerging firms do impose a head-on threat to international equipment suppliers, mainly because the cost of China's domestically made equipment is significantly lower than the counterparts from abroad. Digital switches, for example, cost about 30% lower than comparable equipment in the U.S. market. This Chinese competitiveness has created an important advantage for China in network development, since the price level of different vendors is often slashed below the world average.

Foreign competitors active in China can be roughly categorized into three groups, depending on the corporate size, market position, and business operations. First, large companies like Lucent, Motorola, Alcatel, Ericsson, Nokia, Nortel, Siemens and NEC that have both huge manufacturing facilities and diverse service capacities. Strategically, these international companies hold high stakes in China and are in the forefront of the business activities there. Second, smaller companies that are manufacturers, services providers, or equipment vendors. Their stakes in China are not as crucial and their strategies tend to focus on the Chinese niche market. Third, new entrants such as British Telecom, France Telecom, NTT, MCI, Singapore Telecom, Telstra, Qualcomm, and Sumsung. These firms

---

[289] It was reported that Huawei's share of the switch market in China was more than 20%, second only to Shanghai Bell's in 1997.

do not have a well-established position in China yet, but they aggressively generate a competitive pressure on other foreign players because of their strengths in financial and technological resources.

Foreign competition in China has extended from traditional areas of market penetration in equipment manufacture and supplies to more diversified dimensions of product variety and quality, distribution channel, marketing strategy, project bidding, technology introduction, technical support, managerial assistance, joint R&D, charitable and educational programs, and approaches to form coalitions with different Chinese sectors. In lucrative network service areas, foreign players seem more than anxious to compete with one another if the relaxation of the Chinese regulations ever takes place. Their preliminary efforts are at present focused on the regulatory "gray area" of value-added and managed data network services. Geographically, international firms are expanding their reaches into various Chinese provincial and local equipment vendors and service providers, rather than just concentrating on Beijing, Shanghai, Guangdong and a few other large cities.

Tough competition among international players has significantly increased China's bargaining power and negotiating leverage in its project bidding involving a magnitude of foreign companies. China-US Trans-Pacific Submarine Cable Project stands out as a good showcase.[290]

For many years, China's voice traffic to the U.S. had to travel along a cable system that dips into the sea, surfaces in Japan, and then plunges back under the Pacific to North America. The transmission is expensive and the networks are controlled by AT&T and Japan's KDD. With its rapid economic growth, China's phone traffic and data transmission demand has rocketed. A new and direct China-US cable system is badly needed.

As early as 1990, Chinese policy makers began to look at a project to build a new fiber optic link between China and the U.S. AT&T, a

---

[290] Main source of the case reference is Steve Glain's How Beijing Officials Outnegotiated AT&T on Marine Cable Plans, The Wall Street Journal, July 23, 1997.

dominant owner and experienced operator of most of the submarine cables linking Asia and America,[291] took it almost for granted that the project conceived by China should fall into its hand. AT&T's assumption, however, was shaken up by the US 1996 Telecom Act, as the new law unleashed a horde of competitors who became keen to take a share in the China-US cross-ocean cable project.

When China assembled a consortium for the project, a new competitive arena emerged. China was empowered by the new situation and the Chinese negotiators[292] were given a forceful bargaining tool. The Chinese government insisted that China should have a equal share in the project, not subordinate to any foreign carrier. China's policy was to engage as many international companies as possible on an equal basis. In response to the offer of Teleglobe, NYNEX and C&W to link China directly with North America, AT&T announced it would accommodate China's growing traffic by increasing capacity on an existing cable. This proposal, however, could permit minimal expansion and received no feedback from China. The Chinese officials took a wait-and-see attitude, while keeping in contact with different foreign companies about options available for a direct link to America.

AT&T made another offer to use its cable via a switching station in Guam. AT&T also aggressively promoted a supply contract for the network construction with one of its cable manufacturing units, Submarine Systems Inc. This time, China responded by commenting that a Guam landing would help with AT&T's commitment to Manila to tie in the Philippines to U.S. bound capacity, not benefit Beijing, and that AT&T's maneuver seemed a clear attempt to create a configuration that would allow AT&T/KDD to dominate the project management as well as the operation of the system.

---

[291] AT&T was the only US company that had expertise in operating cross-Pacific telecom services. The company thus had great influence over which companies could subscribe and how the lines were routed. Presently, AT&T and KDD combined own nearly 40% of all cable capacity in Asia.

[292] Two leading Chinese negotiators were Li Ping, 42-year-old MPT deputy director, and Wang Hongjian, 52-year-old MPT director. Both had extensive experience in telecommunications and speak good English.

Then, AT&T's cancellation of a meeting between its chairman Robert Allen and MPT Minister Wu Jichuan produced a harmful impact. Sources speculated that the cancellation was due to Allen's preoccupation with the search for his successor, and Chinese side was given a six-week advance notice. But the Chinese negotiators held that the cancellation delayed talks with other companies and it put off progress on the entire project. The event, to some extent, offered AT&T rivals an opportunity to push ahead.

At about the same time, SBC entered the battlefield. The company approached Teleglobe about jointly proposing a China-U.S. cable project. It also planned for a merger with Pacific Telesis Group and hoped to use Pactel's California network as the main US link to Asia. Unlike AT&T/KDD's indirect route plan, SBC's proposal catered to China's intent for a direct link.

In the late 1996, negotiations went heated between the Chinese delegation and AT&T/KDD, C&W/NYNEX, and SBC teams. Three foreign groups competed with one another in an attempt to meet China's objectives, which gave China a crucial leverage over AT&T. As part of China's ultimate decision for the deal, MPT expanded the international membership of the consortium to a total of 14 companies, including MCI, Sprint, SBC, NTT, SingTel, Hong Kong Telecom, Chung Hua Telecom, Telecom Malaysia, PT Indonesian Satellite Corp., IDC Japan, and Korean Telecom Authority. C&W was only indirectly represented by Hong Kong Telecom, whereas NYNEX was screened out. AT&T, the presumed key foreign player, was confined to a role far less influential than its usual strategic position in such big projects.

Technology Transfer

Two factors account for the importance of technology transfer by foreign companies in China. One, intense competition among foreign players and between foreign and Chinese entities to establish strategic positions for both China domestic and export markets and to create joint ventures or other types of alliances with Chinese enterprises or government organizations has posed a heavy pressure on foreign companies to come to terms on stringent technology transfer arrangements. Two, Chinese government's strong urge for foreign firms to enter into technology transfer schemes as an implicit or upfront prerequisite in exchange for access to the IT and telecommunications market in China.

Critical foreign concerns over technology transfer are that (*i*) some of the advanced technologies they have are of crucial importance to their core business and competitive advantages in the marketplace which, therefore, cannot be given away; and (*ii*) how they can commercialize their technologies in a country that remains weak in legal framework and enforcement without forfeiting their hard-earned knowledge, techniques, and intellectual property rights. The compromise at present, except for technology transfer specified in contracts, seems to be a package of indirect technology transfer mechanisms to the liking of the Chinese side and offered by foreign companies. These mechanisms include:

- Technical assistance in network designing, planning, engineering, and maintenance.
- Joint R&D activities such as joint research, establishment of research labs, and exchange of data and research literature
- Cooperation in network construction, system integration, or equipment installation
- Consulting and after-sale services
- Running technological seminars, workshops, and training sessions

What Are the Key Stakes?

Contextual Factors

Opportunities in China cannot be exploited without a sound and realistic understanding of the dynamic local conditions. Difficulties in conducting business in China are often attributable to the ignorance of apparent and underlying differences in language, culture, history, and changing social, political and legal institutions. Underestimate of the problems of working in China, or overestimate of China's openness in accepting foreign technology and management will both lead to unnecessary discouragement. Failure in business ventures may result from lack of preparedness for China's opacity in political and regulatory mechanisms. It may also contribute to a miscalculation of the Chinese power structure between and at different levels. This refers to the disparity that often exists between the central government and local bureaucracies, or between different government agencies in policy interpretation and enforcement practices.

Many of the problems, difficulties, and frustrations foreign firms are commonly plunged into derive from a broad Chinese socio-economic and political context. Political uncertainty and inconsistency due to the system and leadership transition may significantly influence the future direction of the overall economic development and the policies toward foreign activities in China. Legal and regulatory inadequacies give foreign companies limited legal protection in case of business or property disputes, and underdeveloped financial, banking and communications systems leave them with rather restricted access to local financial support (*e.g.,* working capital) and reliable information resources. The most annoying source of trouble, however, is an obstinate living bureaucracy rooted in China's centuries old political tradition, which is generally manifested in the country's administrative structure, official formalities and procedures, and often confusing and ambiguous rules and regulations governing business activities.

Legal and regulatory environment in China deserves emphatic attention. The Chinese leadership has over the past decade continually struggled to develop a policy and legal framework to meet the country's economic and political needs. Rule of law, not rule of person, has been emphasized time and again, which clearly indicates the leadership's intent to move China from a bureaucracy-base country to a legislation-based one. As a result, laws and regulations have multiplied. To foreign investors in China, legal and regulatory environment is crucial. Foreign investment and multinational companies' operations depend significantly on how China develops its legal and regulatory environment, and how much this country-specific environment is compatible with the international practices.

In this regard, issues foreign investors have to face include the inconsistency between national and local legislation regarding incentives for and regulations on foreign investment, the opacity, vagueness, and arbitrariness of policies and regulations which create uncertainties and risks for business operations, and the weakness of legal institutions which often lures foreign investors to negotiate exceptional treatment for engagement in "irregular" activities. China's legal and regulatory problems have, in part, offered room for cultivation of patronage, guanxi (personal relationship), kickbacks, payoffs, and petty extortion in exchange for special favors on either Chinese or foreign side. Attempts to use informal affiliation with officials or business people to secure a deal or insulate from prohibitive transactions have been common on many occasions.

In terms of business culture, differences often arise by themselves. Foreign companies, American companies in particular, are accustomed to carefully negotiating and drafting contracts on the basis of their business plans. Their priority is given to analysis of business data and to feasibility studies before decisions are made regarding investment in a specific venture. Their Chinese partners, in contrast, often do not regard lawyers and contracts with the same respect, and are less inclined to engage in sophisticated financial analysis. In general, foreign investors tend to be long on wishful thinking, but short on a solid research and planning. Driven by the prospect for profits, many of them envision that China's immense potential will return high profits on investment, and entry is therefore mandatory. Without conducting the normal practice of due diligence, they quickly enter the market only to find themselves lost about how to proceed and where to go. Successful foreign companies, however, are usually those who make constant efforts in understanding the complexities of the Chinese business environment and who stay alert to changes in the policy landscape and are adept in adjustment. They are firm on essentials, and seldom become easily frustrated or desperate in the face of unexpected situations.

Goal Conflict

Foreign firms entering China telecom and IT market usually have in mind a goal clearly defined and profit-oriented: establishing competitive strategic positions to cash in on China's huge domestic market and beat out rivals. Access to market, cost-benefit ratio, sales volume and growth, profit margin, and returns on investment are, almost with no exception, placed on their priority list. China, on the other side, has different strategic interest and objectives. Foreign capital to fuel the development, advanced technology, and management expertise are the three things most wanted and therefore most highly encouraged. The situation here seems like two persons sleeping in the same bed but having different dreams: one dreams of selling products and services for a big flow of profits, the other dreams about getting financial, managerial, and technological resources to eventually hold off outside products and services.

With the fast-track movement of economic and technological integration, different countries are becoming more dependent upon each other. The marketplace of specific countries can no longer be easily segregated or earmarked by political authorities. While the concept of "national interest" remains, it may have to be interpreted, safeguarded, and strengthened by renewed mechanisms. The conventional rhetoric of "foreign interest" and "Chinese interest" is increasingly challenged by the "win-win" business deals. That is, "mutual interest" on bilateral occasions and "common interest" on multilateral settings seem to be making a lot more sense. The same thing applies to "corporate interest" in business deals involving partners from different countries. Gains for one company may not necessarily mean loses for the other, and vice versa. On the contrary, one's gains, more often than not, will generate gains for the other, while loses on one side, most likely, will bring loses to the other. Conflict of goals, or conflict of interest, between Chinese and foreign parties, therefore, may have to be replaced by coordination and reconciliation of goals or interest.

Pitfalls of Alliance

For the tactical purposes of obtaining market penetration in China or for strategic coalition with Chinese partners to acquire long-term benefits, foreign firms are increasingly seen joining hands with various Chinese entities for business alliances in the forms of joint venture manufacture, licensing arrangement, collaborative research, marketing cooperation, and technological assistance and support. Their moves for alliances, unfortunately, are matched by apparent or potential issues and risks. Enforcement of alliance has often been perplexed by complex issues such as selecting the right partners and locations, planning for management team and labor force, negotiating the deal for specified and joint rights and responsibilities, and dispute settlement in case bilateral agreement cannot be reached.

Decision making processes and coordination required between and among the partners for reaching agreements may often turn out as unwieldy and bureaucratic, due to different management structures of the partners involved. Cross ownership and cultural differences may deprive the partners of the flexibility to take timely management actions to adapt to the changing business environment. Cultural incompatibility is frequently reflected in different attitudes toward operation and management problems such as allocation of financial resources, production planning, and approaches to cost-profit accounting. The most difficult part of the Sino-foreign alliance seems to be how efforts can be made on both sides in establishing trust, flexibility, and commitment, even though these things are widely recognized as the key to success. Foreign companies at times involve themselves in an absurd ambivalence between a burning desire to do business and an icy suspicion of their Chinese partners due to lack of trust and confidence, while Chinese firms often keep an over-cautious attitude toward foreign companies' business motives. Business relationship, looked as the cornerstone of business transactions by the Chinese, often appears too ambiguous and bothersome to foreign companies nurtured in Anglo-Saxon oriented cultures. These companies tend to give emphasis on short-term profit that keep prices up, and, as a natural course of action, define business relationships in strict financial terms.

As foreign firms move ahead on their learning curves about China, and as they hire more and more Chinese nationals, the earlier perception to benefit from Chinese partners is becoming weakened. Many foreign corporations, instead, begin to think that the advantages from having Chinese partners are not as great and necessary as originally believed, and benefits may not be quite worth the hassles they have to go through. This has prompted some foreign investors to buy out their Chinese partners' interests to increase their control over the business ventures, or to strive in the first place for sole foreign-funded projects.

At stake with alliances, also, is concerns over illicit technology transfer or release of valuable information to potential competitors and a shift of power over time once the weaker side improves its skills and gets hold of the new products and technology through a process of learning and absorbing. This seems very difficult to control in an environment of collaborative management and joint operation. Local partners' direct access to distribution channels and customers often adds to this concern, because this access may assist local partners to take on an increasingly important role while the alliance progresses. This is one of the reasons why the exit clause to end or renew alliance agreements has to be seriously considered.

Breakthrough: A Puzzle for the Wittiest?

Service provisions and equity ownership in China telecom and information sectors are apparently most important stimulators to foreign investors, but so far, officially, foreign participation is restricted to technology transfer and assistance, in addition to equipment manufacture and supplies. Efforts to make breakthroughs have met with constant resistance from the Chinese central government and the MPT-MII who maintain that foreign companies are welcome to invest in China telecom projects and get their fair share of returns according to the terms agreed, but this has to be under the preconditions that they will not hold equities or be involved in the operation or management of telecommunications business.

According to the MPT-MII minister, China's conditions for liberalization to foreign operators are not yet mature, but this does not mean the country's telecom and information market will never be open. The time may come by 2020, 2010, or earlier, depending on how fast the stated market conditions are met. Built on the official justifications reiterated over the past years that (*i*) foreign operation and management could compromise national sovereignty and security; (*ii*) there is no precedent in the world to allow foreigners to fully operate a country's communication networks; and (*iii*) network management system in China is too premature[293] for Sino-foreign joint operations, Minister Wu specified at length what the conditions are and why the market cannot be open for now:[294]

- Communications and information concern China's national security and sovereignty. They have a high degree of potential risk and vulnerability, therefore, cannot be opened to foreign players.
- China's telecom infrastructure development has been significantly based on the government favorable policies and support. It would be unfair for foreign firms to share the benefits from the Chinese government policies and compete against China's domestic telecom companies for profits.
- China's telecom services are still tied to the country's postal services that operate with deficit and needs to be cross subsidized by telecom sector. This makes it difficult to define and assure the return on investment for foreign investors.
- Sharp regional differences in telecom infrastructure and services development dictates that MPT must undertake the obligations for the development of remote and rural areas,

---

[293] In official usage, "premature" denotes underdevelopment.

[294] MPT Minister Wu Jichuan made these statements when he was interviewed by Mark O'Neill, reporter of China Business Review, *South China Morning Post*, August 28, 1997.

and make a commitment to provide services to those underdeveloped regions where costs of infrastructure construction and providing services are significantly higher. If the market is prompted open, neither foreign nor domestic business companies, whose objective is generally to make profit, will likely make such a commitment or assume such obligations.

- Currently, China lacks an effective legal and regulatory mechanism to regulate the market. Opening up for a complex competition involving foreign firms and Chinese companies could create problems and may not be fair or feasible.
- Non-reciprocity in competition. As networks and communications facilities are far better established in developed countries, China can hardly enter their telecommunications markets to compete. Opening up China's telecom market then is one-sided and not on a fair and equal ground.

MPT's regulatory interpretation did not seem to be in tune with China's top leadership's intention to restructure and liberalize telecom market. MPT faced policy dilemmas when China pushed to explore and experiment with new ways of utilizing foreign direct investment. China's official campaign to develop the country's interior and western regions seems to have produced a higher pressure on MPT's tight position towards foreign investment, because it requires huge sums of investment which could offer foreign firms greater opportunities to do business in many important areas including communications and information.[295] In a number of cases where foreign investment has found a way to penetrate into telecom arena

---

[295] The Chinese government has indicated that plans are being formulated to provide favorable policies to encourage foreign firms to invest in infrastructure projects, including telecom and information projects, in the country's interior and western regions, but foreign investors are concerned about what exactly the favorable policies will be, and if there will be sufficient demand for telecom and information services in those regions to justify and warrant their projects for substantial returns on investment.

due to the existing policy loopholes and gray areas, China's regulatory regime and foreign investors are both challenged by some crucial questions such as:

1. Can the implementation of various revenue-sharing schemes such as Build-Lease-Transfer (BLT), Build-Lease-Service (BLS), or Build-Transfer-Operate (BTO) exclude foreign participation in equity ownership or network management?
2. Do these proposed initiatives indicate or imply a circumvention, or fundamental change in interpretations of the rules and regulations regarding foreign roles in China telecom and information market?
3. Will foreign firms be able to entrench or nibble themselves into equity ownership and services operation, given the distinct Chinese regulatory dynamics and confusions?

As wireless mobile telecom market becomes increasingly open for competition, more and more foreign companies are using joint-venture funding structure to establish their presence in China as financiers and consultants to Chinese domestic players. This creates a rather complex situation for MPT-MII to manage because the line between financing or technical support and equity investment or management involvement is getting more blurred than before. At the same time, assets restructuring or reallocation, as represented by China Telecom's split off into fixed line, mobile, satellite and other sectors and China Telecom (HK)'s acquisition of Guangdong, Zhejian, and Jiansu mobile communication companies, has complicated and obscured the picture of equity ownership. In May 1998, CCT Telecom Holdings Ltd.,[296] a Hong Kong telecom equipment maker, was reported as having negotiations to purchase one fifth of Guangzhou Jin Peng Group, a Chinese firm that makes mobile equipment and offers mobile services, for US$22.3 million. Jin Peng Group has a registered capital of 246.41 million yuan, of which 43% is owned by Guangzhou government and 54% by several former MEI

---

[296] CCT Telecom Holdings Ltd. is also reported to own 3.7% of China Unicom.

companies. Jin Peng owns 14.3% of Unicom and is authorized to develop mobile networks in Guangdong, Shanxi, Hunan, and Jianxi.

Two things, however, seem as clear as they stand. One, MPT-MII's firm stance on not opening telecom service market to foreign companies, for the time being at least, has a great deal to do with its economic interest or financial gains. It makes no sense for MPT-MII to invite rivals to grab or drain its already established source of cash influxed from telecom and information services.[297] Two, the Chinese policy makers face a constant question of to what degree and extent foreign involvement should be permitted in China's telecom and information sector, which meets the country's development needs but does not undermine its political, economic and security framework.

While the Chinese government is constantly reviewing the situation and slowly edging toward experimentation with build-lease-transfer (BLT), build-lease-operate (BLO), and build-lease-service (BLS) options, in attempts to dig out and use more foreign funds and technology, it has shown no interest whatsoever in giving over the stringent control. The unclear distinctions between the telecoms network equity and the ownership of the production facilities, and between "help build/construct/provide" and "build/construct/provide" seem to have caused confusions, even though they appear merely as a matter of semantic wordplay. No wonder both foreign firms and the Chinese government have often been puzzled by the evolutionary terms such as equity-like, equity-type, near-equity, management support, or operation assistance. These terms create confusions as well as speculations that relate to foreign stakes in equity ownership and network operations.

Ambiguities, on the other hand, tend to stimulate operational innovations. For example, foreign carriers may take technology cooperation as an initial step to gain a foothold in network management, or treat non-equity investment as "loans which are paid

---

[297] Timing, perhaps, is a crucial factor in determining China's opening up of telecom services. A Chinese official stated in September 1999 that "it is impossible for China to give away its interests to foreigners before it makes sure its own stakes are safeguarded."

back at interest rates calibrated to the profits booked by the Chinese partner." The trend seems to be that foreign firms are gradually allowed to enter into network equity arrangement even though network operation or management by foreign companies remains a no-no. Ambiguities also provide foreign players with a wide spectrum of access to Chinese local and non-MPT firms that may have political, economic, and/or technical backings to conduct deals at a certain level of independence.

China's continued policy to prohibit foreign firms from taking network equity ownership and management control, or from having market access to offering telecom services, has largely dispirited many international telecom service operators. For those having set up offices in China, the strategy of "wait-and-see" or "wait-and-push" seems to face a tough wisdom test of stay or leave. The critical stakes involved is that if they stay in China too long without making any revenues, they probably cannot afford the heavy cost of running representative offices year after year, but if they uproot and go away, they risk losing the world largest telecom and information market when it is opened at a time unpredicted.

Clouds over and gray areas in China's telecom and information policy and regulations, though, have provided a ground for entrepreneurial adventures. Many international players have cautiously tested the waters, few have made much headway.[298] Those who have managed to forge MOUs[299] for joint-venture arrangements associated with services have not been able to make concrete progress the way they expected. AT&T, Sprint International, BellSouth, Ameritech, SBC, C&W, Hong Kong Telecom, McCaw International, Singapore Telecom, Siemens, Deutsche Telekom, and Metromedia, to name a few, have been stuck by the current prohibitive regulations. The risk they face is that if they are too bold in breaking or bypassing the

---

[298] Some foreign firms attempt to exploit China's regulatory loopholes by installing V-Sat facilities to offer international call or data communication services to users with satellite dishes. MPT currently appears to be relatively tolerant of this practice, perhaps because it is small in scale and it does not require connection with MPT networks.

[299] Memorandum of Understanding.

regulatory boundaries, they may alienate themselves from the Chinese regulator and decrease their chances of getting operation licenses when the market is finally open. Their aggressive initiatives and business relations have seldom escaped the definition of technical consultancy, network development, system integration, engineering advisory assistance, or network services for multinational corporations operating in China via partnership with Chinese firms.[300]

Jogging around the critical regulatory borders are a number of business cases headlined by international media as follows,[301] but the questions everyone asks are: Do these ventures really involve any kind of foreign equity ownership? How can foreign firms jointly offer services to Chinese customers without holding a certain degree of operational control?

- In December 1997, a US-based Internet service company, Prodigy Inc., was reported to be teaming up with China North Industries Co. (Norinco),[302] a state-run conglomerate in Shanghai, and Shanghai Municipal Commission of Foreign Relations and Trade to become the first government-approved foreign Internet service provider. The official approval was granted after more than nine months of negotiation with the Chinese government. Prodigy would own 80% of the JV (Shanghai Prodigy Telecom Inc.) stake by initially investing US$50 million. The service planned would include on-line services with Chinese language content

---

[300] It is said, for example, that CompuServe has a partnership with Jitong to offer Internet services to foreign companies operating in China.

[301] When media sources report foreign firms' business advances due to China's policy "liberalization" in telecommunications, they almost always draw a similar conclusive statement, such as "The deal circumvents China's ban on direct foreign involvement in telecoms equity investment and network management/operation stakes. It serves as a sign that China is on the way toward a change or relaxation of its strict policy grip on foreign players."

[302] Norinco is a Chinese defense company producing tanks, missiles, and AK-47 assault rifles, but has branched in recent years into civilian businesses such as motorcycles.

at a tentative monthly charge of 267 yuan (US$34) for 30 hours of access for hotels and the general public. Its business would expand from Shanghai to nine other Chinese cities with the use of satellite to download data to locally located servers. Prodigy would differentiate itself from China's domestic ISPs by offering business-related content and by bundling introductory service with certain brands of PCs and modems.

- Hutchinson Whampoa Ltd., Hong Kong's largest company controlled by Hong Kong's property tycoon Li Ka-Shing, as reported, may take a 50% share in a JV with the Chinese Liberation Army and MPT to expand its mainland telephone business. Chung Kiu Telecom (China) Ltd., a company offering consultancy and engineering services, may act as a vehicle for this venture.
- Israeli ECI Telecom Ltd. obtained Chinese government blessing for a US$60 million network development project with Chinese Jitong and China National Technical Import and Export Corporation on designing, installing, and commissioning WAN networks (Golden Bridge Network) to offer Internet linked data communications services to major Chinese cities. The project will deploy ECI's NCX 1E6 Multiservice ATM and NCX FRS800 Frame Relay technologies and the financing will be provided by both Chinese and Israeli governments.
- Sprint International claimed that it would hold a 38% share of a JV with Unicom Shanghai to jointly build networks and offer fixed line services, the approval is given from the State Council. In addition, Sprint and Metromedia would join Unicom for the construction of networks in Tianjin and Chong Qing.[303]
- AT&T would act as the front runner to build and operate a US$1 billion broadband telecom network in Pudong, a special

---

[303] Metromedia was reported in May 1998 to invest US$25 million for these projects.

development district of Shanghai where telecom services are badly needed because of the rapid growth of commercial and financial activities. AT&T's 5-year effort appeared to have come to fruition in March 1999, prior to the Chinese premier's U.S. visit. A framework agreement was signed by Shanghai telecom administration, Shanghai Information Investment Corporation and AT&T for a joint venture to offer Internet telephony and value-added data services in Pudong.[304] The significance of this agreement seems that it is the first time China shows its willingness to broach the idea of foreign company's involvement in China's telecom operations, but the exact implementation still needs Beijing's formal approval. In the similar fashion, Deutsche Telekom, as reported, would team up with a local Chinese PTA to carry out a project in Anhui province to provide value-added telecom services.

- Singapore Telecom signed contracts with various subsidiaries of the MPT and the Beijing Municipal Government to build a nationwide paging network. Singapore Telecom claimed it would hold equity ownership stakes of the network. Its investment would be recovered via a percentage of future profits. Besides, Singapore Telecom agreed to invest US$300 million to help build local telephone networks and GSM mobile systems in Shanghai and Suzhou.
- Hong Kong Telecom concluded the first phase of a US$300 million agreement with the MPT to build a fiber optic cable linking Beijing and Hong Kong, and to expand the Beijing GSM network.
- GTE formed a joint venture with Guangdong Resources Corporation in Guangzhou to build a wide-area paging network covering Beijing and 24 Chinese cities. The initial investment by GTE for the project would be US$28 million. GTE would jointly operate the network for 30 years and

---

[304] According to some reports, AT&T would build a network in Pudong, operate it for 20 years, and turn it over to Shanghai.

     provide expertise in R&D, managerial consulting, and personnel training.

- The Japanese government signed a US$5 billion frame agreement in March 1995 with the Chinese telecom authorities calling for a consortium of Japanese companies to carry out "build-lease-transfer" telecom infrastructure projects in the Yangtze Delta. The arrangement would permit equity-like returns for overseas operators and some degree of management participation.

- Ameritech would help build and operate GSM and fixed networks in Shanxi province by establishing a joint venture with China Unicom Shanxi Branch. The ownership of the network would remain with the joint venture partners until Unicom repays off Ameritech's investment, which is expected for completion within 7-8 years. Ameritech's initial 80 percent stake in the venture would be gradually reduced to 49 percent over the 15-year term of the agreement. Ameritech would exert control by providing the chief executive and chief financial officer for the venture, in addition to giving financial and management advice to Unicom.

As is well noted, Ameritech's China venture ended up a failure. The Chicago-based regional Bell Company was the first U.S. telecom operator to sign a joint-venture service agreement. With a total investment of US$20 million, the company agreed to construct and supervise a subscriber GSM digital cellular system and switched telephone network in Taiyuan, the capital of Shanxi province in north-central China. Ameritech was supposed to reduce its 80% initial stake in the project to 49% as defined by the specific contract. The company hoped to recoup its investment in seven years and its pioneering effort would help achieve a first mover advantage in China.

Like BellSouth[305] that withdrew from an agreement to tie up with Unicom to provide cellular services in Beijing and Tianjin, Ameritech lost its patience entirely in August 1997 after less than 2 years of waiting and trying. It wrote off one million US dollars spent on advertising, staffing and promises, and pulled out of all its operations in China. The official reasons given by the management were (a) delays in the project that increased the costs to the point where returns on investment became unrealizable and dismal, and (b) the prevailing regulatory atmosphere that held off foreign service providers from the market entry. The case of Ameritech in China is quite provocative since the company made its China presence with a high profile and stated that since China was its long-term strategic priority in Asia, the company would pursue China market diligently and persistently.

Nothing, perhaps, is more demonstrative of the confusing situation in China than the country's Internet related services. For years China's Internet service providers (ISPs and ICPs) have forged ahead in murky waters. The door for them to reach foreign players has remained half open and half shut. No clear definition or regulation has ever been officially issued concerning foreign investment or involvement in network or content development, even though a mish-mash of the institutional forces has endeavored to get involved in the process of policy making and implementation. The IPO of "China.com" helped raise millions of dollars abroad for the firm's growth, "Sohu.com," "Sina.com" and several other most influential Chinese ISPs/ICPs engaged themselves both financially and technologically with foreign companies and were enthusiastically expanding these ties when suddenly, in September 1999, MPT-MII Minister proclaimed for the first time that China's Internet services, both access facilitating and content provision, fall into value-added telecom service category, therefore, no foreign investment or

---

[305] US West, Nynex Corp. and Bell Atlantic all had the similar experience in China and pulled out from their ventures there.

involvement is allowed.[306] MPT-MII's stance was widely speculated as (a) a tactic gesture to gain more bargaining leverage in China's WTO negotiation; (b) reaffirmation of control over network and information resources; and (c) reflection of MPT-MII's attempt to clarify its authority for Internet related services; (d) increased government concern over foreign companies gaining strategic position in China's Internet sector.

If China does shut itself off from foreign investment in the Internet sector, in an effort to protect the market for domestic players, the country runs the risk of losing the capacity to leapfrog and catch up with the advanced nations by missing out on benefits emerging from the global Internet economy. These benefits will likely dwarf any short-term gains China may reap from its stiff close-door practice. China's online business was about US$43 million in 1999, but the value may become three or four times as large in 2000. Within a 5-year period, China's Internet online transactions may climb up to over US$11 billion.[307] Whether such a growth can materialize will largely depend upon China's regulatory framework and the degree to which China becomes a global Internet player and innovator. Some Chinese policy makers and Internet executives have argued that in the high technology area, capital itself is no longer a controlling power. Instead, it is knowledge, expertise, human resources, and the

---

[306] In defiance to the MPT/MII's policy statement, China's major ISPs/ICPs pinpointed that the concept of foreign investment and sino-foreign joint ventures in IT industries should be renovated, given several important factors, which include (a) the capital invested is not only from foreign nationals, but also significantly from overseas Chinese; (b) China's foreign invested ISPs/ICPs are managed and operated by the Chinese who make business decisions and policies in conformity with the Chinese rules and regulations; (c) overseas capital and technology not only provide resources necessary for ISPs/ICPs operations, but also bring in opportunities for international exposure, broad market access, new management expertise, quality human resources, and international legal and economic practices, none of which will be available without overseas involvement.

[307] Data taken from International Data Corp., a global market research firm.

prevailing legal and economic systems that matter more. Foreign investment not only brings in capital, but also provides Internet players in China with access to all these crucial elements. They concluded that China can benefit, not lose, if its Internet sector is more liberalized.

Foreign investment and equity ownership in China's rather loosely-knit yet highly entrepreneurial ISPs/ICPs are murky and almost impossible for MPT-MII to discern. A freeze or ban on foreign investment in this field is extremely complex and difficult to enforce. Plus, conflicts of interest between MPT-MII and other Chinese institutions and business entities involved in Internet operations will most likely build up strong resisting "firewalls" to MPT-MII's policy implementation. Pragmatically, MPT-MII may have a more positive and compelling effect on China's Internet development if it endeavors to establish a regulatory system by which foreign firms and investors can register their investment and operations legitimately with the relevant departments, and receive requisite licenses for ISP/ICP services or cooperation with Chinese companies.

When U.S. and China reached a bilateral accord on November 15, 1999 for China's WTO accession, the Chinese government made a significant concession in permitting foreign equity investment in telecom and Internet services, which seems to override MPT-MII's pledged ban just two months earlier. Once China formally enters WTO, according to the announced agreement, China will allow foreign investors to hold a significant proportion of the equity shares of the Chinese telecom companies.[308] However, there is no precise clarification yet on what the stated percentages mean,[309] especially when the numbers are applied with specific implementation timeframe to specific areas of value-added, wireless paging, mobile cellular, data communications, Internet, and basic telecommunications services.

---

[308] This permitted foreign equity ownership after China's WTO accession can also be interpreted as the listed shares of the Chinese telecom companies held by foreign or overseas investors.

[309] MPT-MII may use its power to claim the right to make interpretations about the items governing telecom and Internet services in the bilateral U.S.-China agreement.

Over-optimism has no ground, as the actual enforcement of WTO rules are still years away. Foreign investors may yet have to conquer many policy constraints and contextual problems before they can compete in the Chinese market. WTO will not work magic that opens China's long-closed telecom door overnight.[310]

True as always, devil is in the details. In his interviews with *the Wall Street Journal* and a Chinese magazine, MII Minister elaborated on foreign investment in China's Internet. His comments suggested that 50% may be a maximum limit, whereas going beyond it would be dealt with "appropriately" and "rationally." The official supposition is that Internet service providers in China ought to be classified into network access providers (ISP) and content providers (ICP), each regulated by different government organizations. ISPs will be overseen and regulated by MII that sets technological criteria and issues licenses for operation while ICPs will be supervised and monitored by government authorities other than MII, with jurisdiction over information resources. These authorities may include China's media and publishing regulators, the radio and TV broadcast administration, and public security agencies. All ISPs, as MII indicated, are under MII's administration and must apply for licenses. MII's approval and granting of licenses to ISPs will be based on the applicants' capital structure, technology strength, capability for long-term services, and management readiness. All foreign investors involved in China's ISPs cannot have their shares go above 50%. They must get official approvals or licenses before taking stakes in China's Internet ventures.

Policy dilemmas and ambiguities, however, are again self-evident when MII Minister emphasizes that foreign investors' stakes in ICPs are not confined to 50%, but regulated by non-MII content control authorities. That seems to imply that foreign shares in China's ICPs are not yet capped but could be lower or higher than 50%, depending on the specific deals with China's content regulators. MII seems to

---

[310] Some observers call the US-China WTO agreement a psychological boost that sets China's economic reform in stone and throws light on perilous gray policy areas.

be making a great effort to concentrate on network service regulations while it tries hard to get its hands free from the ICP business. MII's position on Internet is then seriously questioned. To what degree of feasibility and practicality can China's Internet service providers be clearly divided into ICPs and ISPs? What is the policy guideline on foreign investment in ICPs, in case where an ICP does not exist independently of an ISP?[311]

Stories go on and zigzag all the way. The WTO framework agreement, or the WTO statement in principle, paves the way for an optimistic prospect ahead, but it does not assure a solid ground on which to step forward. The end of one negotiation may only mean the beginning of another. What matters most is the underlying details and the actual practice of executing the broad theoretical strokes agreed or committed. Barriers may continue to exist, but in more subtle or sophisticated forms, such as cumbersome and unclear rules and regulations, obstinate demands for approvals and licenses, tough supervision and rectification, and slack legal enforcement.[312] The mist over foreign investment cannot be cleared off by WTO alone. There is still a long way to go. The issue of foreign equity ownership and

---

[311] In the Spring 2000, MII stated that China's Internet portals must have their content-tied assets striped of from their network facilities before their could get official approvals for listing their shares in the stock market, because ICP part of the assets were not allowed to go public and the capital raised from the stock market should not be used for ICP development.

[312] Press reports have been around saying that China will encourage foreign investors to enter value-added and Internet related services while access to mobile and fixed line markets will be highly restricted. China will stipulate that foreign partners in telecom joint ventures should have a minimum of US$1 million in fixed assets and an annual business turnover of US$500,000. The Chinese partners, on the other hand, should have a yearly revenue of RMB2 billion (US$240 million). In mobile and fixed line sectors, large foreign firms can enter into joint ventures only with China's state-own telecom giants that have adequate telecom business experience and annual revenues of RMB3 billion (US$370 million). The joint venture management, as sources say, will be formed in Chinese favor: the Chinese side will be entitled to appoint the board chairman and recommend who the general manager should be.

foreign services operation in China's telecommunications market remains far from solved. It will linger on as an intricate puzzle that requires the wittiest to rack their brains for a real solution.

Conclusion

In a world of network superiority, information and knowledge are replacing the conventional notion of wealth and strength. National interest of all countries now seems to have a greater stake in communications and information than in any other sectors. A networked economy embeds an ever-divergent paradigm of manpower, investment, industries, operations, marketplace, and regulatory regime. With increased deployment and continuing penetration of electronic communications and information technology (IT), China's traditional agrarian and pre-industrial economy is on the verge of transformation. The stage on which China plays is no longer bordered, but is fast becoming international. The rapid build-up of communications and information infrastructure in China will not merely bring about technological changes, but more fundamentally, a multitude of social, political, and economic reshaping and reorganization.

There are ten major regulatory issues that have strategic implications. The competition among China Telecom, China Unicom and other emerging Chinese firms, sources of investment that should be sustainable, coordination and harmonization of institutional interests, network security and integrity, and broader market access for international investors and operators are among the most crucial and urgent issues to be tackled.

As Internet infrastructure and services continue to grow with high momentum, information through the Internet will have a profound impact on China's economic, political, social, educational and individual lives. Freer and faster flow and sharing of information resources will lead to a restructuring and redistribution of materials, capital and human resources. As a result, cultural pluralism will increase, and productive and social forces will be reorganized. Something utterly new, confusing, and exhilarating will likely emerge. While China will benefit from the Internet-based information age and network-supported economy, how the Chinese cultural traditions and its political philosophy, such as the concepts of nationhood and sovereignty, will be changed remains unclear and unpredictable. It is possible that China's nationalist impulse will encourage the development of a Chinese oriented vista of the Web, exerting more influence on the world. Through a wide-spread interconnectivity by the Internet, China will learn more from the outside, and China's culture and assumptions will have a subtle and important effect on the outside world, adding new attitudes and perspectives.

The expansion and regulation of the Internet in the face of the dramatic technological convergence give the Chinese government an unprecedented challenge. Suggestions have been made to set up a cross-organizational semi-government committee to take on Internet related issues if significant differences in opinion and lack of institutional synergy proceed. Knowing that western experience is not a model China can readily emulate, the Chinese government is trying hard to figure out how to best foster and regulate the emerging Internet-based information industry. China's consolidation of regulatory regime, restructuring of IT and telecom industries, increased open market access, and national informatization program are remarkable pioneering maneuvers that demonstrate the nation's firm resolve and strategic direction.

In the process of development, China is confronted with numerous country-specific challenges, including heavy and still growing population, lack of a robust investment mechanism, limited resources and infrastructure, required economic and industry restructuring, increased regional economic disparity, narrow access to education, relatively low levels of productivity, efficiency and technology, under-developed regulatory and legal framework, and high international competitive pressure. The question to ask is, "will electronic networks, digital revolution, virtual realities, cyber society, and information and knowledge flows provide China with strategic incentives and remedial instruments to meet these challenges?"

Many in China recognize the power and importance of information technologies and knowledge-based economic systems. They believe knowledge economy represents a brand new age, in which information resources (*e.g.,* data, image, symbols, and even values), not land, labor, capital, or raw materials, act as an essential catalyst for China's development. Others argue that China should not overlook but keep awake on the possible information "bubble" effect that produces an illusion in which "concrete" economy is no longer important. The power of information, they believe, may also turn out bitter fruits of social instability, uncertainty and anxiety, if not sensibly managed. Human societies that depend entirely upon network systems for operations appear to be security fragile: they are potentially exposed to disruption or breakdown once technology is, for one reason or another, abused, attacked, or mismanaged. The instances of computer hacking, viruses, Y2K and cyber terrorism are among the most apparent indications of threat. Network and data security concerns not only the government organizations, but also businesses and individuals who access electronic networks for political, commercial, or personal information and communications.

Information-technology based economies may, apart from its blessings, generate various risks and dangers: (a) Knowledge systems may get split off due to an ever-increasing specialization, or fragmentation, which makes distribution of knowledge asymmetrical and the basis for consensus damaged. Information "explosion" may lead to a seemingly ironical situation, in which information-based human knowledge and wisdom are devalued or lost. (b) Information age may bring about new economic, political and psychological uncertainties different from those in previous human societies. (c) Network-based financial and credit systems are inclined to a high degree of potential risk in case of technology collapse. (d) Information intensifies market competition and industry restructuring, and it shortens the duration in which certain market competitiveness and industry structure are otherwise sustained. This may expedite and polarize the dynamics of the job market and, therefore, undermine the employment environment. (e) If the gap between the information rich and the information poor grows larger, the world that is already twisted by this disparity will become further out of balance as the stronger nations take the advantage of the weaker countries in terms of economic development and international politics.

This observation has good values. Information generates knowledge, while knowledge, more than ever before, makes grounds for power and wealth. The network-based information revolution, however, may also expose the human race to vulnerabilities and risks. China, as a nation and a state, seems to be at a vital crossroads where conventional wisdom and modern intellect meet. The most crucial concern, then, is which path, pace, and options China should adopt for its communications and information development, that fits into a global framework for progress and, at the same time, accommodates China's best national interest.

Index

D

E

H

I

M

About the Author

Xing Fan has been working at the International Communications Studies Program and Asian Studies Program, Center for Strategic and International Studies (CSIS), Washington, D.C., and as a Cyber Century® Research Fellow at the Center for Information Infrastructure and Economic Development (CIIED) under the auspices of the Chinese Academy of Social Sciences in Beijing. In these capacities he has undertaken in-depth research and analysis on China's policy, regulatory and market issues involving telecommunications, information infrastructure, Internet and electronic commerce. He has played an instrumental role in coordinating a number of joint research projects under CIIED's multi-ministry, multi-industry aegis.

Prior to joining CSIS, Xing Fan was a postgraduate research associate at the Harvard Program on Information Resources Policy, where he undertook extensive research on the political, regulatory and technology dynamics of China's telecommunications and information sector. Major publications of Xing Fan include: *"China's Strategic Moves Towards Electronic Commerce: Progress, Performance Prospects;"* *"China's WTO Accession and Its Telecom Liberalization;"* *"Foreign Stakes in China Telecommunications;"* *"Scaling the Great Wall of E-Commerce: Strategic Issues and Recommendations"* (with the Hon. Diana Lady Dougan); and *"China Telecommunications: Constituencies and Challenges."*